The ABCs of
FrontPage 97

The ABCs of
FrontPage™ 97

Gene Weisskopf

SYBEX®

San Francisco · Paris · Düsseldorf · Soest

Associate Publisher: Amy Romanoff
Acquisitions Manager: Kristine Plachy
Acquisitions & Developmental Editor: Dan Brodnitz
Editor: Kim Wimpsett
Technical Editor: Mark H. Butler
Book Design Director: Catalin Dulfu
Book Designer: Design Site
Electronic Publishing Specialist: Alissa Feinberg
Production Coordinator: Anton Reut
Indexer: Ted Laux
Cover Designer: Design Site
Cover Illustrators: Harumi Kubo, Gene Weisskopf

Screen reproductions produced with Collage Complete.

Collage Complete is a trademark of Inner Media Inc.

SYBEX is a registered trademark of SYBEX Inc.

TRADEMARKS: SYBEX has attempted throughout this book to distinguish proprietary trademarks from descriptive terms by following the capitalization style used by the manufacturer.

The author and publisher have made their best efforts to prepare this book, and the content is based upon final release software whenever possible. Portions of the manuscript may be based upon pre-release versions supplied by software manufacturer(s). The author and the publisher make no representation or warranties of any kind with regard to the completeness or accuracy of the contents herein and accept no liability of any kind including but not limited to performance, merchantability, fitness for any particular purpose, or any losses or damages of any kind caused or alleged to be caused directly or indirectly from this book.

Photographs and illustrations used in this book have been downloaded from publicly accessible file archives and are used in this book for news reportage purposes only to demonstrate the variety of graphics resources available via electronic access. Text and images available over the Internet may be subject to copyright and other rights owned by third parties. Online availability of text and images does not imply that they may be reused without the permission of rights holders, although the Copyright Act does permit certain unauthorized reuse as fair use under 17 U.S.C. Section 107.

Copyright ©1997 SYBEX Inc., 1151 Marina Village Parkway, Alameda, CA 94501. World rights reserved. No part of this publication may be stored in a retrieval system, transmitted, or reproduced in any way, including but not limited to photocopy, photograph, magnetic or other record, without the prior agreement and written permission of the publisher.

Library of Congress Card Number: 96-72106
ISBN: 0-7821-2012-1

Manufactured in the United States of America

10 9 8 7 6 5 4 3 2 1

To Miss Hetzner, my high school typing teacher, who taught me a valuable, life-long skill.

Acknowledgments

When a project spans more than three years, it can be a bit difficult to remember all the people who played a part in it. On the other hand, when a project such as this book must be completed in a matter of months, it's not hard at all!

I'd like to thank *everyone* at Sybex for all their talent, good spirits, and willingness to help out when needed. Producing a book with them is always a very gratifying experience.

There are several at Sybex who worked with me directly and played a major role in bringing this book to life. My thanks go to Kristine Plachy, acquisitions manager, and to Dan Brodnitz, acquisitions & developmental editor (and just what is this Duke Nukem stuff anyway?).

Kim Wimpsett, editor, did a wonderful job of taking my writing and turning it into an actual book. I especially appreciated her almost instantaneous responses to my e-mailed questions and her pleasant, professional demeanor in the midst of a very tight schedule.

Mark Butler, technical editor, gets more than just my thanks. His understanding of the Internet and related issues helped steer this book safely through the jargon-strewn straits of networking. I'd also like to thank Alissa Feinberg, electronic publishing specialist, and Anton Reut, production coordinator, for their skilled contributions to this book.

It's also important to remember all of these folks were working on other books simultaneously. From my perspective, however, I'm happy to say it didn't seem like it. Many thanks.

Contents at a Glance

Introduction xix

Chapter 1: Publishing a Web with FrontPage 3
Chapter 2: Working with Webs in the Explorer .23
Chapter 3: Managing Webs in the Explorer 45
Chapter 4: Creating Pages in the Editor 69
Chapter 5: Using Files, Wizards, and Templates 91
Chapter 6: Adding Structure to Your Pages 109
Chapter 7: Formatting Your Pages 125
Chapter 8: Linking Your Pages to the World 145
Chapter 9: Displaying Images in Your Pages 173
Chapter 10: Automating Your Web with WebBots 203
Chapter 11: Arranging Data within Tables 221
Chapter 12: Letting the Reader Interact with Forms 241
Chapter 13: Getting Fancier with Frames 265
Chapter 14: Administering Web Sites 287
Appendix A: Installing and Starting FrontPage .311
Appendix B: Glossary of Terms 319

Index 331

Table of Contents

Introduction xix

Chapter 1: Publishing a Web with FrontPage 3

Understanding the Internet, the WWW, and Intranets 4
    Clients, Servers, and the Global Network 4
    The Language of the Internet 5
    The World Wide Web 5
    Web Sites, Pages, and Links 7
    The Internet versus an Intranet 8
Publishing Pages on the Web 8
    The Hypertext Markup Language 9
    The Essentials of a Web Page 10
    Learning HTML 11
    Keeping a Web Site Together 12
The FrontPage Solution to Web Publishing 13
    The Personal Web Server 14
    The FrontPage Server Extensions 15
    The FrontPage Explorer 16
    The FrontPage Editor 17
    The FrontPage To Do List 19
    Image Composer 20

Chapter 2: Working with Webs in the Explorer 23

Working in the Active Web 24
Creating a New FrontPage Web 25
    Choosing a Template or Wizard 26
    Choosing a Location for the Web 29
    The Folders in a FrontPage Web 31

Opening and Closing an Existing Web 31
Creating a FrontPage Web from an Existing Web Site 32
Importing and Exporting Files 34
    Importing Files 35
    Exporting Files 36
Publishing a Web to a Server 37
    Publishing a Web to a FrontPage Server 37
    Publishing a Web to a Non-FrontPage Server 39
Renaming, Moving, or Deleting a Web Site 42
    Renaming a Web Site 42
    Moving a Web Site 43
    Deleting a Web Site 43

Chapter 3: Managing Webs in the Explorer 45

Displaying Your Web in the Hyperlink View 46
    The Left Pane (Outline) of the Hyperlink View 47
    Expanding the Hyperlink View 49
    The Right Pane (Map) of the Hyperlink View 50
Seeing All Files in the Explorer's Folder View 52
Manipulating Files and Their Properties 54
    Using Commands on Web Files 55
    Renaming or Moving a File 56
    Viewing and Revising File Properties 57
Specifying Web File Editors 58
Finding Text and Spell-Checking throughout the Web 60
    Finding and Replacing Text in Your Web 61
    Checking the Spelling in Your Web 63
Keeping Track with the To Do List 63
    Opening the To Do List 64
    Viewing Tasks 64
    Adding and Modifying Tasks 65
    Completing and Removing Tasks 67

Chapter 4: Creating Pages in the Editor 69

Starting the Editor 70
   Creating a New Page 71
Pretend You're Using a Word Processor 72
   Microsoft Word's HTML Sibling 72
   Basic Editing Procedures 73
   Inserting Paragraphs and Line Breaks 75
Inserting Special Characters 76
Checking Your Spelling 76
   If the Word Is Spelled Correctly 77
   If the Word Is Misspelled 78
Finding and Replacing Text 78
HTML and Browsers—The Start and End of Your Work 80
   Seeing the HTML Source Code 80
   Inserting Extended HTML Code 82
   Previewing Your Work in a Browser 84
Printing Your Page 86
   Defining the Page Layout 86
   Previewing the Printout 87

Chapter 5: Using Files, Wizards, & Templates 91

Creating a New Page in the Editor 92
   Creating a Page from a Template 92
   Creating a Page with a Wizard 94
Opening an Existing File 99
   Opening a Page from the Active Web 100
   Opening a Page from Outside the Active Web 100
   Opening Other File Types 101
   Inserting a File into a Page 102
Saving a Page 103
   Saving a Page as a File 104
   Saving a Page as a Template 104
Browsing Pages in the Editor 106

Chapter 6: Adding Structure to Your Pages ...109

Creating Sections with Horizontal Lines ...110
    Changing the Look of a Line ...111
    Using Images of Lines ...111
Creating a Hierarchy with Headings ...114
Organizing Data within Lists ...115
    Creating a List from Existing Text ...115
    Creating a List As You Type ...117
    Working in a List ...117
    Changing the Look of a Bulleted or Numbered List ...118
    Creating a Nested List within a List ...120
    Creating Other Types of Lists ...121

Chapter 7: Formatting Your Pages ...125

Setting Character Properties ...126
    Choosing the Text to Format ...126
    Accessing Font Properties ...127
    Changing Font Properties ...127
    Changing the Special Styles Properties ...131
Setting Paragraph Properties ...132
    The Formatted Paragraph Style ...133
    Setting Paragraph Alignment ...134
    Indenting Paragraphs ...135
Setting Page Properties ...135
    Changing the Title and Other General Options ...136
    Changing the Background Color ...137
    Specifying a Background Image ...139
    Getting Background Options from Another Page ...140
    Setting Page Margins ...141
    Creating Meta Page Information ...142

Chapter 8: Linking Your Pages to the World 145

- Understanding Links 146
  - Text or Image Hyperlinks 146
  - Target Files and Bookmarks 147
  - Absolute and Relative URLs 148
- Creating a Hyperlink 150
  - Linking to an Open Page 151
  - Linking to a Bookmark 151
  - Specifying a Target Frame 152
  - Linking to a Page in the Current FrontPage Web 153
  - Linking to a Page on the WWW 153
  - Linking to a New Page 154
- Revising, Deleting, and Following Hyperlinks 155
  - Revising a Hyperlink 155
  - Deleting a Hyperlink 156
  - Following Hyperlinks in the Editor 156
- Working with Bookmarks 156
  - Defining a Bookmark 157
  - Revising, Deleting, and Going to Bookmarks 158
- Creating Clickable Image Maps 158
  - Choosing the Type of Image Map 160
  - Defining the Hotspots 162
  - Specifying a Default Hyperlink 165
  - Viewing Hotspots 165
  - Revising Hotspots 166
- Fixing and Verifying Links in the Explorer 167
  - Fixing Target Names Automatically 167
  - Verifying Links in the Explorer 168

Chapter 9: Displaying Images in Your Pages 173

The World of Image Formats 174
    The GIF Format 174
    The JPEG Format 175
Inserting an Image into a Page 175
    Inserting a Video Clip 177
    Saving New Images in a Page 177
Selecting an Image 178
Setting Image Properties 179
    Specifying the Image Source 179
    Specifying the Type of Image 180
    Specifying an Alternative to the Image 182
    Specifying Video Properties 183
    Specifying Image Alignment 184
    Specifying Image Size 185
Donning Your Beret with Image Composer 186
    Starting Image Composer 187
    Working with Sprites in Compositions 187
    Saving the Workspace or Composition Guide 190
    Picking Colors for Your Web 191
    Creating a Sample Composition 193

Chapter 10: Automating Your Web with WebBots 203

What's a WebBot? 204
The FrontPage WebBots 205
Including Another Web Page Automatically 207
    How FrontPage Encodes a WebBot 209
    Revising a WebBot 210
Inserting a WebBot for Your Comments 210
Automating Text Entry with the Substitution WebBot 211
    Referencing a Variable in a Page 212
    Creating a Configuration Variable 213
Creating a Table of Contents 215
Stamping Your Page with the Date and Time 217

Chapter 11: Arranging Data within Tables .221

- The Structure of a Table 222
- Creating a New Table 224
  - Using the Insert Table Button 224
  - Using the Insert Table Command 224
- Working within a Table 225
  - Selecting Table Elements 226
  - Formatting a Table's Contents 227
  - Adding and Aligning a Caption 228
- Changing the Look of a Table 229
  - Changing a Table's Alignment and Layout 230
  - Setting a Table's Background and Border Colors 231
- Changing the Look of Cells 232
  - Changing a Cell's Alignment and Layout .233
  - Creating Header Cells 234
  - Setting a Cell's Background and Border Colors 234
- Changing the Size of a Table 235
  - Changing the Table's Width 235
  - Changing a Column's Width 236
  - Adding and Removing Cells 237
  - Merging and Splitting Cells 237
  - Changing Cell Span 238

Chapter 12: Letting the Reader Interact with Forms 241

- Working with Forms 242
  - Form-Building Basics 243
  - Selecting Form Controls 244
  - Aligning Fields in a Form 245
- Telling the Server How to Handle the Data 246
  - Choosing the Form Handler 246
  - Configuring the Save Results Form Handler 247
- Creating the Sample Form 249
- Adding Fields to a Form 251

Changing the Properties of a Control 252
    One-Line Text Box Properties 253
    Text Box Data Validation 254
    Drop-Down Menu 257
    Radio Button 259
    Check Box 259
    Scrolling Text Box 260
    Push Button 260
Filling Out the Form in a Browser 261

Chapter 13: Getting Fancier with Frames 265

Dividing a Page into Frames 266
Creating a Frame Set from a Template 266
    Starting the Frames Wizard 267
    Choosing a Frame Set Template 268
    Specifying an Alternate Page 270
    Saving the Frame Set 271
Viewing a Completed Frame Set 272
Creating a Custom Frame Set 273
Modifying a Frame Set 274
    Changing the Number of Frames or Their Sizes 274
    Specifying a Name and URL for a Frame 277
    Changing the Appearance of a Frame 279
Specifying a Target Frame in a Link 280
Delivering a Message with a Marquee 281

Chapter 14: Administering Web Sites 287

Testing and Refining Your Web Site 288
Keeping Your Web Secure 291
    Assigning Permissions 292
    Assigning Unique Permissions for a Web 293
    Assigning Permissions to Users 294
    Assigning Permissions to IP Addresses 297

Working with the Personal Web Servers 299
    Running the FrontPage Personal Web Server 300
    Running the Microsoft Personal Web Server 300
    Registering Users in the Microsoft Personal Web Server 301
    Running the FrontPage Server Administrator 304
    Migrating to the Microsoft Personal Web Server 306
Changing the Name of the Home Page 307
    Changing the Home Page Name with the Microsoft PWS 308
    Changing the Home Page Name for the FrontPage PWS 308

Appendix A: Installing and Starting FrontPage 311

Running the Setup Program 312
Starting FrontPage 316
Getting Help 317

Appendix B: Glossary of Terms 319

Index *331*

Introduction

Back in the early days of the PC revolution, if you wanted to underline or boldface text in a document, you might very well have had to look up the control codes for those effects in your printer manual. Unless you were something of a programmer type (and there were plenty of them back then by necessity), your word processor was often less than conducive to getting jobs done quickly and creatively.

Then, the Internet, the World Wide Web, and the Hypertext Markup Language (HTML) sparked the computer revolution in an entirely new way (the twenty-ninth rebirth of this revolution, by my count). But once again, the early users of Internet technology had to be akin to code crunchers in order to create pages for the Web, using nothing but a text editor and their knowledge of the HTML language.

Thankfully, those early days are waning quickly, and Microsoft FrontPage 97 is one of the primary reasons. With FrontPage in hand, you don't need a deep understanding of HTML in order to produce attractive and informative Web pages and entire Web sites that work from the start. With *The ABCs of FrontPage 97* in your other hand, you'll be well-prepared to set out on the Infobahn.

Who Should Read This Book

The ABCs of FrontPage 97 will introduce you to Microsoft FrontPage 97 while at the same time introducing you to the process of creating Web sites and Web pages. Whether you're building a home page for your personal Web site on the Internet or a departmental Web site on your corporate intranet, this book and FrontPage will help you get the job done quickly and easily—and best of all, your site and pages will work.

This book will work especially well in two ways:

- If you are new to publishing on the Web, you'll get a solid grounding in the basics while learning how to use FrontPage.
- If you are already familiar with Webs and HTML, you'll see how to implement them within FrontPage, taking advantage of its highly regarded Web-site management and page-editing tools.

You certainly don't need to be a computer expert to use this book, but you should have a general working knowledge of Windows. You will see that creating Web pages in the FrontPage Editor is really not all that different from creating documents in your word processor. With the FrontPage Explorer, creating and managing Web sites become very straightforward tasks.

What's Inside

The best way to start reading this book is from the beginning. Chapter 1, "Publishing a Web with FrontPage," is an introduction to the Internet and the World Wide Web. It explains how FrontPage is a well-rounded solution to the issues involved with creating, running, and managing a Web site, and creating Web pages for that site.

Chapter 2, "Working with Webs in the Explorer," shows you how to create new Web sites in the FrontPage Explorer and how to manage its files and folders. Chapter 3, "Managing Webs in the Explorer," also discusses the Explorer and the ways it helps you understand the hyperlinks in the files in your site. If you aren't working with entire sites but want only to create HTML pages, you might skim over these two chapters and save them for later.

Then go to Chapter 4, "Creating Pages in the Editor," which gives you an overview of the FrontPage Editor, where you create your Web pages. You can save your pages in a FrontPage web, or use them elsewhere. Chapters 5 through 13 all cover various page-creation issues in the Editor.

Chapter 5, "Using Files, Wizards, and Templates," shows you how to create new pages in the Editor from templates or Wizards. In Chapter 6, "Adding Structure to Your Pages," you'll learn how to organize a page with standard HTML features such as headings, horizontal lines, and lists. Chapter 7, "Formatting Your Pages," discusses the ways you can change the appearance of a page by formatting text, paragraphs, or the entire page.

Perhaps the most important feature of any Web site—hyperlinks—is covered in Chapter 8, "Linking Your Pages to the World." You'll learn how to create hyperlinks from text or images, specify the target files and bookmarks, and create image maps that contain multiple, clickable links. You'll also learn how the Explorer keeps track of and manages all the links in your FrontPage web.

Chapter 9, "Displaying Images in Your Pages," covers another important feature in any Web site, the images it displays. You'll learn the differences between GIF and JPEG image files, and you'll learn how to convert images to other formats. You'll see how to insert images and video clips into a page and how to change their size and appearance. You'll also take a grand tour through Microsoft Image Composer, the hot new image-editing program that comes with FrontPage.

Chapter 10, "Automating Your Web with WebBots," covers FrontPage WebBots. These unique Web page components let you add automated features to your Web pages simply by inserting a WebBot into them. You'll learn how to create a table of contents page that links to every page in your Web, how to include a page automatically in another page, and more.

The HTML table is discussed in Chapter 11, "Arranging Data within Tables." You can use tables to organize data within its orderly rows and columns. You will also learn how to take advantage of the structure of a table for organizing a page without actually showing the table.

Chapter 12, "Letting the Reader Interact with Forms," introduces you to building forms in Web pages. You'll see how easy it is in the FrontPage Editor to create text fields, check boxes, radio buttons, drop-down menus, and other form controls.

In Chapter 13, "Getting Fancier with Frames," you'll learn about the frame set, which is a single page that displays other pages, each within a separate frame, or window. You'll also learn about the marquee, which is a scrolling message that walks right across the screen.

Finally, Chapter 14, "Administering Web Sites," covers some of the Web administration tasks you can perform in FrontPage, such as assigning access rights to a Web site. Following this chapter is Appendix A, "Installing and Starting FrontPage," which discusses the issues you'll need to consider when installing FrontPage.

I used plain language whenever possible in this book, which was a pretty daunting task considering the language of the Internet is mostly acronyms and jargon. Appendix B, "Glossary of Terms," will help you over the humps.

Other features you'll find in this book include helpful Notes, Tips, and Warnings, which serve as adjuncts to the main body of text. All the sample Web pages and examples of HTML features in this book are simple, uncluttered, and to the point. You won't have any trouble following along with the exercises and explanations.

This book utilizes some typographical elements you'll find useful to help distinguish certain aspects of the text. Text you enter with your keyboard is in **boldface,** while file names and URLs are in a monospaced `program font`. All letters in file names are capitalized when the name appears within a paragraph, but when the name appears within a path or URL, the letters are lowercased.

The figures in this book were taken from a computer screen at a resolution of 800 by 600 while running FrontPage with its default settings. You may notice small differences between the screens in this book and your own screen if your computer is running at a different resolution or you have modified FrontPage's standard settings.

I hope you find *The ABCs of FrontPage 97* to be helpful as well as enjoyable to read and that it becomes a valuable tutorial and reference guide as you build your Web sites and pages. If you have any comments about this book, please send them to me in care of Sybex; they will be much appreciated.

Chapter 1

PUBLISHING A WEB WITH FRONTPAGE

FEATURING

- Understanding servers, clients, and networks
- Accessing the World Wide Web (WWW)
- Using an intranet as an in-house web
- Publishing Web pages
- Using the Hypertext Markup Language (HTML)
- Connecting pages with hyperlinks
- Using FrontPage as your Web site–publishing solution

The explosive growth of the Internet in the past few years is ample evidence of how a simple concept—a network that could connect every computer on Earth—can fulfill countless needs.

This chapter first introduces you to the Internet, the World Wide Web, and a subset of the Internet called *intranets*. Then you'll see how Microsoft FrontPage 97 offers the tools you'll need to set up and manage a site on the Web, create pages on the Web, and leap over many of the hurdles you'll encounter while publishing on the Web.

If you want to get right to work in FrontPage, you can skip ahead to Chapter 2, "Working with Webs in the Explorer," to learn about creating a new Web site or opening an existing one. Chapter 3, "Managing Webs in the Explorer," shows you how to work with the files and hyperlinks in a Web site using the FrontPage Explorer. To start creating Web pages with the FrontPage Editor, turn to Chapter 4, "Creating Pages in the Editor." If you need help installing FrontPage, turn to Appendix A, "Installing and Starting FrontPage."

Understanding the Internet, the WWW, and Intranets

As strange as it may seem, the Internet was conceived, designed, and implemented so Aunt Fiona, a Macintosh user who lives in Oxford in Britain, can post the latest pictures of her pesky kittens Naomi and Lucille on a computer in London that runs the Windows NT operating system. Then, her niece and nephew, Amanda and Alan, who live in Sausalito in the United States and use a PC running Windows, can connect to a computer in San Francisco that runs the Unix operating system and have that computer connect to the computer in London. All so they can view those cutest-of-cute pictures.

Of course, the original designers of what has become the Internet did not actually have dear Aunt Fiona herself in mind; they were more interested in Department of Defense contractors and university research centers. But the need to make any sort of file—such as those kitten pictures—available to the world is exactly why the Internet was created as an open network to which any computer could connect, and through which all connected computers could communicate.

Clients, Servers, and the Global Network

The Internet consists of three fundamental elements (along with several hundred other ones that are slightly less fundamental):

Server: A computer program that makes data available to other programs on the same or other computers—it "serves" them.

Client: A computer that requests data from a server.

Network: A means by which multiple computers can communicate with one another, such as clients requesting and receiving data from a server. The communication may be via copper wire, coaxial cable, fiber-optic cable, satellite transmissions, and so on.

> **NOTE** When you connect to a server halfway around the world, you may be using any or all of these network communication methods. Of course, it won't really matter to you; the system simply follows the most advantageous route over the network. From your perspective, your computer merely connects to the server in a fraction of a second (on a good day).

The Language of the Internet

Although the Internet is a network, you shouldn't think of it as a single network. It's really a collection of countless smaller networks, all of which agree to "talk the same language" in order to communicate across the Internet.

Transmission Control Protocol/Internet Protocol (TCP/IP) is the means by which these networks communicate. It's this network *protocol* (the rules of the road) that makes the Internet the Internet.

The bottom line is that a client computer in Sausalito, such as Amanda and Alan's, can connect to a Unix server in San Francisco, which then connects over the Internet to a Windows NT server in London and receives information such as Aunt Fiona's kitty pics.

There are many ways to access data on the Internet, such as by using the File Transfer Protocol (FTP), a program that transfers files from one computer to another. But there's one method for accessing the Internet that has taken the world by storm; it allows companies and individuals to publish newspapers and magazines, open online retail stores, offer online catalogs and reference material, and yes, even publish their favorite cat pictures—the World Wide Web.

The World Wide Web

The rocket fuel for the Internet's dizzying rise is the World Wide Web (WWW, or simply, the Web). The creation of the Web in the early 1990s vastly improved the way you access data on the Internet.

> **NOTE**
>
> In this book, you'll see the word *web* used frequently in different contexts. The word *Web* (capitalized) refers to the World Wide Web; the term *Web site*, or just plain *site*, refers to a collection of files on the Web that you access with a browser. A *FrontPage web* (lowercase), or simply a *web*, is a Web site that you've created in FrontPage. Realize that it's not always easy, or even necessary, to distinguish between a Web site and the Web because the network and the computers connected to it must all function together.

The network language of the Web is called the *Hypertext Transfer Protocol*, or HTTP. Each file, or resource, on the Web is identified by its *Uniform Resource Locator* (URL), which is its address, or location on the Web. URLs begin with a protocol name, such as HTTP, and look something like this:

```
http://www.sybex.com
```

The software by which you access data on the Web is the *browser*, which is essentially a file viewer. There are several popular browsers available, including Microsoft Internet Explorer and Netscape Navigator.

Here's the nutshell overview of how you open a resource (file) on the Web:

- In your browser, specify the URL of the Web resource you would like to access.
- The browser sends that request to the server with which you're communicating.
- The server then forwards the request to the server at the URL you specified.
- That server sends back the resource to your server.
- Finally, your server sends the resource back to your browser.

This may sound complicated, but all this usually happens in less than a second, no matter where on the Internet the resource may be located. It's really no different (at least, from your own perspective) than picking up the telephone, dialing a phone number (URL), and having the worldwide phone system make the connection.

Once you have opened a resource in your browser, you can view it, print it, or save it to your local disk. Basically, it's yours to play with.

Note that when a Web browser receives a file it cannot handle (a file type with which it is not familiar), it may ask you if you'd like to save that file to disk, in which case you could work with the file later on. Otherwise, it will pass the file along to the computer's operating system, which will then open the appropriate program (assuming there is one) for that file.

Web Sites, Pages, and Links

When you want to create documents, or *pages*, that Web browsers can read, you use the *Hypertext Markup Language* (HTML). By encoding a file in HTML, you can create the content and define the structure and format of the Web page.

HTML files are always just plain text files, so you can send a page to virtually any type of computer in the world (as long as it's connected to the Internet, of course). The trick is that when a browser opens a page, it interprets the HTML code and displays the page as you intended.

> **NOTE** You will actually find that the same page may not appear quite the same when it's displayed in different browsers. This is because the "look" of a page is not hardwired into the HTML language. Rather, the look is merely "described" and the browser is responsible for coming up with a suitable representation. This may sound like a weakness in the Web, but it's actually a great strength—browsers on completely dissimilar computers will still be able to present reasonably similar renditions of the same page.

The very best aspect of the World Wide Web is the ability to embed links within pages. A *hyperlink*, or *hotspot* or just plain *link*, is text (usually signified by being underlined and in a different color) or a graphic image that you can click with your mouse to access the target resource of that link anywhere on the Web. Hyperlinks are a quick, easy, and very effective way to let you jump from one URL to another.

The term *Web site* describes a collection of resources that all relate to one topic, and should therefore be considered as one body of information. The resources in a Web site are often all located on one server, but they don't need to be.

A *home page* is the initial page that you see when you access a Web site without specifying the name of a specific file at that location. The home page often serves as a welcome mat or a table of contents, or it might give instructions for accessing the other resources in the site.

> **TIP** If this book's plethora of jargon begins to obfuscate your cerebral faculties, you might find some assuagement with the glossary in Appendix B.

The Internet versus an Intranet

All of the issues discussed in the previous sections relate to the global Internet and the World Wide Web. But you can also set up a local, browseable TCP/IP network that takes advantage of HTML pages, links, URLs, Web sites, and the rest but isn't necessarily connected to the global Internet. Such a network is called an *intranet*, and differs from the Internet only because it is not accessible to every Internet-connected computer in the world.

In this day and age, it's quite likely that the computers on a local network already have Web-browsing software installed; that's all that's needed from the client end of things. And the users of those computers are probably already familiar with browsing the WWW and would therefore be just as ready to browse an intranet.

Once you've set up an intranet, it would be easy to open up just part of it to the Internet at large because all the resources on the intranet would already be in a WWW-ready format.

Finally, the browsing and linking concept of the Web is amazingly effective at letting multiple client computers share the same resource via their browsers. And it works as well for communications between offices within a company as it does between countries on separate continents.

Publishing Pages on the Web

Because you create HTML-encoded files with ordinary text, you can do so in any text editor, such as Windows Notepad or the DOS program Edit. You'll find that creating simple Web pages in this way is not at all difficult and can be a rewarding experience as well. For creating more elaborate pages—those beyond just "simple,"—the job is much better left to a dedicated HTML editor (see "The FrontPage Editor" later in this chapter).

Now we'll take a quick look at HTML, and you'll see just how straightforward this language really is.

> **TIP**
>
> Remember that we're talking about the raw, ungarnished language of the Web. When you create Web pages in the FrontPage Editor, you'll usually be well-shielded from the underlying HTML code.

The Hypertext Markup Language

A Web page is made up of different *elements*, each of which is defined by an HTML code, or *tag*. A tag is always enclosed in angle brackets, and most tags come in pairs, with an opening and a closing tag. The closing tag is the same as the opening tag but starts with a forward slash.

For example, to define text as a first-level heading in HTML, you use the <H1> tag, as in:

    <H1>This is a Main Heading</H1>

A browser will interpret these tags and display the text within the tags appropriately (as shown here). The tags themselves are not displayed within a browser, unless there is a problem with a tag. Most browsers will ignore any codes within angle brackets that they do not recognize but will display what should have been a code if, for example, one of the angle brackets was mistakenly left out.

Some tags have optional or required attributes. For example, the heading tag can take an optional alignment attribute:

    <H1 ALIGN=CENTER>This is a main heading that is centered</H1>

Note that the case in which you write a tag does not matter; the tags <H1> and <h1> are equivalent.

Browsers also ignore multiple spaces within a Web page, displaying them as a single space. All hard returns within the HTML code are ignored as well so any blank lines you create in the code by hitting Enter a few times will not be displayed in the browser.

The Essentials of a Web Page

Every Web page must include a few tags that define the page as a whole when a browser receives the page it will recognize it as such. Shown here is an example of a complete (although quite short) HTML page. You could create this page in Notepad and save it to disk under a name such as SAMPLE.HTM:

```
<HTML>
<HEAD>
<TITLE>Greetings from the Web</TITLE>
</HEAD>
<BODY>
<P>Hello, world!</P>
</BODY>
</HTML>
```

You could then open the resulting file in a Web browser, such as in Microsoft Internet Explorer (see Figure 1.1). You can see the text *Hello, world!* in the browser's main window, and the page's title *Greetings from the Web* in the browser's title bar. All the other text in the previous code consists of HTML tags, which define the Web page but do not actually appear in the page when you view it.

Of course, there are many, many HTML tags you can use to create pages for the Web; the previous example was just the bare minimum needed to define a page.

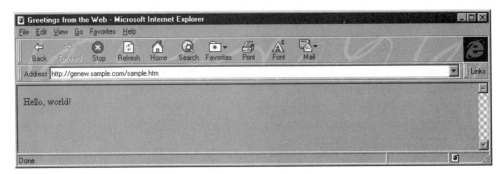

FIGURE 1.1: The sample page displayed in a Web browser

> **NOTE** Keep in mind that HTML is an evolving language, with new tags being proposed (practically every day) as additions to the accepted language. You'll find that FrontPage supports the most commonly recognized and popular tags so the pages you create can be read by virtually any browser on the market. However, FrontPage does offer just a few tags that are Microsoft's own invention, which can be interpreted only by Internet Explorer (although by the time you read this, they may have already been accepted as standard HTML).

Learning HTML

You'll find snippets of HTML code appearing throughout this book; although, you won't need to remember them, study them, or grow weary of them to be a successful Web publisher. That's why FrontPage is the solution to Web publishing—it can handle the subtle nuances (as well as the drudgery) of the language.

In fact, that's exactly what you do when you type a document in a word processor. You simply tell the program to display a word in boldface type, for example, and that's how the word will appear in the printout. You avoid having to know the special code that the word processor actually sent to the printer to print that word in boldface type.

> **TIP** Even though we'll leave the bulk of the coding to the software, understanding the basics of HTML will make your Web publishing jobs a lot easier, just as understanding the concepts of files and folders makes navigating your hard disk easier.

You can learn a lot about HTML by seeing the tags that underlie the document you are either creating or viewing:

- In the FrontPage Editor, use the View ➤ HTML command, which displays in a separate window the actual HTML code for the page you are editing.

- Most Web browsers also allow you to look at the underlying HTML code for the page you are viewing. For example, in Microsoft Internet Explorer, the View ➤ Source command displays the code in Notepad, as shown here.

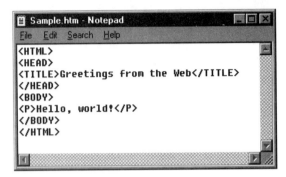

Although you don't have to spend a lot of time studying the source code for HTML pages, I encourage you to become familiar with the more common tags, and see them in the context of a page full of HTML code. That will prepare you to learn more about the HTML language and to understand how the FrontPage Editor produces a Web page.

When the time comes that you want to add a new, as yet unsupported HTML tag into a page in the FrontPage Editor, you'll find the job a snap (as described in "Inserting Extended HTML Code" in Chapter 4).

Keeping a Web Site Together

Publishing an HTML page on the Internet or your intranet is a pretty straightforward task, except that you almost never publish just a single page all by itself. The beauty (and complexity) of the Web lies in its interconnections (links) and the way one page can refer to many others and, with the click of a mouse, actually bring them to you.

A robust Web site will contain many interconnected resources, including HTML pages, graphical images, multimedia sound and video files, and other documents that you might save on your hard drive. Tying all those Web resources together are the links you create in the pages, which are called *internal* links when they target resources within the current Web site. You will also have many *external* links, via URLs, to resources outside of your Web site.

One of the most important, yet time-consuming, Web-site management chores is keeping all those links intact:

- If you delete a resource from your Web site, you must remember to eliminate or revise any links to it from any of the other pages.

- If you rename a resource in your Web site, you darn well better revise the name in any links to it.
- You must test links to external resources on a regular basis to ensure that those links are still valid.
- When you bring a new page into your Web site, you must remember to bring along any other resources it needs, such as image files.

A Web site with numerous "dead" links, or links that go nowhere, is a sure sign of a soon-to-be dead Web site. But as you'll learn later, you can let FrontPage handle these issues with its Explorer, and you can use its To Do List to keep track of all the chores that need to be done.

The FrontPage Solution to Web Publishing

All of the issues discussed so far in this chapter have traditionally made the job of creating and running a Web site difficult and time consuming. Enter the Web-smart components of FrontPage 97:

Personal Web Server: Two "personal-sized" Web servers that allow you to create, test, revise, and host a Web site while under server control.

Server Extensions: Add-on programs for Web server software that make the server "FrontPage-aware" and able to interact more closely with FrontPage webs.

Explorer: A Web-site management tool that shows you all the resources in the site, lets you add, remove, and rename resources, and keeps all the hyperlinks up to date.

> **NOTE** Don't confuse the FrontPage Explorer with all the other Explorers that Microsoft produces—its Internet Explorer is a Web browser, and its Windows Explorer is the disk and file navigation tool for Windows.

Editor: A powerful HTML editor that lets you produce Web-ready pages while working in what is really an easy-to-use word processor.

To Do List: A convenient way to keep track of all the large and small tasks that need to be completed on your FrontPage web.

Image Composer: An image editor that allows you to create images for any Web site, import them, modify them, adjust them, embellish them, and otherwise slop paint on the old e-canvas.

In the sections that follow, we'll take a short look at these FrontPage components so you can see how each one simplifies your task of creating and running a Web site.

The Personal Web Server

FrontPage 97 comes with two personal Web servers (PWS) that can host your Web site as you build, test, and maintain it. The FrontPage Personal Web Server has always been a part of the FrontPage package. The Microsoft Personal Web Server is a newer, more sophisticated server that is actually a subset of the Internet Information Server (IIS) that comes with Windows NT. It will eventually supplant the FrontPage PWS.

Both of the servers fulfill three important functions:

Local Server: With a PWS running on your PC, you can build and test your Web site on a single computer, without being connected to a network and a server. This means you are free to work on your Web site on a portable computer, for example, seated comfortably in a beach chair miles from any telephone lines.

Server Functions: A PWS works hand-in-hand with the other components in FrontPage while you build your Web site. For example, it lets the FrontPage Explorer access any of the Web sites that are located under the PWS and provides password security, as well.

Host Server: You can host your site with a PWS, which may be all the server you need.

With a PWS acting as the server, you can use a Web browser to test your Web site on your local computer. The PWS will check a user's access authorization if needed, fetch requested pages, respond to clicks on image maps, and respond to FrontPage WebBots when they are activated (WebBots are FrontPage automation tools that are discussed in Chapter 10).

You'll take best advantage of all that the FrontPage package has to offer when you run a FrontPage-aware server, such as a PWS, every time you work on a FrontPage web. In fact, if you're using the FrontPage PWS, the FrontPage Explorer will start it automatically when the server is needed, such as when you want to open a FrontPage web. By default, the Microsoft PWS starts when you start your computer (see Chapter 14 for more on these servers).

> **NOTE** The corollary to this is that you should avoid making changes to a FrontPage web or its pages, links, or other files while outside of a server and the FrontPage Explorer. At best, those changes would go unnoticed by FrontPage; at worst, they could throw the web into disarray and cause real problems for FrontPage.

The FrontPage Server Extensions

You'll get the most out of your FrontPage webs when your Web server is FrontPage-aware. For example, the two personal Web servers discussed in the previous section are FrontPage-ready. Microsoft offers the FrontPage Server Extensions to add FrontPage capabilities to many widely used servers, such as Windows NT 4 Server with the Internet Information Server (IIS), Apache, O'Reilly WebSite, and Netscape Communications Server. Some of the benefits of the Server Extensions include the ability to

- Automate common Web page and Web site tasks with FrontPage WebBots.
- Enable Web site security for both Web authors and browsers.
- Copy an entire Web site and all of its FrontPage facilities from one FrontPage-aware server to another.
- Import a Web site into the FrontPage environment from a non-FrontPage–aware server.

FrontPage comes with versions of the Server Extensions for several different servers, and you can find more versions on Microsoft's Web site

```
http://www.microsoft.com/frontpage/
```

where they are available for free.

You will also find an updated list of operating systems and Web servers for which the FrontPage Server Extensions are available. If your server cannot support the FrontPage Server Extensions, keep the following in mind:

- By default, FrontPage uses the name `INDEX.HTM` for the home page in a web under the FrontPage PWS, and `DEFAULT.HTM` under the Microsoft PWS; you may need to change either FrontPage or your server so they each use the same home page name (see "Changing the Name of the Home Page" in Chapter 14).

- You can still include many of FrontPage's WebBots in your Web pages, but you should not use those that require server interaction. These include the WebBots named Confirmation Field, Discussion, Registration, Save Results, and Search.
- To create clickable image maps in the pages in a web, choose one of the non-FrontPage image map styles for that web, such as client-side image maps (see "Creating Clickable Image Maps" in Chapter 8).
- When you copy a FrontPage web to a non-FrontPage Web server, such as by using the Web Publishing Wizard or FTP, you can exclude any folders in your site whose names begin with `_VTI_`. These folders are FrontPage-related and are not needed when a server does not have the FrontPage Server Extensions.

If the host server does not support the FrontPage Server Extensions, you should still take advantage of their capabilities when you create your Web site by working under one of the Personal Web Servers.

The FrontPage Explorer

You use the FrontPage Explorer for creating, revising, and managing a Web site; it is covered in detail in Chapters 2 and 3. The Explorer works in conjunction with a FrontPage-aware server, such as the Personal Web Server.

From the Explorer, you can open any FrontPage web to which you are allowed access on any of the servers available to the Explorer. Figure 1.2 shows the Explorer in its Hyperlink view with an open web.

The left side of the Explorer lists all the pages and other files that make up the resources of the web. It displays either their page titles or, if they have no titles, their file names. At the top of the list of Web resources is the home page, such as the file named `INDEX.HTM` when the server is the FrontPage PWS.

The resources are arranged in a hierarchical manner, based on the links each page contains. You can manipulate the outline in the usual Windows manner—click on the plus sign to expand a level of the outline to show more detail or click on the minus sign to hide the detail.

The right side of the Explorer in Figure 1.2 displays a graphical representation of the web, with lines connecting a page to any resources it either includes or links to. This is a real peek behind the scenes of your web because it reveals the normally hidden relationships among its resources.

Publishing a Web with FrontPage   17

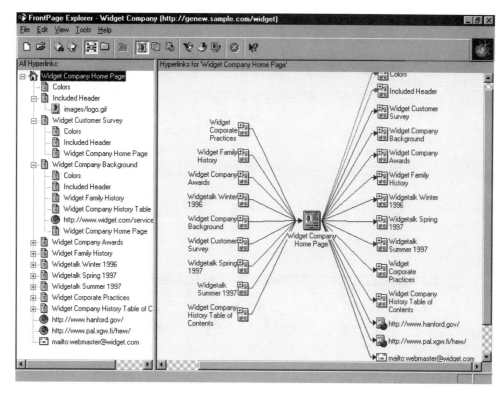

FIGURE 1.2: The FrontPage Explorer lists the files in a Web site and displays them as a map based on their links.

You can also display a Folder view in the Explorer, which lists each folder and file in the web, along with its size, the date and time it was last modified, the person who modified it, its URL, and any comments that have been attached to it.

Together, these views let you see and manipulate the FrontPage web as a whole, instead of your having to work with and keep track of separate and seemingly unrelated files.

The FrontPage Editor

As you learned earlier, you create an HTML document by using tags to define the structure and format of a Web page. When someone views that page in a Web browser, the browser displays the contents of the page in accordance with the HTML tags you used.

The FrontPage solution for creating Web pages is the FrontPage Editor; it is discussed starting in Chapter 4. It is essentially a WYSIWYG word processor that has two important Web-authoring virtues:

- It is designed to work specifically with HTML pages and offers you just about all the page-layout options that are available in the most recent version of HTML.
- When you create a page in the Editor, you are assured the HTML tags in that page will be compliant with the HTML standard and can therefore be viewed in any Web browser (assuming the browser supports the version of the HTML tags you included in the page).

Figure 1.3 shows the Editor and a Web page open for editing. The Editor has many of the tools and features you have come to expect in a Windows word processor. For example, you can open multiple documents in the Editor, and copy and paste data between them in the usual ways.

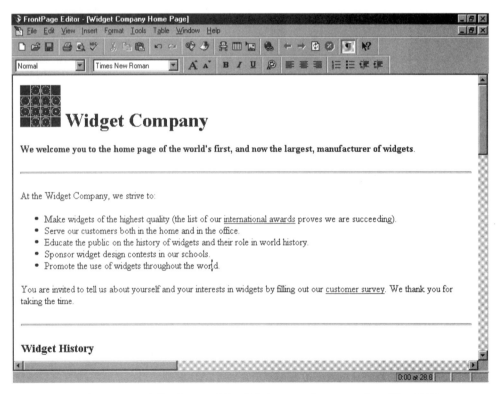

FIGURE 1.3: The FrontPage Editor is essentially a Windows word processor for editing HTML pages.

> **NOTE** If you use Microsoft Word or other programs in Microsoft Office, you'll find that the Editor is carved from the same block of granite. You'll recognize many of its features and commands, and should find it a comfortable place in which to get right to work. The Editor even shares the Office spelling dictionary and thesaurus.

The FrontPage To Do List

Creating and maintaining a Web site is no small feat, at least not if you want to do the job well. You will need to attend to countless Web-related tasks, large and small. To help you keep track of these tasks, FrontPage offers the To Do List, which is discussed in Chapter 3 and shown in Figure 1.4.

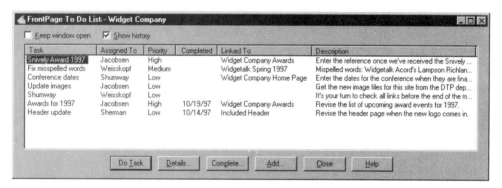

FIGURE 1.4: The FrontPage To Do List helps you manage Web-related tasks.

When you invoke the Edit ➤ Add To Do Task command in either the Explorer or the Editor, the task you create in the To Do List is automatically linked to the page or file that is active in the Editor or selected in the Explorer. When you later select the linked task in the To Do List and click the Do Task button, the linked file will automatically open for you to complete the task.

There is one To Do List for tracking tasks in every FrontPage web. Anyone working on the site can create a new entry for a task and include information such as a name for the task, to whom it's assigned, its priority, the resource to which it is linked, and a description of the task. You can sort the items in the To Do List by clicking a column-title button at the top of any of the columns.

When you actually finish a task, you can mark it as completed in the To Do List, and either delete it from the list or retain that task as a history of jobs completed.

Image Composer

A Web site without a few images is like a, well, you can fill in the rest. Essentially, the World Wide Web would not be the exciting place that it is if it weren't for the rich and varied use of graphical images in the millions of pages on the Web.

Because images play such a crucial role in bringing a Web site to life, FrontPage comes with Microsoft Image Composer. With this program you can create images, add clip art and photos, open many different image file formats, and add a wide range of special effects to your work. You'll find it discussed in Chapter 9.

Now that you've had an introduction to the Internet, the World Wide Web, Web sites, and FrontPage, we'll look at how you can create and manage Web sites in the FrontPage Explorer.

Chapter 2

WORKING WITH WEBS IN THE EXPLORER

FEATURING

- **Working with the active web in the Explorer**
- **Creating a new web from a template or Wizard**
- **Specifying the location for the new web**
- **Opening an existing web**
- **Closing the active web**
- **Creating a web from an existing, non-FrontPage Web site**
- **Importing and exporting files**
- **Publishing a FrontPage web to a server**
- **Renaming, moving, and deleting a web**

The FrontPage Explorer is your Web site navigation center, the place where you start and finish your work on a site. This chapter shows you how to work with a FrontPage web as a whole, along with, of course, a FrontPage-aware server such as FrontPage's Personal Web Server.

Working in the Active Web

In the FrontPage Explorer, you work with one FrontPage web at a time, which is called the *current* or *active* web. When you use the File ➤ Open command in the FrontPage Editor, for example, you can choose to open one of the Web pages from the active web in the Explorer. Any new pages you create and save in the Editor will become part of the active web, unless you specify otherwise.

One bonus of the FrontPage Explorer is that you don't have to worry about saving your work. Unlike the individual Web pages you work on in the FrontPage Editor, there is no File ➤ Save command in the Explorer. Any changes you make to a web are saved automatically.

> **NOTE** Because the Explorer saves changes to a web automatically, you should always exit from the Explorer only *after* you have exited from the FrontPage Editor. That way, the Explorer will be aware of any changes you make to pages in the Editor.

Each FrontPage web can have one home page. When the FrontPage Personal Web Server (PWS) is hosting this site, the home page is named `INDEX.HTM` by default. When a browser accesses the web (the folder on the server) without specifying a particular page or other resource, such as

```
http://www.host.com/web_site/
```

this home page is the page that will open automatically.

If the server that will ultimately be hosting your web expects a different name for a home page, you can change the default name that FrontPage uses (see "Changing the Name of the Home Page" in Chapter 14).

One thing you'll need in order to create, open, or otherwise modify a FrontPage web is permission to do so—not from your mother, but from the server that hosts that web.

When you start the Explorer and try to create a new web, you will be prompted for your name and password, as shown here. Both the name and password are case-sensitive, so be sure to enter them exactly as you created them. If your entries match those stored on the server, your new web will be created. Otherwise, you'll have another chance to enter your name and password again.

> **NOTE** If you're running FrontPage under a server other than the Personal Web Server that comes with FrontPage, access rights to the web will be determined by that server. The password and logging in procedure will vary from server to server.

When you first install FrontPage, you will need to assign access rights to an administrator for the FrontPage *root web*, which is usually the folder `\FrontPage Webs\Content`. The administrator has full access rights to all webs within the root web. In "Keeping Your Web Secure" in Chapter 14, you'll read about adding other administrators, authors, and users to the root web or to individual webs within the root web.

Creating a New FrontPage Web

You'll tap into the power of FrontPage if you use it from Day One to build your Web site, especially when you use it hand-in-hand with a FrontPage-aware server. Doing so will simplify much of your Web site building and maintenance tasks.

Here are the steps you follow to create a new FrontPage web; each is discussed in the following sections:

1. In the FrontPage Explorer, choose File ➤ New ➤ FrontPage Web (Ctrl+N) or click the New FrontPage Web button on the toolbar.

2. In the New FrontPage Web dialog box, choose a template or Wizard on which to base the new Web and click OK.
3. Next select a server on which to create the web, enter a name for the web, and click OK.

The Explorer builds the new site in a folder off of the root web, which will contain all the FrontPage-related folders and files needed for the new site. So if you create a new web named `MyWeb` under the Personal Web Server, a folder called

```
\FrontPage Webs\Content\MyWeb
```

will be created. Under a different server, the path to `MyWeb` could be different.

> **NOTE** Under the control of the Personal Web Server, you must have the permission level of an administrator in order to create a new FrontPage web. If you have not yet provided your name and password during this session in the Explorer, you will be prompted to do so before the new web is created. Permissions are discussed in "Keeping Your Web Secure" in Chapter 14.

When you start the FrontPage Explorer or close a FrontPage web in the Explorer, the Getting Started with Microsoft FrontPage dialog box is displayed by default (shown in Figure 2.1). To create a new web, select one of the three options in the Create a New FrontPage Web group. The first and third options are discussed in the next section; the Import Wizard is discussed later in this chapter in "Creating a FrontPage Web from an Existing Web Site."

You can also open an existing FrontPage web with either of the two choices in the Open a FrontPage Web group. The first option opens the web that you most recently opened in the Explorer. The second option displays the Open FrontPage Web dialog box, as though you had used the File ➤ Open FrontPage Web command, which is discussed later in this chapter in "Opening and Closing an Existing Web."

Choosing a Template or Wizard

FrontPage's templates and Wizards make creating a Web site as easy as you can get. The process is similar to creating a new Web page in the FrontPage Editor. In the Explorer, choose File ➤ New ➤ FrontPage Web or click the New FrontPage Web button on the toolbar to display the New FrontPage Web dialog box (shown in Figure 2.2).

Working with Webs in the Explorer 27

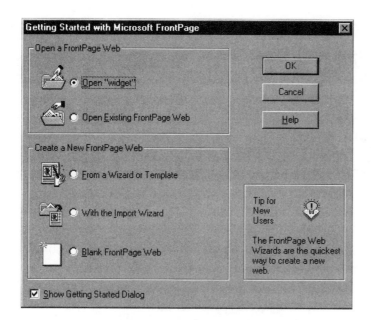

FIGURE 2.1:
The Getting Started with Microsoft FrontPage dialog box lets you open an existing Web or create a new one.

FIGURE 2.2:
You can choose a template or a Wizard in the New FrontPage Web dialog box.

> **NOTE** When you already have a web open in the Explorer, the New FrontPage Web dialog box offers an option called Add to the Current Web. If you select this option, all the pages associated with the new web will be imported into the current web. If an incoming file has the same name as an existing file, such as `INDEX.HTM`, you will be asked to choose which one you want to keep.

Each FrontPage web template contains a set of pages that can serve as the basis for the web you build (you'll know if a new web is based on a template if its name doesn't end with *Wizard*). For example, a new web based on the Project Web template can help you and other members of a team oversee a specific project:

- The Members page lets you keep track of who's involved in the project and includes a place for a picture of each member.
- The Schedule page lets you keep track of the project's schedule.
- The Status page offers you a place to create links to monthly, quarterly, and annual status reports for the project.
- The Search page lets you search all of the pages in the web for text you specify.
- The Archive page is a storehouse of links to related resources that may reside outside of the web.
- The Discussion page provides a central place to link to discussion groups in the web.

The Project Web contains a home page that includes a What's New section, a send mail link, a header and footer that are shared with the other pages in the Web site, and links to the other pages.

But using a template is not as restrictive as it may sound; when you start a new FrontPage web from a template, you are free to revise any of the pages, add new pages, or remove pages from the site. The template simply serves as a helpful and convenient way to get started.

Besides the Project Web, here's a quick rundown of the other templates:

Normal Web: Creates a web that contains only a blank home page that serves as a starting point.

Working with Webs in the Explorer

Customer Support Web: Creates a web that gives your customers a place to come to get information or help with your products.

Empty Web: Contains all the necessary folders for a new FrontPage web, but contains no pages or other resources.

Learning FrontPage: Contains all the Web resources you'll need to work through the FrontPage tutorial, which you access with the Learning FrontPage topic in the Help system's table of contents.

Personal Web: Creates a web that an individual in a company could use to provide personal and job-related information.

> **NOTE** Remember that each new FrontPage web has many other files and folders that are used only by FrontPage and are an essential part of the web. This is also discussed later in this chapter in "The Folders in a FrontPage Web."

When you choose a Wizard in the New FrontPage Web dialog box, the Wizard will ask you a series of questions about the content of the new Web site. For example, it may ask you about the type of pages you want in the web, the contents of the home page, and the contents of a feedback form page. It will then build the pages accordingly.

Here are the Wizards for creating a new FrontPage web:

Corporate Presence Wizard: Helps you design a web that can be the basis for your company's debut on the Web.

Discussion Web Wizard: Helps you design a web that lets visitors leave messages or respond to messages, and organizes the messages in related threads.

Import Web Wizard: Helps you import an existing, non-FrontPage web into a FrontPage web; this is the same as choosing File ➤ Import in the Explorer.

Choosing a Location for the Web

When you select a template or Wizard on which to base your web and then click OK in the New FrontPage Web dialog box, the dialog box shown in Figure 2.3 prompts you for a location and name for the new web.

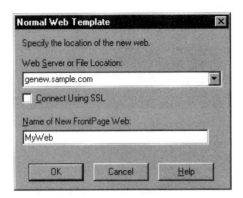

FIGURE 2.3:
When creating a new web, you need to specify a location and name.

The dialog box offers the following choices:

Web Server or File Location: Choose to create the FrontPage web either under the control of a Web server or on disk but outside of any Web-server control. You can type in a server location or a folder name, or choose one from the drop-down list.

Name of New FrontPage Web: Enter a name for the new web, which will be the actual name used for the site's folder within either the root web (usually \FrontPage Webs\Content) or the folder you selected outside of Web-server control. Therefore, the name must conform to the naming conventions used by the server or the operating system. The name you specify will also be used for the new web's title. Once created, you can change either the name or the title, as discussed later in this chapter in "Renaming a Web Site."

When you click the OK button, the new Web site will be created under the name and server or folder you specified. However, if you usually must provide your name and password to modify webs in the Explorer and you have not yet done so in this session, you will be prompted to do so before the server will create the new web.

> **NOTE** Don't worry if you make a mistake in any of the choices you've made so far—you can always just delete the web in the Explorer and start another new one (deleting a web is discussed in "Renaming, Moving, or Deleting a Web Site" later in this chapter).

The Folders in a FrontPage Web

A FrontPage web contains not only the files you create in it, but several other folders and files, as well, that are created when you create a new web. These are used by FrontPage to manage and run your web under a FrontPage-aware server. The names of most of these folders begin with an underscore, such as _VTI_PVT (shown here), and will be invisible in the FrontPage Explorer, as well as to a Web browser under a FrontPage-aware server.

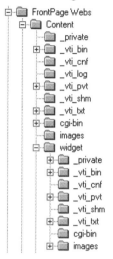

Most of these folders are strictly for FrontPage's own use, and you should therefore *not* change or delete them. But there are three folders that you are free to use as you need them:

Images: This is a convenient folder in which to store image files, such as GIF and JPEG files. When you create a new FrontPage web, you may find that this folder already contains some image files for use in the web. For example, you can include the file UNDERCON.GIF in Web pages that are still under construction.

_Private: This folder will be not be visible to browsers so any files in it will be invisible, as well. The contents of this folder will be visible in the FrontPage Explorer, however, unlike the other FrontPage folders that begin with the underscore character.

Cgi-Bin: Use this folder for CGI scripts or other Web-executable files.

Opening and Closing an Existing Web

To open an existing FrontPage web in the Explorer, use the File ➤ Open FrontPage Web command or click the Open FrontPage Web button on the toolbar. The Open FrontPage Web dialog box is similar to the one you find when you are creating a new web, as discussed earlier in this chapter in "Choosing a Location for the Web."

In this case, you can select a server or folder, or type in the name of one, and then click the List Webs button. This displays a list of the titles of all the available FrontPage webs on the chosen server or folder. Select the one you want and then click the OK button to open that web.

> **NOTE** If a FrontPage web's title is different from its actual folder name, the folder name will appear in parentheses after the title in the Open FrontPage Web dialog box.

As always, if you have not yet entered your username and password during this session in FrontPage, you will be prompted to do so before the web can be opened.

You can choose File ➤ Close FrontPage Web at any time to close the active FrontPage web in the Explorer. You don't have to worry about losing any changes you've made because the Explorer saves them automatically. Because you can only have one web open at a time in the Explorer, the active web will be closed when you open another one.

Let me emphasize once more that before you close a FrontPage web in the Explorer, you should first close any pages from that web that you are working on in the FrontPage Editor. This will ensure that the Explorer can update the web with any changes you've made to the pages.

> **NOTE** If you plan to create a new web or open an existing one, you may want to jump over the rest of this chapter for now, and go on to Chapter 3. There you will learn how to work with the links and files of your web in the Explorer. If you're not yet working with an entire Web site but are ready to create some individual HTML Web pages, you could move ahead to Chapter 4.

Creating a FrontPage Web from an Existing Web Site

The FrontPage Explorer and Personal Web Server aren't much use if you already have a Web site that was not created in FrontPage. You can certainly use the FrontPage Editor to edit the pages in that Web site, but you can't open the site in the Explorer, update its links automatically, include FrontPage WebBots, and so on.

But it's easy to create a new FrontPage web from an existing site, which will allow you to continue your work on the site within FrontPage:

1. Start in the FrontPage Explorer without a web open. If a web is already open, choose File ➤ Close FrontPage Web.
2. Choose File ➤ Import (you can also use this command to import files into the active web in the Explorer, as discussed later in this chapter in "Importing and Exporting Files").
3. You will see the Import Web Wizard dialog box (similar to the one shown earlier in Figure 2.3), in which you specify a location (either a server or a folder on disk) and name for the new Web site. Then click OK, which will create the necessary FrontPage folders in the specified location for the incoming Web files.
4. Now the Import Web Wizard will prompt you to enter the directory (folder) in which the existing Web site resides. Click the Browse button, select that folder, and choose OK.
5. If there are folders within that folder that should also be imported, be sure to select the Include Subdirectories option in the Wizard. Then click the Next button.
6. The Wizard then offers you a list of all the files in the existing Web, and lets you select the ones to import (see Figure 2.4). All the displayed file names will be imported; to exclude one or more files, just select them in the list and click the Exclude button. You can select multiple file names in the usual way—click and Shift+click to select a group of contiguous files, or Ctrl+click to select noncontiguous files. When you are ready, click the Next button.
7. The last step offers you the chance to go back to a previous step or cancel the operation, if necessary. Otherwise, choose Finish.

The files from the existing Web site will be imported into the new one, which is now ready for you to continue working on it from within FrontPage.

Note that if there was not already a folder within the existing Web site called `Images`, FrontPage will create a new folder with that name. It will not, however, move any of the existing image files into it.

If you'd like to keep all your image files there, which is one of the FrontPage standards (a convenience but not required), you are free to do so within the Explorer at any time. You can read about this later in this chapter in "Renaming, Moving, or Deleting a Web Site."

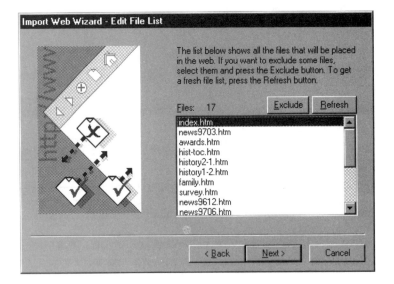

FIGURE 2.4: You can exclude any files that you do not want to import into the Web site.

Importing and Exporting Files

In the course of building and maintaining your FrontPage web, you will need to bring in many different types of files. You will incorporate images into your pages, where each image is a separate file. You may also have a page that plays a tune or makes an announcement when that page is opened, which would be handled by sound files in your web.

Of course, the beauty of the Internet and the WWW is that you can build a Web site whose contents (pages and other files) reside anywhere on the WWW; they need not all reside in the same location. Nonetheless, even if a file is accessible outside of your site, if you want to be sure that the file will always be available you should keep it within the confines of your own site.

> **TIP**
>
> You can import files into the active FrontPage web in the Explorer, and you can also export files from the site so copies of the files are sent to the locations you specify. In the FrontPage Editor, you can open a wide variety of file types that will be converted into standard HTML Web pages as they are opened. These types include rich text format (RTF), text, Microsoft Word, and WordPerfect. Chapter 5 discusses opening and saving files.

Importing Files

You can import any file into the active FrontPage web with the File ➤ Import command. This is the same command that was discussed earlier in this chapter in "Creating a FrontPage Web from an Existing Web Site." But in this case with a web already open, the command allows you to bring existing files into the active web.

Not only will the imported files be copied into the web's location on the server, but FrontPage will also parse any incoming HTML pages in order to keep track of any hyperlinks they contain.

The Explorer will warn you if an imported file will overwrite an existing file of the same name. You can choose whether to import the file and replace the existing one. Here's how you import one or more files into the active web:

1. Choose File ➤ Import, which will display the Import File to FrontPage Web dialog box. This is shown in Figure 2.5, with a list of files already in it.
2. Click the Add File button, which displays a standard files dialog box. If you choose the Add Folder button, you can select a folder and all the files and subfolders within it; they will be imported into a folder of the same name in your web.
3. Select a folder and then choose the files you want to import from this folder; you can select multiple files with the Shift+click or Ctrl+click method.
4. Click the Open button, which will once again display the Import File dialog box.

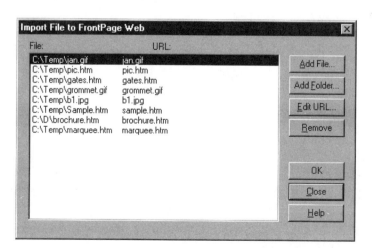

FIGURE 2.5:
The dialog box that lists the files you have selected to import into the active Web.

You will see the files you selected listed in the dialog box. At this point, there are six different buttons from which you can choose:

- **OK:** All file names that are currently in the dialog box will be imported into the active Web. To eliminate files from the list, select the files and click the Remove button. You can use the Shift+click and Ctrl+click methods for selecting multiple files.
- **Add File:** Selects more files to add to the import list.
- **Add Folder:** Selects a folder and all the files and subfolders in it to add to the list.
- **Edit URL:** Edits the URL (file name and location) of the selected file; you might need to rename an incoming file so that it does not overwrite an existing file of the same name. You can also add a folder name to the URL of an incoming file so that the file will be imported into that folder in the active Web.
- **Remove:** Removes the selected file names from the import list, but does not actually delete the files from disk.
- **Close:** Closes the dialog box without importing the files; the list of files will still be there and waiting the next time you choose File ➤ Import, until you close the current Web or open another.

The Explorer will track all the links in the HTML pages you import and incorporate them into the FrontPage web. For example, if an incoming page links to a page named `SUMMARY.HTM`, and a page of that name already exists in the current web, then the incoming page will now link to that page.

All incoming files are placed in the active web's primary folder, unless you have edited the URL of an incoming file and specified a different folder for that file. Once they are in the web, you can move the files to other folders and let the Explorer automatically adjust any links to those files, as described later in "Renaming, Moving, or Deleting a Web Site." For example, you may want to move all GIF and JPEG image files into the folder named `Images` within the current Web site.

Exporting Files

You can select a file name or icon in the Explorer's right-hand pane and export it to another location outside of the Web site. For example, you might want to send a page or image file to a coworker for her to incorporate into the site she is working on.

1. Select the file you want to export.
2. Choose File ➤ Export.

3. In the dialog box, choose the location for the file and enter a file name for it.
4. Click OK to finish the job.

A copy of the file will be created under the name and location you specified. The original file will remain untouched in the current Web.

Publishing a Web to a Server

If you create your FrontPage web on the same server that is hosting it, then the world might be seeing your work virtually as you do it. When you create a FrontPage web somewhere else, however, at some point you'll need to get the finished web onto the host server.

In FrontPage lingo, *publishing* your web is the process of copying it either to a different server or with a different name on the same server. You use the File ➤ Publish FrontPage Web command to do the job.

If you want to publish a web to a server that does not have the FrontPage Server Extensions installed, you will have to follow a somewhat less elegant process (see "Publishing a Web to a Non-FrontPage Server" later in this chapter).

NOTE Publishing your web to a server can be a convenient way to back up the entire web with all its folders and files. The resulting copy will be a fully functional FrontPage web so you could make changes and perform testing on that web while leaving the original unchanged.

Publishing a Web to a FrontPage Server

It's easy to publish (copy) a Web to a FrontPage-aware server—one that includes the FrontPage Server Extensions. For example, when you've been building a Web site on a local PC using a Personal Web Server, you can use the Explorer to copy the site to the Internet or intranet server that will host this site. Just like creating a new web, you must have administrator-level permission to publish a web.

You might also publish a web when you simply want to update the files in the destination site with those you've been creating or revising in FrontPage.

Here's how you copy the active FrontPage web in the Explorer to another FrontPage-aware server:

1. In the Explorer, open the web you wish to publish.
2. Choose File ➤ Publish FrontPage Web.
3. In the Publish FrontPage Web dialog box, shown in Figure 2.6, select the server, or a folder on disk, to which you want to copy the web.

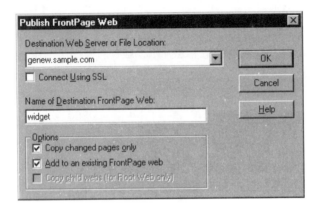

FIGURE 2.6:
You specify a server or folder destination and a name in the Publish FrontPage Web dialog box.

4. Enter a name for the web in the Name of Destination FrontPage Web field. Remember that the web's name will also be used to name the folder in which it resides so the name must follow the naming conventions used on that server.
5. If there is already a FrontPage web of that name, you can choose to combine the current web into the existing destination web. To do so, select the Add to an Existing FrontPage Web check box.
6. If you are only updating the files in an existing web, select the Copy Changed Pages Only check box.
7. If you are copying a FrontPage root web, you can select the Copy Child Webs check box so that all webs within the root web will be also be created at the destination.
8. When you're ready, click OK to finish the job.

If the destination web name you entered did not yet exist within the server's root web, a new folder of that name will be created and the web will be copied there. All the files and folders within that new web will be duplicates of the current web.

Publishing a Web to a Non-FrontPage Server

You can publish a FrontPage web from the Explorer to a server that does not have the FrontPage Server Extensions and is therefore not FrontPage-aware. You can do so either with the traditional File Transfer Protocol (FTP) or with Microsoft's Web Publishing Wizard.

> **NOTE** If you have not yet installed the Web Publishing Wizard, you can do so from the setup program on your FrontPage disk. You can also download it for free from Microsoft's Web site. Go to `http://www.microsoft.com`, and search for it by name.

Of course your Web site won't offer all the FrontPage features that are available under a server with the FrontPage Server Extensions, as discussed in "The FrontPage Server Extensions" in Chapter 1.

Publishing a Web with FTP

You can copy your FrontPage web to any server that supports FTP, just as you can copy any other files to that server. Windows 95 and NT have FTP built-in, but its command-line interface is all too reminiscent of the dog days of DOS.

You'll find an easy-to-use interface on many FTP programs that are on the market. They can make copying files from your system to another virtually painless. Some of these programs are even available free of charge; you can find many FTP programs listed on Yahoo if you search for "FTP software."

As mentioned in Chapter 1, when you are copying a FrontPage web to a server that is not running the FrontPage Server Extensions, you need not include any folders whose names begin with `_VTI_`. These are used only by FrontPage and are not needed outside of it.

Using the Web Publishing Wizard

You can copy your web to a non-FrontPage aware server with Microsoft's Web Publishing Wizard (WPW). This tool will help you copy your web to just about any of the popular Web servers, as long as they're able to run an FTP session. The WPW is a separate program that you can start either from within the FrontPage Explorer or as a stand-alone program.

1. Start in the Explorer and open the web you wish to publish. Follow all the steps for publishing to a FrontPage server that were described in the previous section, "Publishing a Web to a FrontPage Server."
2. When you click OK in the Publish FrontPage Web dialog box (see Figure 2.6), the Explorer will connect with the server you specified. When it finds that the FrontPage Server Extensions are not installed on that server, the Explorer will automatically start the Web Publishing Wizard (WPW) and pass control to it.

> **NOTE** If you know that you will be publishing to a non-FrontPage–aware server, you can run the WPW as a stand-alone program, outside of FrontPage. You should find it on the Windows Start menu under Programs ➤ Accessories ➤ Internet Tools.

3. The WPW walks you through the process of copying your web to the server. It starts by letting you select the folder or just a file that you want to copy (shown in Figure 2.7).
4. Either type in the name of the folder or file that you want to copy, or click the Browse Folders button and select a folder in the usual way. You can instead click the Browse Files button and select a single file.

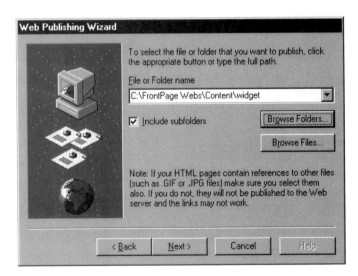

FIGURE 2.7: The Web Publishing Wizard starts by letting you select the folder and files you want to copy to another server.

5. If you selected a folder, you will probably want to select the Include Subfolders check box in the WPW dialog box. This will ensure that your `Images` and `_Private` folders will be included in the copy.
6. Click the Next button to continue, and pick the Web server to which you will be publishing your web (see Figure 2.8).
7. If you've already defined the destination Web server, just select it from the list and click the Next button. Otherwise, click the New button to define a new server. Here are some of the things you'll need to know about the server:
    - The name of your Internet Service Provider (ISP), if you use one to access the WWW. The list of choices includes AOL, CompuServe, and GNN; choose Other Internet Provider if yours is not listed.
    - The URL of your ISP, such as `http://www.host.com`, so the WPW can find the site.
    - The type of connection you make to access the destination Web server, either Network or Dial-Up Networking. If you choose the latter, you then select the connection settings to use.
    - The protocol that the WPW should use to send your web files, either FTP or Windows File Transfer. Select FTP if you're not sure.
    - Your username and password for the destination Web server.
    - The name of the FTP server on the destination server.
    - The name of the destination subfolder on the server, as well as your own root folder on that server (which usually is restricted only to you).

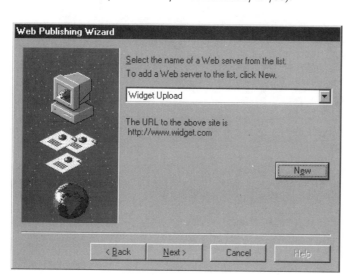

FIGURE 2.8: You specify the server that you wish to send your web to or define settings for a new server.

> **NOTE** If all this sounds a little daunting, don't worry, you're right. It's the Internet and networking in general at its most perplexing. If things go well, the WPW will proceed without even needing to ask you for most of this information.

8. Once you've selected a Web server, click Next to reach the last step.
9. If the Wizard has everything it needs, it will prompt you to click the Finish button. If you want to change any of the information you've entered so far, click the Back button; otherwise click Finish.

The WPW will begin to copy the folder or file you selected to the destination server; a progress meter will give you an idea of how much more there is to go. When it is finished, the WPW will close.

Renaming, Moving, or Deleting a Web Site

You can perform several Web management tasks on the active web from within the Explorer.

> **NOTE** You should only perform these procedures from within the FrontPage Explorer so it can complete the entire job and update its own indexes of your web.

Renaming a Web Site

You name your web when you create it, and that name is also used to name the actual folder on the disk where the web resides. You can rename your web at any time within the FrontPage Explorer.

Select Tools ➤ Web Settings, and choose the Configuration tab in the FrontPage Web Settings dialog box. You'll find two edit fields:

Web Name: The actual name of the web's folder on the server. Any name you enter here must be compatible with the file-naming conventions on that server.

Web Title: The descriptive title of the web that is used only by FrontPage.

You can change the web's title at any time, but because a web's name is part of its URL, you should avoid changing the name once the web has been in service.

Moving a Web Site

There is no specific command for moving a web to another location, but you can do so in two steps. First, copy the web to the new location with the File ➤ Publish FrontPage Web command, as discussed earlier in this chapter. Then use File ➤ Delete FrontPage Web (discussed next) to delete the original Web site.

Deleting a Web Site

You can delete a FrontPage web from its server by opening that web in the FrontPage Explorer and choosing File ➤ Delete FrontPage Web. You will be asked to confirm your decision—for the obvious reasons! If you choose Yes, the web, with all its folders and files, will be erased from the server's disk—completely and irrevocably. So use caution, and be sure you really want to delete a web before you proceed.

In this chapter, you've seen how the FrontPage Explorer can help you create a Web site, add files to it, publish it, and generally maintain it. The next chapter will show you how you can view and manage the links and files within a web in the Explorer, and keep track of ongoing chores with the FrontPage To Do List.

# Chapter 3

MANAGING WEBS IN THE EXPLORER

FEATURING

- Working in the Explorer's Hyperlink view
- Working in the Folder view of your web
- Updating links when you rename or move a file
- Working with file properties
- Associating files with editors or viewers
- Finding text and checking the spelling in the entire web
- Organizing chores with the To Do List

The Explorer gives you an inside look at your FrontPage web and reveals the relationships among all its files. With its ability to update hyperlinks automatically, you are free to add, move, or rename files in your web without worrying about keeping track of every link to them.

If you're not yet working with an entire Web site but are ready to create some individual HTML Web pages, you could move ahead to Chapter 4, which begins the discussion about the FrontPage Editor. You can save your Web pages in the Editor to any location; so you don't have to have a FrontPage web up and running.

However, even if you're not building an entire web at the moment, a quick perusing of this chapter will give you a look at how FrontPage manages the files and hyperlinks in a web, clarifying many issues that can arise when you're creating individual pages in the Editor.

Displaying Your Web in the Hyperlink View

The most important aspect of a Web site is its interconnected "Webness" so to speak. Without the outline and map of the Hyperlink view, this would be pretty much hidden from casual observation—you would have to dig to find out who links to whom.

You can display the active FrontPage web in the FrontPage Explorer in either the Hyperlink or Folder view and switch between the two at any time. In either view, the Explorer window is divided into two panes; drag the vertical divider left or right to change the size of the panes.

When you choose View ➤ Hyperlink View, or click that button on the toolbar, the web is displayed hierarchically, like an outline, according to the hyperlinks in its pages.

The left pane displays a list of all the pages and other files and URLs that are part of the current web (see Figure 3.1). The right pane displays a graphical representation of the web—a map of sorts, which starts with the resource currently selected in the left pane. Pages and other resources are shown as icons in this map view, with arrows connecting a page to the targets of any links it contains or files it includes.

The Explorer also has a Folder view, which is very much like Windows Explorer. The left pane displays the folders contained in the Web site, and the right pane displays all the files in the selected folder, along with detailed file information for each one. (For more about the Folder view, go to "Seeing All Files in the Explorer's Folder View" later in this chapter.)

Managing Webs in the Explorer

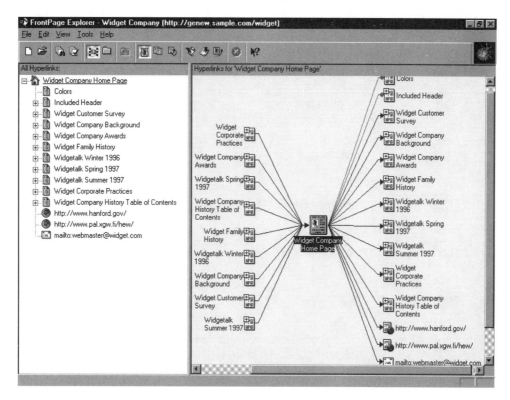

FIGURE 3.1: In the Hyperlink view, the FrontPage Explorer displays your web in a hierarchical view, based on the hyperlinks in its pages.

The Left Pane (Outline) of the Hyperlink View

The left pane of the Hyperlink view lists Web pages by their HTML page title. File names are displayed for graphic images and other files that don't have titles, and URLs are displayed for links to other Web resources.

Each resource has a relevant icon to the left of its name. You can see some examples in Figure 3.1; they're described in Table 3.1.

The resources in the left pane are grouped in a hierarchical manner, where the structure is based on the hyperlinks each page contains. If page A has a link to page B, page B will appear as a subordinate of page A (indented beneath it in the list). Resources included in other resources, such as graphic images displayed in a Web page, will also be shown as subordinate to that resource.

Table 3.1: The Icons Used in the Explorer

Icon	Description
🏠	The Web's home page
📄	A Web page
🖼	A graphic image file (GIF or JPEG)
✉	A link to an e-mail address
🌐	A link to a URL
📋	A broken link that is no longer valid
▲	An error in a Web page, usually in a WebBot

A resource will appear more than one time in the list if it is included in multiple resources or is the target of links in other pages. In the previous example, if page B also contains a link back to page A, such as <u>Return to page A</u>, then you'll see page A also appearing as a subordinate of page B.

> **NOTE** The home page in a FrontPage web running under the FrontPage Personal Web Server is named `INDEX.HTM` by default (a home page in a Web site under a different server may have some other name). That page always appears at the top of the list in the left pane of the Hyperlink view. Because Web sites generally branch out from links in the home page, there may be many resources that are subordinate to that page.

You can navigate through this resource outline and expand or collapse its levels, just as you can with the levels of folders and files in the Windows Explorer:
- A web in the list that has a plus or minus sign to its left has subordinate resources that it either contains or links to.
- Click the plus sign to expand that level and show the subordinate resources, or select the page and press →.
- Click the minus sign at the left of a web to hide its subordinates, or select the page and press ←.
- Double-click on a page to hide or display its subordinates.
- Press Home or End to go to the top or bottom of the list, respectively.
- Scroll through the list using the vertical scroll bar or ↓ or ↑.
- Scroll the list from side to side using the horizontal scroll bar or Ctrl+→ or Ctrl+←.

Later, in the section named "Manipulating Files and Their Properties," you'll see how you can copy, move, rename, delete, open, and change the properties of files in the FrontPage Explorer. In Chapter 8, the section named "Fixing and Verifying Links in the Explorer" shows you how the Tools ➤ Verify Hyperlinks command can check all the links in your Web site to be sure that they are still active (not broken).

Expanding the Hyperlink View

You can expand or contract the scope of the Hyperlink view with three commands on the View menu (or their buttons on the toolbar). Each serves as a toggle that either turns on or off the option.

Choose View ➤ Hyperlinks to Images, or click that button on the toolbar, to hide or display image files in both panes of the Hyperlink view. If a site contains many image files, you can turn off this option so that you get a better view of the other resources. Even though this option was turned on in Figure 3.1, no image files are displayed. Therefore, you can see that the home page for the Widget Web does not contain any image files (as opposed to Figure 3.2 in the next section).

Choose View ➤ Repeated Hyperlinks, or click that button on the toolbar, to hide or display multiple links from one Web page to another resource. You will generally work with this option turned off so only a single link will be shown from a page to a resource, such as an image file that serves as a button in dozens of places within the page.

Choose View ➤ Hyperlinks Inside Page, or click that button on the toolbar, to hide or display links to the same page that contains the link, such as when a link refers to a bookmark in the same page.

> **NOTE**
> You may often have multiple hyperlinks within a page, such as when you have a table of contents at the top of the page that contains links to locations within the page. In this case, you could use both the Repeated Hyperlinks and Hyperlinks Inside Page buttons to see all the links. You can read about bookmarks and other types of links in "Understanding Links" in Chapter 8.

Remember that you can turn on or off these view options at any time, either to see more of the details of your site or to unclutter the display.

The Right Pane (Map) of the Hyperlink View

The right-hand pane of the Explorer's Hyperlink view, as seen earlier in Figure 3.1, reveals in a map-like display the underlying link relationships among the pages and other resources in a web. The resources are represented by larger icons than in the outline of the left pane and have their page titles, file names, or URLs displayed, as well.

The resource you select in the left pane is given the center of focus in the right pane's map view. You can also right-click on an icon in the map view and choose Move to Center from the shortcut menu, which shifts the center of focus to that icon.

Figure 3.2 shows another example of the map view of a web, in which the page whose title is Widget Company Background has been selected in the outline in the left pane so that it has been given the center of focus in the map view in the right pane.

This map view shows you a vast amount of information at a glance—information that would be very difficult to glean and organize by combing through each page in the web. Here's what the right pane of the Hyperlink view in Figure 3.2 shows you:

- Pages that contain hyperlinks to the resource at the center of focus are shown to the left, with arrows pointing to that center resource. In Figure 3.2, there are two pages in this web that contain hyperlinks to the Widget Company Background page: the Widget Company Background page itself and the Widget Company Home Page.

> **NOTE**
> Notice that the Hyperlinks Inside Page button has been enabled, which allows you to see that the Widget Company Background page contains a link to itself, such as a bookmark.

Managing Webs in the Explorer   51

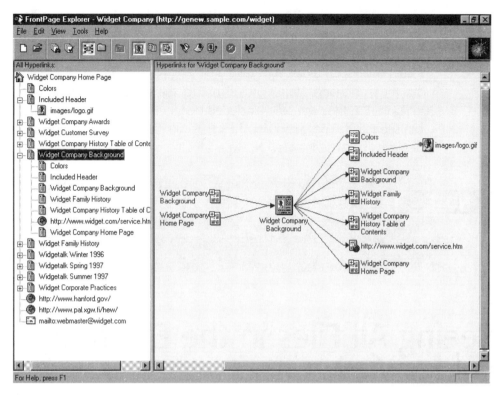

FIGURE 3.2: The Hyperlink view shows you the chain of links among the pages and resources in the web.

- The Widget Company Background page contains hyperlinks to other pages, which are represented by arrows that run from the page's icon to each target icon at its right.
- A link arrow that ends in a bullet indicates that the target is included in the page. The Widget Company Background page has two links to included resources, both of which are Web pages. The page called Colors is used to define the background color of other Web pages (see "Setting Page Properties" in Chapter 7). The page called Included Header contains the information that will appear at the top of other pages, and it is inserted in those pages with an Include Bot (see "Including Another Web Page Automatically" in Chapter 10).
- A link arrow that ends in an arrowhead indicates a clickable hyperlink that opens the target of the link. The Widget Company Background page in Figure 3.2 has five hyperlinks that open other resources. Four of these are

pages within the current web (internal links), and one is a link to a URL outside of the current web (an external link).
- The icons for pages that contain links (other than the one at the center of focus) will display a plus sign. Click a plus sign to expand and display the links, and the plus changes to a minus sign. Click the minus sign to hide the links. In Figure 3.2, the page called Included Header has been expanded, and you can see that this page contains the image file called `LOGO.GIF` (which is displayed because the View ➤ Hyperlinks to Images command was enabled).

> **NOTE** Don't forget that you can view more or fewer icons with the three commands on the View menu—Hyperlinks to Images, Repeated Hyperlinks, and Hyperlinks Inside Page. These were described earlier in "Expanding the Hyperlink View."

Seeing All Files in the Explorer's Folder View

To view your web's folders and files in the Explorer, choose View ➤ Folder View or click that button on the Explorer's toolbar. The left pane displays the folders contained in the Web site, and the right pane displays all the files in the selected folder. Figure 3.3 shows the Folder view of the Widget Web site used in earlier examples.

The Folder view is very much like the Windows Explorer view of a disk drive. You can expand a folder in the left pane to display the folders it contains by clicking on the plus sign to the left of that folder. To hide the folders within a folder, click on its minus sign. The contents of the selected folder are displayed in the right pane.

The right pane of the Folder view includes the following columns of information for each file in the web: file name, page title, file size, file type, date and time modified, author, and comments. This is the same information that you can view and modify in the Properties dialog box for each resource in the Explorer, as discussed in the next section.

Managing Webs in the Explorer 53

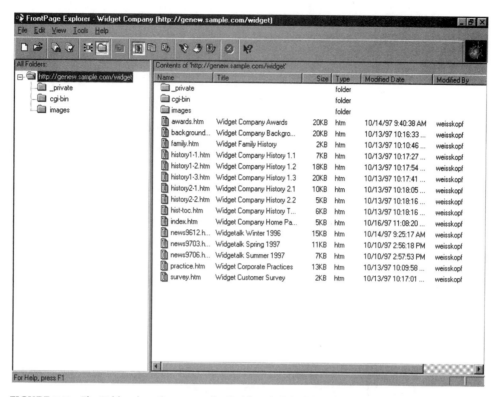

FIGURE 3.3: The Folder view gives you a detailed list of all the files in your web.

> **TIP**
>
> The shortcut menu for a selected file in the Folder view has a choice called Show Hyperlinks. Selecting this command displays the Web site in the Hyperlink view, with the selected file as the center of focus.

You can manipulate the list of files in the usual Windows ways:
- Click one of the column titles to sort the list of files by that column. For example, click the Modified By column title to sort the list alphabetically by author. Click the Modified Date column title to see the most recently edited files at the top of the list.
- Resize a column by dragging its column title's right-hand border to the left or right.

- Select multiple files with the Shift+click or Ctrl+click method, such as when you want to delete several files in one operation.

You can create new folders in Folder view, as long as you have administrator-level permission. Just select the folder in which you want to create the new one and choose File ➤ New ➤ Folder.

You can use subfolders to organize a Web site in the same way that you organize files within subfolders on your disk drive. For example, by default the Explorer creates a folder called `Images` within a new web, in which all image files can be stored.

Suppose your Web site includes many pages and images that make up a reference manual. You could put those files out of the way by placing them all in a subfolder, such as `/MyWeb/Manual` and `/MyWeb/Manual/Images`.

If you include a file named with the default home page name for this site, such as `INDEX.HTM`, in a subfolder, you now have something that can be called a subweb. When someone browses to that folder without specifying a resource name, such as `/MyWeb/Manual/`, the server will send the browser the file `INDEX.HTM` from that folder.

Now let's look at the many ways with which you can work with the resources in the Hyperlink and Folder views in the Explorer.

Manipulating Files and Their Properties

There are several commands that affect the files in the Explorer. You can either select a file and choose a command from the Edit menu, or right-click on a file in the Explorer's right-hand pane and choose a command from the shortcut menu.

Each file has its own set of properties. You can change a few of them, such as the file's name or comments about that file. The rest are updated automatically when the resource is modified, such as the file's size, the date and time the file was created or last modified, and the name of the author who last worked in the page.

> **NOTE** When others are working concurrently on the same site as you are, the changes they make will not be displayed in your copy of the Explorer. That's when you can use the View ➤ Refresh command, which will cause the Explorer to read the Web again from the server and update its view of it.

Using Commands on Web Files

Here are the commands you will find on the Edit and shortcut menus; the commands that are available depend on which view you're using in the Explorer (Hyperlink or Folder) and the type of resource you have selected:

Open: Opens a Web page for editing in the FrontPage Editor; opens other types of resources in the program that is associated with that file type. For example, a GIF or JPEG image file might be opened for viewing in your default Web browser or for editing in your preferred image editor, such as Microsoft Image Composer (see "Specifying Web File Editors" later in this chapter).

Open With: Lets you choose the editor or viewer in which to open the selected resource (again, see "Specifying Web File Editors" later in this chapter).

Delete: Deletes the resource and removes it from your Web (only if it is a file within the Web and not a URL to an external file); you will be asked to confirm the deletion.

Properties: Displays the Properties dialog box for the resource (see "Viewing and Revising File Properties" later in this chapter).

Cut/Copy/Paste: In Folder view, these commands let you copy or move a file. The Cut command removes the resource from the Web and copies it to the Windows Clipboard; the Copy command only copies the resource to the Clipboard; the Paste command places the contents of the Clipboard into the selected folder in the active Web.

Rename: In Folder view, this command lets you change the file name of the selected folder or file; you can also select the file and click a second time to edit its name (but don't double-click or you'll open the file for editing). See the next section for more on renaming or moving a file.

Add To Do Task: Creates a new entry in the FrontPage To Do List that will be linked to the selected file (see "Keeping Track with the To Do List" later in this chapter).

The file icons in the right pane of the Explorer's Hyperlink and Folder views give you quick access to the following tasks:

- Double-click an icon to open that file, so that you can double-click a Web page to open it in the FrontPage Editor, or on an image file to open it in an image editing program.
- Drag a page icon onto the Editor's desktop (not into a page) to open it there.

- Drag an icon into an open page in the FrontPage Editor to create a link there to the resource represented by the icon.

Renaming or Moving a File

Before you rename or move a file, be sure that the file is not open in another application, such as a Web page open in the FrontPage Editor or an image file open in the Image Composer. This will avoid any conflicts that can occur when two programs try to access the same file or when a file that is open is moved from its original location on disk.

In the Explorer's Folder view, you can move a file to another folder simply by dragging it there, or by using the Edit ➤ Cut and Paste method. For example, when you have imported an existing Web into a new FrontPage web, as discussed earlier in "Creating a FrontPage Web from an Existing Web Site" in Chapter 2, you could move all the image files into the Images folder in your web.

To copy a file, hold down the Ctrl key while you drag it, or use the Edit ➤ Copy and Paste method. You can also drag a file with the right mouse button instead of the left, and then pick a command from the shortcut menu that is offered. You can perform these same operations on folders although the need to do so may never arise.

> **WARNING** Never change a file name's extension (the characters after the period) unless you are certain that you need to do so. The extension is the standard means by which programs and operating systems identify a file's type. If you were to change an image file's extension from GIF to HTM, for example, FrontPage and just about every other program would now consider this file to be an HTML Web page and might not be able to open this file correctly.

Note that renaming or moving a file can have a huge impact on the Web site, as there may be one or more pages that link to this file—by name and location! But you don't have to worry about fixing any links that go nowhere, because the Explorer will quickly update any links to that file.

When you rename a file, you will see the Rename dialog box, shown on the opposite page. It lets you know that the Explorer is on the job, watching over your web, and tells you how many other resources are linked to the file whose name you are changing. At this point, you can do any of the following:

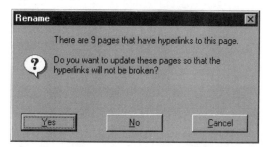

- Click Yes to have the Explorer automatically revise the links to this file so they will refer to the new name.
- Click No if for some reason you want to rename the file without having the links to it revised; this will "break" the links so that there targets no longer exist.
- Click Cancel to cancel the renaming operation.

You can read more about the Explorer's link-maintenance abilities in the section called "Fixing and Verifying Links in the Explorer" in Chapter 8.

Viewing and Revising File Properties

You can view or modify the properties of a file in the Explorer's right pane by right-clicking on the file name or icon and choosing Properties from either its shortcut menu or the Edit menu. Figure 3.4 shows both tabs of the Properties dialog box.

The General and Summary tabs display all the properties of a resource, such as the file name, type, size, and the date and time it was last modified. These are the same properties that you see in the columns in the right pane in the Folder view. You can also revise two of the properties:

Comments: Enter comments about the file, such as its purpose in the web or when it should be updated.

Title: For files that are not HTML Web pages, such as image files, you can enter a more descriptive page title here that FrontPage will use (and only FrontPage) to identify the resource.

NOTE To change the title of a Web page, open it in the FrontPage Editor, right-click on the page, choose Page Properties from the shortcut menu, and enter the title in the Page Properties dialog box.

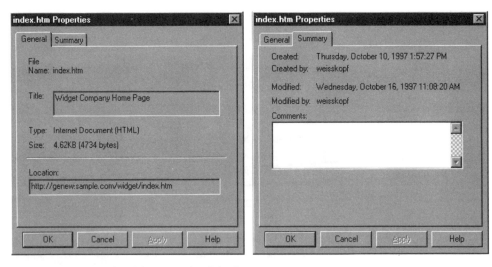

FIGURE 3.4: Both tabs of the Properties dialog box

You will also see a Location field in the General tab of the Properties dialog box, which displays the resource's URL, such as

```
http://genew.sample.com/widget/index.htm
```

Specifying Web File Editors

In the right pane of the FrontPage Explorer, you can open a Web page for editing in several different ways, such as by double-clicking on its name or icon or by selecting it and choosing Open from the Edit menu or its shortcut menu.

By default, a Web page is opened in the FrontPage Editor, but as you'll read in this section, you can choose to use a different editor if you prefer. You can also specify the editor or viewer that will be used to open file types other than HTML pages.

A file type is defined by its file name extension so FrontPage will open a resource with whichever program is assigned to the extension. FrontPage comes with several file types already associated with an editor. For example, files with either HTM or HTML extensions are assigned to the FrontPage Editor; files with no extension are assigned to Notepad, the Windows text editor; image files, such as those whose extension is GIF, JPG, or BMP, are assigned to Microsoft Image Composer, the graphics-editing program that comes with FrontPage.

You can add or change file and editor associations at any time in the FrontPage Explorer. For example, you could specify that a file whose extension is XYZ should be opened by your favorite ExWhyZee editor, or that files with no extension should be opened by a text editor other than Notepad. Understand that the program you associate with a file can be any program you choose for that file type; it need not be an actual editor.

> **NOTE** If a file type is not associated with an editor in FrontPage, you may still be able to open that file in the usual ways if there is a program association for that type with Windows. In that case, double-clicking a file in FrontPage would produce the same results as doing so, for example, in the Windows Explorer.

Let's create an association for sound files with a WAV extension. In a typical Windows installation, this file type is already associated with the program SNDREC32.EXE, so we shouldn't have any problems creating the same association in this exercise in FrontPage:

1. In the Explorer, choose Tools ➤ Options, and then select the Configure Editors tab. This displays the current list of file and editor associations, which is shown in Figure 3.5.

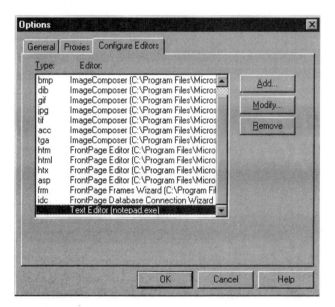

FIGURE 3.5:
You assign a program to a file type in the Configure Editors tab of the Options dialog box.

2. Click the Add button, which displays the Add Editor Association dialog box, shown here.

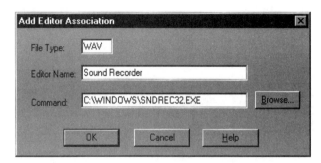

3. In the File Type field, enter the file name extension **WAV**.
4. In the Editor Name field, enter a descriptive name, such as **Sound Recorder**.
5. In the Command field, enter the path and program name, such as **C:\WINDOWS\SNDREC32.EXE** or click the Browse button and select the program in the Browse dialog box.
6. Click OK when you are finished, and click OK again to close the Options dialog box.

Now when you double-click a file in the Explorer whose extension is WAV, that file will be opened for editing in the program you specified.

You can remove a file association from the Configure Editors list by selecting it and clicking the Remove button. To change an association, select it in the list and click Modify. You can also use this method simply to see the entire command for an association, which is often not displayed in full within the width of the Options dialog box.

Instead of relying on the association of the file extension, you can choose the program with which to open a file in the Explorer. Use the Edit ➤ Open With command, or the Open With command on the shortcut menu. This will display the Open With Editor dialog box, which lists all the current associated programs in FrontPage. Just pick the program you want to use to open this file and click OK.

Finding Text and Spell-Checking throughout the Web

In your word processor, you have probably used commands named something like Find, Replace, and Spelling, many, many times. These are quick and easy ways to seek out a word, sentence, or just a few characters in the document, replace text with other text, and check the spelling of all the words in the document.

You can perform these same tasks in a Web page in the FrontPage Editor, which you'll read about in Chapter 4. But FrontPage offers an even more powerful way to utilize these commands—you can invoke them in the Explorer to have them start the process across every page in your entire web. This is yet another example of how FrontPage brings huge Web-management tasks down to a simple operation.

Finding and Replacing Text in Your Web

Suppose that Jamie Doe, the assistant to the junior mailroom clerk in your company, has been promoted to a new position, and that Ralph Emerson has taken his place. Fine for them, but now you, as the overlord of your Web, have to look through every page in the Web to find each occurrence of Jamie's name, and replace it with Ralph's. Here's how to let the Explorer help you in the search:

1. Before you perform this operation, you should close any pages that are open in the FrontPage Editor. This will ensure that the pages that are searched on disk by the Replace command will be the most recently saved.
2. If it is not already open in the Explorer, open the web now.
3. Choose Tools ➤ Replace, which displays the Replace in FrontPage Web dialog box, shown below.
4. Enter the text **Jamie Doe** in the Find What field.
5. Enter **Ralph Emerson** in the Replace With field.
6. In this case, choose the All Pages option so that FrontPage will search every Web page. If you had selected only a few pages before invoking this command, you could choose the Selected Pages option to search just those pages.
7. Click the OK button to start the process.

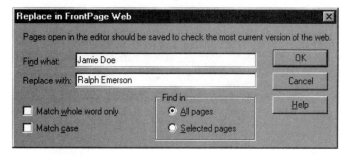

The command starts its search through every page in your web and displays its progress in the dialog box shown in Figure 3.6. You'll see the page title for each page in which the search text has been found, the number of occurrences in that page, and a status indicator that is red when the file is first listed, but turns to yellow once you've edited the page or added a task for that page to the To Do List. You can click the Stop button to halt the procedure, and later click Resume to continue.

> **NOTE** Don't worry, the Replace command won't automatically replace the text it finds; you'll be able to verify each change within the page itself. This allows you to see exactly what should be changed; perhaps Jamie Doe's name has already been entered on a page under his new job title, which you would not want to replace in this procedure.

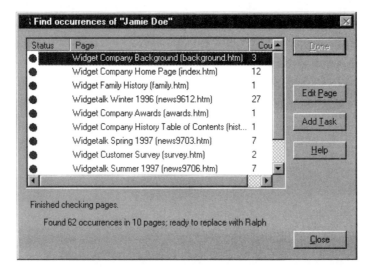

FIGURE 3.6: When finding or replacing text in your Web, this dialog box lists all the pages in which the text was found.

When the job is finished or you have stopped the process, you can select the first page listed in the dialog box (or any page on which you want to start) and click the Edit Page button. This will open that page in the Editor and run the Replace command in that page, as though you had started it manually while editing the page (as discussed in "Finding and Replacing Text" in Chapter 4). When the routine is finished, you can have the command save the file and continue on to the next page.

Instead of running through the Replace routine for each page, you could instead select a page in the list and click the Add Task button. This creates a task in the FrontPage To Do List that is linked to that page so you will remember to return to it later on to complete the job.

Checking the Spelling in Your Web

You can check the spelling of all the pages in your web by opening the web in the Explorer and choose Tools ➤ Spelling or clicking the Cross File Spelling button on the toolbar. As with the Replace command discussed in the previous section, you can choose to check all pages or just those you have selected in the Explorer. You can also choose to have the pages with misspellings automatically added to the To Do List for later action.

When you click the OK button to start the command, you'll see a dialog box similar to the one in Figure 3.6, which lists all the pages in which misspelled words have been found. To correct any misspellings, select a page and click the Edit Page button to open that page in the Editor and run through the spell-checking routine (which is discussed in "Checking Your Spelling" in Chapter 4). When you're finished with one page, the next one will open and you can continue.

You can also select a page in the list and click the Add Task button to create an item in the To Do List that will remind you to check the spelling on that page.

Keeping Track with the To Do List

The number of files and links in a Web site can grow to an astounding size, and each may require many tasks, both large and small, to make it ready for the site. The fact that multiple authors can all work on the same Web site means that you need some way to keep track of who is responsible for doing what tasks.

On top of this profusion and ever-present danger of confusion, there is also the fact that a Web site is never really finished. In days of old, the act of publishing something meant that you were absolutely and completely done with it, at least until the next edition. But when you publish electronically on the Web, there's just no such thing as a final draft. What you finish on Friday afternoon may be fodder for your Monday morning projects!

Now you'll see how the FrontPage To Do List can help you keep track of the myriad and ever-changing tasks in a Web site.

Opening the To Do List

The FrontPage To Do List is just what its name implies—a convenient way for you to keep a list of things that need to be done in the current web (see Figure 3.7). You can add tasks to the list, remove tasks, sort the list, and mark tasks as being completed at any time.

Anyone working on a Web site can open the To Do List from either the FrontPage Explorer or the Editor in two different ways. To display the list, choose Tools ➤ Show To Do List or click that button on the toolbar.

To display the To Do List and also create a new task in it that is linked to the currently selected resource in the Explorer or to the active page in the Editor, choose Edit ➤ Add To Do Task.

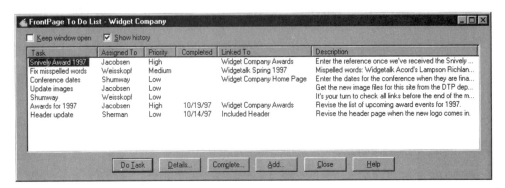

FIGURE 3.7: You can use the To Do List to keep track of tasks for the current Web site.

Viewing Tasks

There are six fields that define a task in the To Do List, four of which you can modify when you create or revise a task. Each field is represented by a column in the To Do List:

    Task: The name you want to call the task

    Assigned To: The person who is responsible for completing the task

    Priority: The order of the task's importance—Low, Medium, or High

    Completed: The date on which the task was marked as being completed (see the Show History option)

    Linked To: The resource to which this task applies

    Description: Your comments about the task

Managing Webs in the Explorer 65

> **TIP** You can sort the items in the To Do List by clicking on a column-title button at the top of a column. For example, click the Linked To button to sort the list by the Web resources to which the tasks are linked. Or click the Priority button to put all the highest priority tasks at the top of the list.

There are two check boxes in the To Do List window that affect its display:

Keep Window Open: When selected, the To Do List will remain open while you are doing a task (after you have clicked the Do Task button).

Show History: When selected, the Completed column appears in the list, along with any tasks that have been marked as completed.

Besides the Close and Help buttons, there are four other buttons in the To Do List window:

Do Task: Opens the Web resource that was linked to this task, using the associated editor (as discussed in "Specifying Web File Editors" earlier in this chapter).

Details: Opens the Task Details dialog box where you can view or revise a task's settings.

Complete: Lets you mark the selected task as being completed; if the selected task has already been marked as completed, the button will be labeled Remove and will let you remove the task from the list.

Add: Lets you add a new task, one that will not be linked to a Web resource.

Adding and Modifying Tasks

You can add a new task to the To Do List in two ways:

- In the Explorer or Editor, choose Edit ➤ Add To Do Task; this will open the To Do List and its Add To Do Task dialog box, which is shown in Figure 3.8. The task you create will be linked to the file that was selected in the Explorer or open in the Editor.
- When the To Do List is already open, click its Add button to open the Add To Do Task dialog box; the task you create will not be linked to a resource.

In the Add To Do Task dialog box, you can enter a name for the task, choose a priority for it, revise the name of the person responsible for the task (by default, it will be

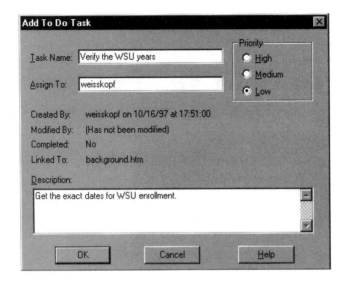

FIGURE 3.8:
You create a new task in the Add To Do Task dialog box.

the name of the person creating the task), and enter descriptive comments. The other information about the task is not editable, such as the date the task was created and the resource to which it is linked.

> **NOTE** If you enter a new name or revise the name in the Assign To field, be sure to spell that name consistently for all the other tasks assigned to that name. Otherwise, sorting the To Do List by the Assigned To field won't produce very useful results.

When you are finished, click the OK button and the new task will appear in the To Do List.

To modify an existing task, select the task in the list and click the Details button. This will display the same dialog box that you use to add a new task. You can then view or edit the information as needed.

Completing and Removing Tasks

When you actually finish the job that is described in a To Do List task, you can select that task in the list and click the Complete button. The Complete Task dialog box offers you two ways to handle the task:

- Mark the task as being completed and leave it in the To Do List, where the date of completion will appear in the Completed column when you have selected the Show history check box in the To Do List window.
- Delete the task from the To Do List so it no longer appears there.

It's a good idea to take advantage of the first option, so that all tasks that have been created will always appear in the To Do List, even when they're completed.

> **NOTE** When you mark a task as being completed, FrontPage will not check to see that you actually did the work described by the task. You're on the honor system!

When you select a task in the list that has already been marked as completed, the Complete button will now be labeled Remove. Choosing that button lets you remove the task from the list. Again, don't rush to remove all completed tasks; you may want to show someone just how many tasks you Web authors have accomplished!

In this chapter, you've learned how the FrontPage Explorer can help you understand and manage the links and files in your Web sites. You will also read about the Explorer's tremendous link-handling abilities in Chapter 8, and about its security tools in Chapter 14. In the next chapter, we'll begin the discussion of how you edit Web pages in the FrontPage Editor.

Chapter 4

CREATING PAGES IN THE EDITOR

FEATURING

- Starting the Editor
- Working in the Editor
- Inserting special characters
- Checking the spelling in a page
- Searching for and replacing text in a page
- Working with a page's HTML code
- Previewing a page in a browser
- Printing a page

This chapter begins the discussion of the FrontPage Editor, the tool you use to build your Web pages. This overview of the Editor and its features will prepare the way for the chapters that follow, where you'll learn about a wide variety of HTML elements that you can create in your pages.

Starting the Editor

You will usually use the FrontPage Editor in conjunction with the FrontPage Explorer and a Web server such as a Personal Web Server. For example, you will open HTML pages from the active web in the Explorer, modify them in the Editor, and then save them back to that web.

> **NOTE** Chapter 2 introduced you to the concept of the *active* web, which is the web currently open in the FrontPage Explorer. When you open an existing page in the Editor, it offers you any of the pages in the active web by default. The same is true when you save a page in the Editor—it will offer to save the page in the active web by default. (File operations are discussed in Chapter 5.)

There are several ways to start the FrontPage Editor. From within the Explorer you can choose Tools ➤ Show FrontPage Editor or click that button on the toolbar. If the 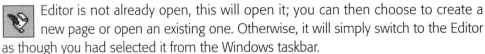 Editor is not already open, this will open it; you can then choose to create a new page or open an existing one. Otherwise, it will simply switch to the Editor as though you had selected it from the Windows taskbar.

You can also open an existing page into the Editor from the Explorer's right-hand pane, in either Hyperlink or Folder view:
- Select the page name or icon and then choose Edit ➤ Open (Ctrl+O), or choose the Open command from the page's shortcut menu.
- Double-click on a page name or icon.
- If the Editor window is visible on the screen, drag the page name or icon into the Editor's desktop (not into another open document, which would create a link within that document).

You can also run the Editor as a stand-alone HTML editor by starting it from the Windows Start menu. The Editor will open with a new blank document ready for editing, or you can open an existing one. In this way, you can work on any HTML page. However, you should avoid working on the pages in a FrontPage web unless the Explorer is open and able to track the changes you make to it.

When you are working in the Editor, you can switch to the Explorer at any time by choosing Tools ➤ Show FrontPage Explorer or by clicking that button on the toolbar.

 Of course, you can switch to either program in the usual Windows ways, such as by selecting it from the Windows taskbar.

When you are finished with the Editor, you can close it with the File ➤ Exit command. As recommended in Chapter 1, you should close any open documents in the Editor *before* you close the active web in the Explorer or close the Explorer itself. This ensures that the Explorer keeps its web up to date by recording any changes you make to the pages in that web.

Creating a New Page

Chapter 5 covers the many ways you can work with files in the Editor, but let's take a quick look at how you create a new page in the Editor, so you'll have plenty of "scratch paper" on which to practice.

To create a new blank page, just click the New button on the toolbar and you're ready to get to work. Remember you can have multiple documents open at the same time, switching between them as needed.

You can also create a new page from a FrontPage template, which is a ready-built page that serves as the basis for the new page. You choose a template when you use the File ➤ New command. The Normal Page template is the standard blank page that opens when you click the New button. Templates are discussed in Chapter 5.

> **NOTE** Just as you do in your word processor, you must save your work in the Editor in order to keep it. You can choose to save a document either to the active web in the Explorer or to another location. Again, this topic is discussed in Chapter 5.

To close the active document, choose File ➤ Close or click that document's Close button on the right side of its title bar (or on the right side of the menu bar if the document's window is maximized).

Pretend You're Using a Word Processor

The FrontPage Editor looks very much like a typical WYSIWYG word processor where "what you see is what you get." In this case, what you see in the Editor is pretty much what the rest of the world will see in their Web browsers when they view the current page on your Web site (see Figure 4.1).

If you are a Microsoft Word user, you may notice the Editor looks suspiciously similar to Word. The similarities are not accidental.

Microsoft Word's HTML Sibling

Microsoft has worked very hard to have all its Office products (such as Word, Excel, and PowerPoint), and now FrontPage, share the same look and even the same

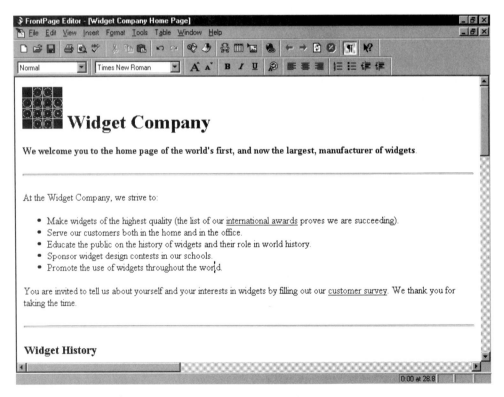

FIGURE 4.1: You create your Web pages in the FrontPage Editor.

program resources. For example, you'll find the same toolbar buttons for commands such as New, Open, Cut, and Paste. Those commands also appear in the same menus, so if you're already familiar with Microsoft Word, you won't have any trouble getting right to work in FrontPage.

Let's take a quick look at some of the features of the Editor in Figure 4.1:

- At the top of the screen, beneath the Editor's title bar, is its menu, its Standard toolbar, and its Format toolbar. Several other toolbars are available, as well. You can turn on or off the display of a toolbar by selecting it from the View menu.
- At the bottom of the screen is the Editor's status bar, which displays useful information as you work in the Editor. For example, the left side of the status bar displays a description of the currently selected command on the menu, and it displays the target address of a hyperlink when you point to a link in the page.
- The document (Web page) that you're editing appears in the window beneath the toolbars. You can open multiple documents (pages) in the Editor, and you can switch between them in the usual ways, such as by selecting a document name from the Window menu or pressing Ctrl+F6.
- The horizontal and vertical scroll bars offer one way to scroll through your document; you can also use the usual keyboard keys, such as PgUp and PgDn. If your mouse has a scrolling wheel, such as Microsoft's IntelliMouse, you can use the wheel to scroll up or down through the page.

Basic Editing Procedures

The best way to familiarize yourself with the Editor is to start typing. You'll find that most of the basic procedures you've already learned in your word processor are applicable in the FrontPage Editor:

- You can have multiple documents open at the same time in the Editor, but only one is the active document. This is the one that will receive any text you enter and will be the target of any commands you issue.
- In the active document, enter text just as you would in your word processor; press Enter only to create a new paragraph.
- Press Del to delete the character to the right of the insertion point; press Backspace to delete the character to its left. Press Ctrl+Del to delete the word to the right of the insertion point; press Ctrl+Backspace to delete the word to its left.

- Press Ctrl+Home to go to the top of the document and Ctrl+End to go to the bottom.
- Using the standard Windows commands, you can change the size of the active document's window, minimize it to an icon, or maximize it so it's as large as possible.
- Select text or graphic images by dragging over them with your mouse or by pressing the Shift key while you use a keyboard arrow key to select the material.
- Once you have selected a portion of the document, you can invoke a command from the menu or toolbar to act on that material. For example, choose Edit ➤ Cut, or click that button on the toolbar, to remove the selection from the document and send it to the Clipboard.
- You can transfer text or images between FrontPage and other programs in the usual ways, such as with the Edit ➤ Copy command in the Editor (or by clicking that button on the toolbar) and then with Edit ➤ Paste in the other program.
- Choose Edit ➤ Undo (Ctrl+Z), or click that button on the toolbar, to undo your most recent action in the document. You can "undo an undo" by choosing Edit ➤ Redo or by clicking that button.
- To change the properties of an object in a page, such as selected text or a horizontal line, select the object and choose Edit ➤ *Object* Properties or press Alt+Enter. You can also right-click on the object and choose *Object* Properties from the shortcut menu.

> **NOTE** The name of the Properties command will change depending on what you have selected; for example, when you have selected a horizontal line, you'll see the Horizontal Line Properties command on the Edit menu.

You can add comments in a page with the Insert ➤ Comment command. The text you enter will be displayed in the page in the Editor, but not when the page is viewed in a browser. A comment can explain an area in the page, serve as a reminder to you or another author, or provide a more detailed explanation of a task that needs to be completed than the short description in the FrontPage To Do List.

You can access the To Do List just as you do in the Explorer. If you choose Edit ➤ Add To Do Task, you will create a task in the To Do List that is linked to the current page. You can also choose Tools ➤ Show To Do List, or click that button on the toolbar, to display the To Do List without creating a linked task.

Inserting Paragraphs and Line Breaks

When you want to create a new paragraph in a document, simply press Enter, just as you would in your word processor. Behind the scenes, this will insert a new `<P>` and `</P>` opening and closing tag in the underlying HTML code, defining the beginning and end of the new paragraph.

A new paragraph not only begins on a new line, it also has its own formatting. For example, if you press Enter at the end of a left-aligned paragraph (the default alignment), you can make the new paragraph centered.

> **NOTE** The Editor also places the HTML code for a non-breaking space between the two paragraph tags, so the new line created when you press Enter looks like this: `<P> </P>`. If you add nothing to this new paragraph, the non-breaking space will force a browser to display a blank line, where it might otherwise ignore the "empty" paragraph. See the next section to learn more about placing these special codes in your pages.

You can force a break between lines without creating a new paragraph by pressing Shift+Enter instead of Enter. This inserts the single line-break tag, `<BR>` (you can also choose Normal Break from the dialog box of the Insert ➤ Break command). The text that follows the line break will appear on a new line but will otherwise still be a part of the current paragraph and carry all of its formatting.

Most browsers insert some extra space between two paragraphs of text, so there will be instances when you will not want to use the `<P>` tag to create a new line. For example, when you display your name and address in a page, you would not want extra space between each line of the address.

Shown below are two addresses in a table in the Editor. In the address on the left, Shift+Enter was pressed at the end of each line to insert a line break. In the address on the right, Enter was pressed.

John and Joan Doe ↵ Widgets, Inc. ↵ 123 S Proton Dr ↵ Hanford, WA 98765	John and Joan Doe Widgets, Inc. 123 S Proton Dr Hanford, WA 98765

Notice the Editor displays a right-angle arrow for the line break (it displays nothing between regular paragraphs). You can turn on or off the display of line breaks and some other on-screen marks by choosing View ➤ Format Marks or by clicking the Show/Hide Marks button on the toolbar.

Inserting Special Characters

Your computer's keyboard is limited to a standard set of letters, numbers, and punctuation. But there are a lot of other characters "out there" that simply are not included on your keyboard. For example, there's the degree symbol (100°), the copyright symbol (©1997), and the fraction one-half symbol (½).

In the FrontPage Editor, you can insert a variety of these kinds of symbols into your page with the Insert ➤ Symbol command, which displays the Symbol dialog box (see Figure 4.2). Select the symbol you want and click the Insert button to place that symbol into your document at the insertion point as though you had typed it. You can continue to select other symbols in the dialog box and click the Insert button. When you are finished, click the Close button.

Checking Your Spelling

The FrontPage Editor lets you check the spelling in your Web pages, just as your word processor lets you do so in your documents. To check the spelling in the active page, choose Tools ➤ Spelling (F7) or click the Check Spelling button on the toolbar. If you have experience with any of the applications in Microsoft Office, this routine will be quite familiar.

Creating Pages in the Editor

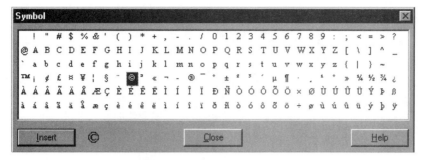

FIGURE 4.2: The Insert ➤ Symbol command lets you pick a symbol to include in your page.

The spell-checker will check the spelling of the active page, starting from the position of the insertion point in the document. Note that the spell-checker will *not* check the spelling of any included pages in the active page. These are pages that appear as the result of the Include Bot, which is discussed in "Including Another Web Page Automatically" in Chapter 10. You must open these pages separately to check their spelling.

> **TIP**
>
> Don't forget you can check the spelling in all pages in the web by choosing the Tools ➤ Spelling command within the Explorer. This was discussed in "Finding Text and Spell-Checking throughout the Web" in Chapter 3.

If the spell-checker finds no misspelled words in the page, a dialog box will notify you of the success. If it finds a misspelled word (or rather, a word not in the spelling dictionary), you will see the Spelling dialog box (shown in Figure 4.3) with the suspect word displayed in the Not in Dictionary field.

If the Word Is Spelled Correctly

The spell-checker flags many words that are actually quite correct, especially names or uncommon technical or medical terms. When the suspect word is correct, you can do any of the following:

- Choose the Ignore button to bypass this word and continue to check the spelling; if the suspect word appears again, it will be flagged again.
- Choose the Ignore All button, bypassing all occurrences of the suspect word during this spelling session.

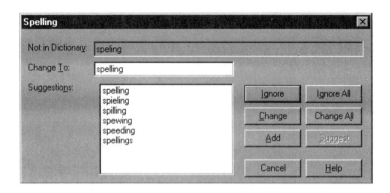

FIGURE 4.3:
The Spelling dialog box displays a suspected misspelled word and offers a list of suggested replacements.

- Choose the Add button to add this word to the custom dictionary. In the future, FrontPage will recognize the word is spelled correctly.

If the Word Is Misspelled

If the word in question is not correct, you can either type the correct spelling into the Change To field or select one of the words from the Suggestions list (which will then appear in the Change To field). At this point you have several options:

- Select a word in the Suggestions list and choose Suggest to get a list of suggestions for that word.
- Choose the Change button to replace the misspelled word with the word in the Change To field.
- Choose Change All to change all occurrences of the misspelled word in the active page.

You can also choose the Cancel button at any time to end the spelling routine.

Finding and Replacing Text

You can use the Edit ➤ Find command to find all occurrences of text you specify in the active page. Again, if you want to search through all the pages in the active web, use this command in the Explorer, as discussed in "Finding Text and Spell-Checking throughout the Web" in Chapter 3.

In the Find dialog box, shown here, you enter the characters you want to find. You can choose to find those characters only when they are a complete word or when the case of their letters exactly matches those you entered. You can also choose to search up or down the page, starting from the insertion point.

To begin the search, choose the Find Next button. The first occurrence of the specified text will be selected in the page. At this point you can:
- Choose Find Next to find the next occurrence.
- Click Cancel to close the Find dialog box.
- Click within the page in the Editor so you can continue to work in it, perhaps to edit the text that was found. The Find dialog box will remain open.

For the Edit ➤ Replace command, you specify the text to search for as well as the text with which to replace it. If you leave the Replace With field empty, the text that is found will effectively be deleted.

NOTE You should practice safe computing by saving the page before you make changes of this type throughout the page.

You perform the Replace operation with three buttons in the Replace dialog box:

Find Next: As in the Find dialog box, finds the next occurrence of the specified text but does not replace it.

Replace: Replaces the text that was found and finds the next occurrence.

Replace All: Replaces every occurrence of the text in one operation.

You can click outside of the dialog box to work within the page or click its Cancel button to close the dialog box.

HTML and Browsers—The Start and End of Your Work

All of your pages in the Editor are built from plain old-fashioned HTML code. The Editor does such a good job of giving you a WYSIWYG view of the page, however, that you will often just work along without even thinking about the code.

Nonetheless, it's there and waiting if you need it, and the more you work with Web pages, the more often you may want to take a peek at the underlying code. The Editor gives you several ways to interact with a page's HTML code; each is explained in the following sections:

- You can view the code at any time, making changes to it as though you were working on the page in a text editor.
- You can insert HTML tags or special characters that the Editor does not support.
- You can view your page in any Web browser you have available on your computer, so you can see exactly how the page will look.

Seeing the HTML Source Code

When you want to see the HTML code on which the active page in the Editor is based, choose View ➤ HTML. A window will open that displays the actual HTML code for your page, the same code that will be saved to disk when you save your page.

Figure 4.4 shows the View or Edit HTML window for the page that was displayed in the Editor in Figure 4.1. If you're just viewing the code and do not want to make any changes to it, you can close the window when you're done and return to the page in the Editor by clicking the Cancel button or pressing Esc. This ensures any accidental changes you might have made to the code will be ignored.

If you make changes you want to keep, click the OK button to close the window. Use caution when you are making changes to the HTML code, as they will be reflected in the page when you return to the Editor. If you accidentally delete one of the angle brackets for an HTML tag, you'll see the result immediately in the Editor.

NOTE Although the Editor's menus are not active while you are in the HTML window, you can still cut or copy text to, or paste text from, the Clipboard—just use the standard shortcut keys for those commands (they are shown on the Editor's Edit menu).

Creating Pages in the Editor 81

FIGURE 4.4: The View ➤ HTML command lets you view or edit the underlying HTML code for a page.

The HTML window not only displays the underlying HTML for the active page, it also helps you interpret it by color-coding it:

- The text you have entered is shown in the normal black.
- HTML tags are shown in purple.
- The attribute or argument names within tags are shown in red.
- The actual attributes you have entered (via the Editor) are shown in blue.

The different colors make it a lot easier to make sense of the code as you scroll through it. You can turn off the colors by deselecting the option called Show Color Coding at the bottom of the window.

There are two other options to choose between at the bottom of the HTML window:

- The default choice, Current, displays the HTML code for the active page in the Editor and lets you make changes to it.
- The Original choice displays the HTML code for the active page as of the last time you saved it to disk; you cannot edit the code in this view.

Either way, viewing the underlying code is always a good exercise that will help you get a feel for the ins and outs of HTML.

> **TIP**
>
> When you want to get your hands onto the HTML code, you can open your Web page in a text editor, such as Windows Notepad (the page should *not* be open in the FrontPage Editor when you do this). Once you have access to the HTML code, you can, for example, search for all occurrences of the `<STRONG>` tag and replace them with the `<EM>` tag. That's something you really can't do within the Editor, because its Edit ➤ Replace command cannot search for HTML tags.

Inserting Extended HTML Code

The fast-paced development of HTML means there will always be some tags accepted by some browsers, even though those tags have not been accepted and incorporated into the official HTML specification (which is under the auspices of the World Wide Web Consortium).

Whatever the reason for certain code not being supported by the FrontPage Editor, you can still include any HTML code in your Web pages by using the Insert ➤ HTML Markup command. This displays a dialog box with a multi-line edit field in which you enter the HTML code you want to include in the page.

> **WARNING**
>
> FrontPage basically ignores the HTML code you enter here and does not check it for accuracy. It's up to you to enter the code without mistakes and ensure it will be interpreted correctly by a browser.

When you click the OK button to close the HTML Markup dialog box, you'll see a small icon in your page that represents the code you added. Even though you won't be able to see how this new material looks in the Editor, you can view this page in a Web browser to see the results (previewing your work in a browser is discussed in the next section).

Creating Pages in the Editor

Another way to add unsupported HTML code to your pages is by adding an attribute to a supported tag, such as for a paragraph, horizontal line, or image. For example, suppose a new attribute called `BGSCENT` comes along for the `<BODY>` tag of a Web page, which tells a browser the scent to exude when this page is opened (don't smirk, in a year or two you might be complaining about just such an exciting new HTML feature). Here's how to add this attribute to a page in the Editor:

1. Choose File ➤ Page Properties.
2. In the Page Properties dialog box, click the Extended button, which displays the Extended Attributes dialog box.
3. Click the Add button and you'll see the Name/Value Pair dialog box shown here.

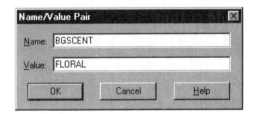

4. Enter the name of the attribute in the Name field, such as **BGSCENT** for this example (note you can use any mix of uppercase or lowercase letters, since the case of the letters is not important in HTML).
5. Enter the value of the attribute in the Value field, such as **FLORAL**. The BGSCENT attribute might have many other possible values, such as ROSE, HAY, or WETPUPPY, just as a page can have many possible colors for its BGCOLOR attribute (see "Changing the Background Color" in Chapter 7).
6. Click OK, and you'll see the new attribute appear in the Extended Attributes dialog box, as shown on the next page. Note the Modify and Remove buttons in the dialog box, which you can use to revise or delete the selected attribute.
7. Click OK, and then click OK in the Page Properties dialog box to complete the job.

The attribute will be entered into the `<BODY>` tag for this page, so its HTML might look like this:

```
<BODY BGSCENT="FLORAL">
```

Remember the FrontPage Editor will ignore this extended attribute.

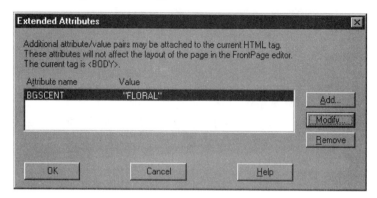

Previewing Your Work in a Browser

The ultimate outcome for a Web page is to be viewed within a Web browser. Although the FrontPage Editor does a very good job of showing you how a page will appear within a browser, it can never offer the final and absolutely definitive view of a page. No editor can.

The primary reason for this is that HTML was designed to be very flexible in the way its pages are formatted. As explained in Chapter 1, you will find that the same HTML code can be interpreted somewhat differently in different browsers.

On top of that inherent flexibility is the fact there are just too many variables out in the real world that could affect the ultimate appearance of a page within a browser. For example, a browser running within a screen resolution of 800 by 600 pixels displays over 50 percent more of a page than a screen resolution of 640 by 480.

> **NOTE** An important part of developing a Web site is testing it with a typical browser. This not only shows you how the pages will appear in that browser, but it also lets you test the links within the site. This process is described in "Testing and Refining Your Web Site" in Chapter 14.

The only way to be sure how your pages will look is to view them within a browser or, preferably, in several of the more popular browsers. But you can also view a single

Creating Pages in the Editor   85

page within a browser, right from the Editor, so you can immediately see how it will appear in that browser:

1. Choose File ➤ Preview in Browser. If this is a new page you have not yet saved, you will be prompted to do so, because the browser will read the file from disk and not from the Editor (see "Saving a Page" in Chapter 5).

    You can instead click the Preview in Browser button on the toolbar to open the browser you last accessed.

2. In the Preview in Browser dialog box, shown in Figure 4.5, select a browser from the list of available browsers.

3. Now select a size for the browser's window in the Window Size group of options. For example, if your computer's resolution is 800 by 600, you can choose the 640 by 480 option to see how the page will look in a browser that has been maximized to full-screen size on a computer whose screen resolution is 640 by 480. Choose the Default option to open the browser without specifying a size.

4. Click the Preview button, and the browser you selected will open and display the Editor's active page.

In the browser, you can see how the page looks when displayed within the specified window size and how the features within the page compare to the way they appear in the Editor. You can switch back to the Editor in the usual Windows ways, such as with Alt+Tab.

When you first install FrontPage, if it finds Internet Explorer on your system, or you choose to install it at that point, it will automatically add it to the list in the Preview in Browser dialog box.

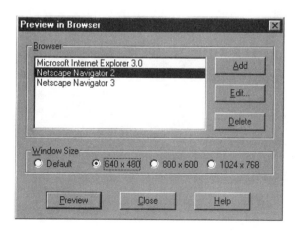

FIGURE 4.5:
You can view your page within a Web browser with the File ➤ Preview in Browser command.

Chapter Four

If you have other browsers available on your computer, you can also add them to the list by clicking the Add button in the Preview in Browser dialog box. You enter a name for the browser, which will appear in the list of browsers, and then enter the command that will open that browser. Use the Browse button to select the program from a typical Windows files dialog box.

Once this browser appears in the list, you can select it to preview the active page in the Editor. You can later use the Edit or Delete button in the Preview in Browser dialog box to revise the settings for a browser or to remove it from the list.

Printing Your Page

You can print the active page in the Editor in the same way you print a document in your word processor. Of course, the need to do so may arise only rarely; a page is meant to reside on a Web site and be viewed by a browser.

Nonetheless, you may wish to print pages in order to proof them for accuracy outside of the computer, or to show them to others who may not have access to a computer.

To print the active page using the current print settings, choose File ➤ Print or click the Print button on the toolbar. This displays the standard Print dialog box, in which you can specify the number of copies to print, the range of pages to print, and the printer to which the job should be sent.

Defining the Page Layout

Before you print, you can modify the page layout via the File ➤ Page Setup command; its dialog box is shown here. You can specify the margins for the printout, as well as the text that should appear in the header and footer on each page.

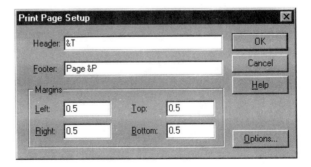

Creating Pages in the Editor — 87

You can enter any text you want in the header and footer, but there are two special codes you can also include, each of which begins with the ampersand (&). Use &T to display the page's title (the same title you specify with the File ➤ Page Properties command in the Editor), and &P to display the page number in the printout (there are no page numbers within the context of the web).

> **NOTE** Unlike your word processor, the settings in the Page Setup dialog box affect all the pages (files) you print within the Editor and will remain in effect until you change them.

Previewing the Printout

Before you print a page, take a few seconds to preview on the screen what your printout will look like on paper by choosing File ➤ Print Preview. The buttons on the preview toolbar perform the following tasks:

Print: Closes the preview but opens the Print dialog box, where you can print as usual to a printer.

Next Page: Displays the next page of a multipage printout; you can also use PgDn. The left side of the status bar shows the current page number.

Previous Page: Displays the previous page; you can also use PgUp.

Two Page/One Page: Toggles between displaying a single page or two pages of the printout.

Zoom In: Magnifies the preview so you can see more detail on the page, but less of the entire page.

Zoom Out: Shows you more of the page but shrinks the size of the characters on it.

> **TIP** Here's a fast way to zoom in on a specific portion of the page without having to hunt for it after the screen is magnified. Just point to that portion of the preview (notice the pointer looks like a magnifying glass) and click to enlarge the display. That piece of the page will be within the preview, so you won't have to search for it.

Close: Closes the preview and returns to the active page; you can also press Esc.

Again, your Web pages are meant to be viewed within your Web site by a browser, so you may need to print pages only when you wish to view them outside of a computer (perhaps in a comfortable chair in front of the television).

This chapter has introduced you to the FrontPage Editor and has shown you some of the basic editing tools it offers. In the next chapter, you'll learn how to work with files in the Editor.

Chapter 5

USING FILES, WIZARDS, & TEMPLATES

FEATURING

- Creating a new page from a template
- Letting a Wizard help you create a new page
- Opening a page from the active web
- Opening a page from another location
- Opening other types of files
- Inserting a file into the page
- Saving a page to the active web
- Saving a page to another location
- Saving a page as a template

The FrontPage Editor offers you many ways to handle the files in your FrontPage web. You'll find its templates and Wizards give you a real boost when creating new pages. If you want to bring in non-HTML files from other sources, you'll learn the Editor can import a wide variety of file types. Of course, you can also create or revise pages that are not part of a FrontPage web, but you won't be able to take advantage of several FrontPage features.

Creating a New Page in the Editor

You create a new page in the Editor with the File ➤ New (Ctrl+N) command. This displays the New Page dialog box (shown in Figure 5.1), which lists the available templates and Wizards you can use to create a new page (a Wizard includes that word in its name). When you select an item in the list, a description of it appears in the lower portion of the dialog box.

> **NOTE** When you later save a new page in the Editor, it will be saved in the active web in the FrontPage Explorer by default. But you can specify another location outside of the web if you prefer (see the section "Saving a Page" later in this chapter).

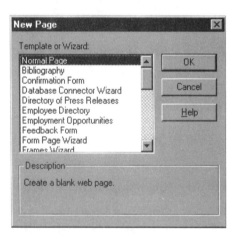

FIGURE 5.1: The New Page dialog box lets you create a new page from a template or with the help of a Wizard.

Creating a Page from a Template

A template is simply a ready-made page you can use as a starting point for a new page, much as a FrontPage web template lets you build a new web. A page template not only makes it easier to get a page going, but it also provides a consistent look when you base several different pages on the same template.

In the previous chapter, you learned how to create a new blank page by clicking the New button on the Editor's toolbar. This button is actually a shortcut for creating a new page from the Normal Page template. If you look back at Figure 5.1, you'll see that the Normal Page template is the first item listed in the New Page dialog

Using Files, Wizards, and Templates   93

box; its description states that it creates a blank page. In other words, when you want to start a page from scratch, either click the New button or choose the Normal Page template.

You'll find a wide variety of templates in the New Page dialog box. For example, there are templates called Employee Directory, Feedback Form, Meeting Agenda, and Table of Contents. At first glance, each template looks like a completed page, with titles, sections, bulleted lists, names, and dates.

At second glance, you'll see that some of the text is instructional comments that help you fill in your own information on the page. Other text will be generic in nature, such as a title that simply says *[Company Name]* and should be replaced by your own text.

Figure 5.2 shows the Office Directory template; you can open it in the Editor with the File ➤ New command to see what's in it.

> **NOTE** When you base a new page on a template, be sure to read the comments for tips on using the page, and be sure to delete any information in the page that is not relevant.

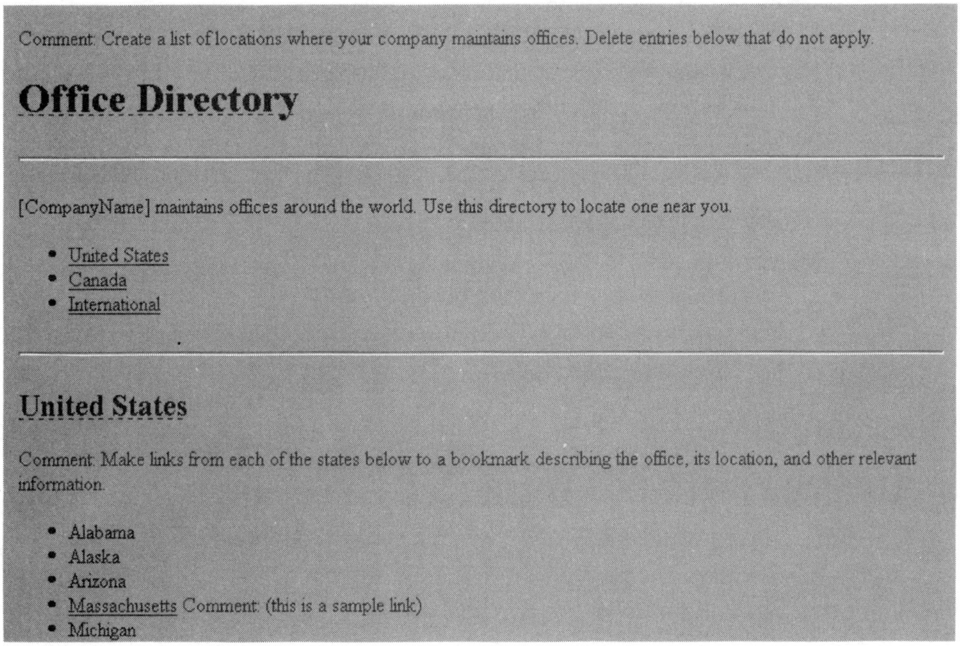

Comment: Create a list of locations where your company maintains offices. Delete entries below that do not apply.

Office Directory

[CompanyName] maintains offices around the world. Use this directory to locate one near you.

- United States
- Canada
- International

United States

Comment: Make links from each of the states below to a bookmark describing the office, its location, and other relevant information.

- Alabama
- Alaska
- Arizona
- Massachusetts Comment: (this is a sample link)
- Michigan

FIGURE 5.2: The Office Directory template helps you set up a page that lists the addresses of your offices.

Here are some points to notice about the Office Directory template:
- The page's title, which you can see in the window's title bar, is a generic one that you should revise appropriately (use the File ➤ Page Properties command).
- There is a descriptive comment at the top of the page (you can create your own comments with the Insert ➤ Comment command, which was mentioned in Chapter 4 in "Basic Editing Procedures").
- You should fill in your own company's name in the line that begins with *[Company Name]*.
- The Office Directory heading has been named *Top* as a bookmark (see Chapter 8 for more on links and bookmarks). Figure 5.3 shows you some of the Back to Top hyperlinks in this page that return you to the Top bookmark at the top of the page.
- Each of the three items in the first bulleted list is a hyperlink to a bookmark in this page, so that United States links to the heading of that name, which you can see below this bulleted list. The Canada hyperlink targets the heading of that name (again, as a bookmark) that you can see near the bottom of Figure 5.3.
- In the section headed United States, there is a list of the 50 states, Puerto Rico, Washington, D.C., and so on. The comment above the list (but below the heading) suggests that you create a link from each relevant item to a bookmark elsewhere in the page (you would delete any items that you don't use). In Figure 5.2, you can see that Massachusetts is a hyperlink because it is underlined. It links to a bookmark of that name at a sample address in the page, which you can see in Figure 5.3.
- The Massachusetts section in Figure 5.3 contains hyperlinks to an e-mail address and to a Web site URL. You would edit the text of each hyperlink to match your own addresses and edit the target addresses of each link, as well (creating and editing hyperlinks are discussed in Chapter 8).

Creating a Page with a Wizard

A Wizard helps you create a new page by asking you a series of questions about the content or layout of the page. It then builds the page based on your responses, and you get to work on the result.

Using Files, Wizards, and Templates

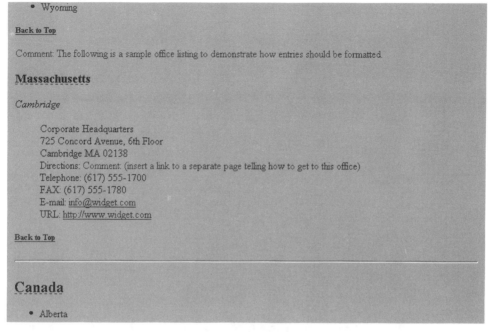

FIGURE 5.3: The lower portion of the Office Directory template

You can choose from many Wizards in the New Page dialog box, which was shown in Figure 5.1. As an example, look at the Personal Home Page Wizard, which lets you customize a home page for your own use.

> **NOTE** To see what Wizards can do, you should experiment with those that interest you. You can always revise the resulting page as needed or delete it if you don't want to keep it. You can also run the Wizard several times, make different choices for each option, and save each page under a different name to compare the results.

The number of steps in this Wizard depends on how many choices you pick in the first step. There can be well over a dozen steps in all, each of which lets you fine-tune the page to your own needs.

Let's look at each step of the Personal Home Page Wizard:

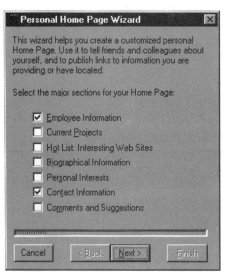

Step 1: In the first step, you pick the main sections that you want to appear in your personal home page. The ones you choose will appear as main headings in the resulting page, with relevant information beneath each one. You can choose any number of headings, from one to all seven; in this example, only two sections are selected.

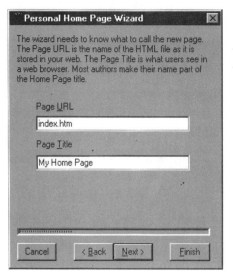

Step 2: Enter a file name (URL) and page title for the new page. Note that the page will not be saved at this time, but the name you specify will be the default name when you later issue the File ➤ Save command.

Using Files, Wizards, and Templates   97

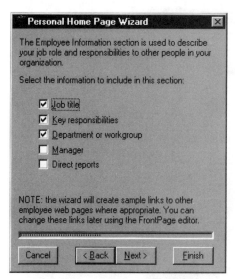

Step 3: Because the Employee Information section was selected in the first step, you are now asked for specifics about what should appear in that section.

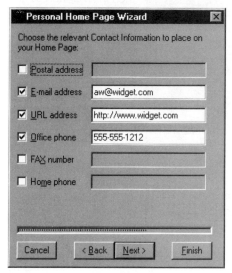

Step 4: You now select what should appear in the Contact Information section, such as your e-mail and URL address, phone or fax number, and mailing address. Remember you can edit any of this information once the page is created.

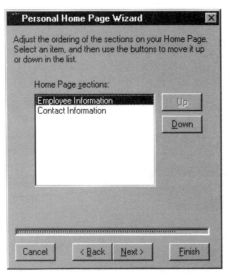

Step 5: You can change the position of the main sections in the page (there are only two in this example); just select one and click the Up or Down button to move it in that direction in the list.

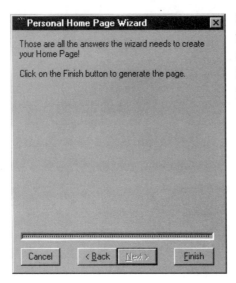

Step 6: In the last step, you can click the Finish button to complete the job and create the page, or you can go back to change any of your choices in the preceding steps.

The result will be a new page like the one shown in Figure 5.4, which contains the sections and information you specified. At this point, you are free to modify the page as you would any other page.

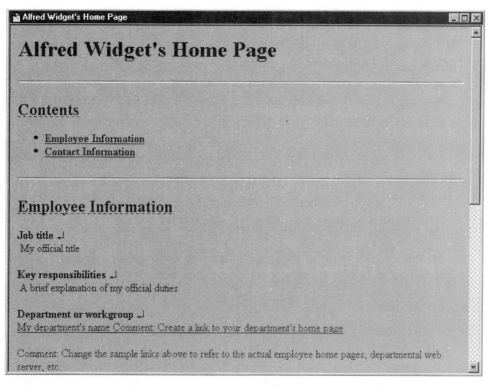

FIGURE 5.4: The customized page that results from your Personal Home Page Wizard

Opening an Existing File

To open an existing Web page or another type of file in the Editor, choose File ➤ Open (Ctrl+O) or click the Open button on the toolbar. This displays the Open File dialog box, from which you can open a page from the active web in the Explorer, or a page or other file type from another location. Instead of using the Open command, you can select a name of a recently opened file from the bottom of the File menu.

> **TIP** Remember that you can also open a Web page from the Explorer's right-hand pane, such as by double-clicking the page name or icon or by selecting it and choosing Edit ➤ Open.

Opening a Page from the Active Web

To open a page from the FrontPage Explorer's active web in the Editor, choose File ➤ Open and then choose the Current FrontPage Web tab in the Open File dialog box, which is shown in Figure 5.5.

This tab displays the file name and page title of every page in the active web. Select a page and choose OK to open it. This will probably be the most common way that you'll open a page in the Editor, because all the pages for the web are usually stored there, as well. Working hand-in-hand with the Explorer and the Editor allows the Explorer to update the web with any changes you make to its pages in the Editor.

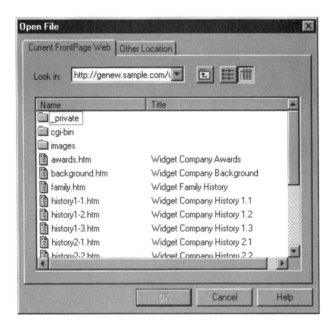

FIGURE 5.5: In the Open File dialog box, you can open a page from the active web in the Explorer.

Opening a Page from Outside the Active Web

Usually you will be opening HTML pages in the Editor from the active web in the Explorer. But you can open pages from other locations, as well. Choose File ➤ Open in the Editor, and then choose the Other Location tab in the Open File dialog box, which is shown in Figure 5.6.

To open a page from disk, enter the path and file name in the From File field. There is a Browse button to help you find the file.

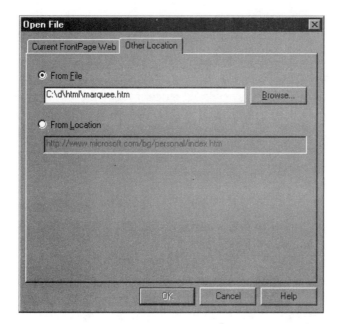

FIGURE 5.6:
You can open a page outside of the active web by specifying the location in the Open File dialog box.

To open a page by specifying its URL, such as from the WWW or your intranet, enter the URL in the From Location field. Using this method, you can open any page from any Web site to which you have access, just as you do in your browser. Once open, you are free to save the page to your local disk or Web site.

Free that is, within the constraints of upright behavior and copyright law. But this is a handy way to bring a page from one Web site into the Editor, where you can revise it as necessary and then save it to a different location.

Opening Other File Types

You can open many types of files in the Editor beyond standard HTML Web pages. The Editor will convert an incoming file from its native format into an equivalent-looking HTML file. You can then save it as an HTML Web page in the usual way.

When you choose a file to open, the Editor will determine what type of file it is and, if it's able to, will convert it as it opens it. To make it easier to find a file, and to see the types of files that the Editor can convert, use the Browse button and look at the Files of Type drop-down list in the Open File dialog box. When you choose one of the file types on the list, only files with the appropriate extension for that type, such as DOC or XLS, will be displayed in the dialog box.

You will find a wide variety of file types in the list, including several different versions of Microsoft Word, Excel, and Works, and also WordPerfect. The more generic Rich Text Format (RTF) and plain text (TXT) file types are also on the list.

If the incoming file contains any graphic images, the Editor will attempt to place them in the document where they belong. Since images are always separate files from the pages in which they appear, when you later save this document as an HTML page, you will be asked if you also want to save the images as separate files (see the section "Saving a Page" later in this chapter). By saving the images, they will be available the next time you open this page, either in the Editor or in a browser on your Web site.

If the file you want to open is of an unknown type to the Editor, it will display the dialog box shown here, asking you how it should convert the file—either as an HTML, RTF, or Text file. This is a last-ditch effort on the part of the Editor, and none of the choices may be appropriate. But in some cases, such as when you want to open a text file whose extension is unfamiliar to the Editor, you can choose the appropriate file type and let the Editor proceed.

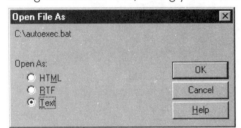

TIP If the Editor can't open a certain file type, you may be able to save that file in the HTML format in the program that created the file. You could then open the HTML file directly into the Editor.

Inserting a File into a Page

You can bring another file into the current page with the Insert ➤ File command. The contents of the other file will appear at the insertion point's position within the page.

NOTE You use the commands Insert ➤ Image and Insert ➤ Video to display an image or video file in your page; these are discussed in Chapter 9. In Chapter 7, you'll learn how to specify a background sound that will play when the page is opened in a browser.

You'll probably find many occasions to bring another Web page into the current one. For example, suppose you have an online user manual that is spread across multiple pages so that each page downloads pretty quickly. But you would also like to have the entire manual in a single page so a visitor to the site could download the complete manual in one operation. You could use the Insert ➤ File command to combine each of the pages into a single page, and then save that page back to the Web site.

Saving a Page

When you have opened an existing page, you can save it back to its original location under the same file name by choosing File ➤ Save (Ctrl+S) or by clicking the Save button on the toolbar. The page will be saved immediately and you can continue with your work.

> **NOTE** In the FrontPage Editor, you must save your work just as you do in your word processor—frequently! A recently saved file on disk is your best protection from power outages and the myriad of other small disasters that seem to occur during our busiest times.

When you are working on a new page that you have not yet named, choosing File ➤ Save displays the Save As dialog box, shown in Figure 5.7. This is the same dialog box you will see when you choose File ➤ Save As, which is how you can save an existing page under a new name or to a different location.

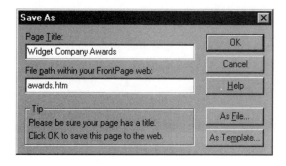

FIGURE 5.7:
You are prompted for a file name and page title when you save a page for the first time or use the File ➤ Save command.

In the Save As dialog box, enter a file name and, if you have not yet done so, a page title (see "Setting Page Properties" in Chapter 7). Then you can click one of the following three buttons to save the page:

OK: Saves the page to the active web in the FrontPage Explorer.

As File: Saves the page to the location you specify.

As Template: Saves the page as a FrontPage template.

If you opened a page that was not a part of the current web in the Explorer, and that page contains one or more graphic images, you will be asked if you want to save

those images when you save the page. In the dialog box shown here, you can enter a new name for the image file if you choose, and then click the Yes or Yes to All button if there are two or more images. Or, you can click the No button and not save the image.

Saving a Page as a File

Choosing to save the current page as a file outside of the active web is one way to export a page to another location; the other way is from the Explorer, as discussed in "Exporting Files" in Chapter 2. When you do this in the Editor, you can also choose to save the page not as an HTML file, but in another file format.

When you choose the As File button in the Save As dialog box, you are offered a standard Windows files dialog box in which you can specify the name and location for the file. Unless you specify otherwise, the file will be saved under its existing name and type.

Saving a Page as a Template

When you create a new page in the Editor, you're not limited to the templates that come with FrontPage. You can add to the list of templates in the New Page dialog box by saving your own pages as templates.

You can create a template from any page that you want to duplicate in the future. For example, if all the employees in your company were going to have a page in your web, you could create a template that would serve as the basis for each of those pages:

- Company name and logo at the top
- A heading for the employee's name
- A generic image that would be replaced by a photo of the employee
- Another heading for the employee's department name
- A generic address section in which would go the employee's e-mail address, telephone extension, and so on
- A bulleted list for information about the employee

The options are endless, but the point is that this employee information template should be generic enough to be used by any employee, yet customized enough so that only the information needs to be revised. The formatting of the page will need no adjusting.

Here's how to save a page as a template:

1. Choose File ➤ Save As.
2. Click the As Template button.
3. In the Save As Template dialog box, shown here, revise the page title and file name as needed, and enter a description in the field provided. All of this information will appear in the list of templates in the New Page dialog box.

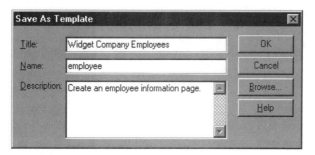

4. If you want to replace an existing template, click the Browse button and choose one from the list.
5. Otherwise, click the OK button to complete the job.

Once you have created the template, it will be available in the New Page dialog box, like any other template. If you'd care to know, each template file resides in its own folder (named with a `TEM` extension) within the Pages folder within the FrontPage program folder, such as

```
C:\Program Files\Microsoft FrontPage\Pages\
Employee.tem\Employee.htm
```

If you delete a template's folder, such as with the Window's Explorer, you will be removing that template from the New Page dialog box.

Browsing Pages in the Editor

You can navigate through the hyperlinks in your Web pages from inside the Editor. To open the target of a hyperlink (that uses the `HTTP` or `FILE` protocol), hold down the Ctrl key and click on the link. Or right-click on the hyperlink and choose the Follow Hyperlink command from the shortcut menu.

When multiple pages are open in the Editor, you can switch between them in the usual ways mentioned earlier, such as by pressing Ctrl+F6. You can also use the Back and Forward buttons on the toolbar to move from one page to another, just as you do in your browser. In this case, the pages are actually open in the Editor.

This chapter has shown you the many ways you can work with files in the FrontPage Editor. To repeat one bit of advice, save your pages frequently as you work on them. The next chapter shows you how to impose some structure on your pages with horizontal lines, headings, and lists.

Chapter 6

ADDING STRUCTURE TO YOUR PAGES

FEATURING

- Dividing a page with a horizontal line
- Changing the properties of a line
- Creating an outline structure with headings
- Creating and working with bulleted and numbered lists
- Changing the look of a list
- Nesting lists
- Creating other types of lists

In this chapter you'll learn how the FrontPage Editor lets you organize your pages into logical sections with horizontal lines, headings, and lists. These features can make your Web page more attractive and easier for someone to browse.

Creating Sections with Horizontal Lines

Perhaps the simplest way to add structure to a Web page is by inserting a horizontal line with the Insert ➤ Horizontal Line command. This invokes the HTML tag `<HR>` and is often referred to as a *horizontal rule*. By default, the line spans the entire width of the page in the Editor or in a browser. It is a simple but very effective way to delineate one section from another, as shown in Figure 6.1.

In this case, the page has a banner headline and graphic across the top with a horizontal line beneath them, separating the banner and graphic from a table of contents of hyperlinks. Beneath the table of contents is another line, followed by the main body of the page (which you cannot see). The lines create obvious divisions between logical sections of the page.

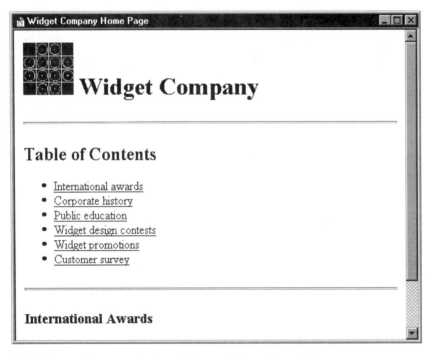

FIGURE 6.1: You can use horizontal lines to divide sections within a page.

Changing the Look of a Line

The default horizontal line is a thin one that spans the entire page. To modify the look of a horizontal line, open its Properties dialog box (shown here) by right-clicking on the line and then choosing Horizontal Line Properties from the shortcut menu.

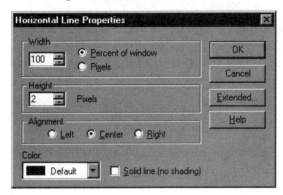

You can change the width, height, alignment, and color of the line:

Width: The width of a default line is 100 percent of the width of the Editor's or a browser's window and changes accordingly. Change the percentage to 50 for a line half the width of the window. Choose Pixels to specify an exact width for the line, no matter how wide the window may be. If the resulting line is longer than the width of window, the portion that extends beyond the edge of the window will simply be hidden from view.

Height: The default height, or the thickness of the line, is 2 pixels; increase or decrease the height as needed.

Alignment: If you specify a width for the line other than 100 percent, you can choose to align the line to the left or right side of the window or center it within the window.

Color: Select a color for the line; you can also choose to have the line displayed with a shadow effect or as a solid line.

Using Images of Lines

Another way to create a dividing line in a page, which you'll find on many Web sites, is with a graphic image of a line. Lines and images of lines both serve the same purpose, but the image can add multiple colors, patterns, or a picture. Working with other kinds of images is discussed in Chapter 9.

> **NOTE** One small disadvantage of using a graphic image is that it takes time to download. But most line image files are small, and if you reuse that image as a horizontal line elsewhere in the page or in the Web site, the browser only needs to download it once.

FrontPage comes with a collection of clip art images, several of which are suitable for horizontal lines. You'll read more about using clip art for page backgrounds in Chapter 7 and for images within your pages in Chapter 9.

Figure 6.2 shows an example of an image being used in place of the standard HTML horizontal line in a page.

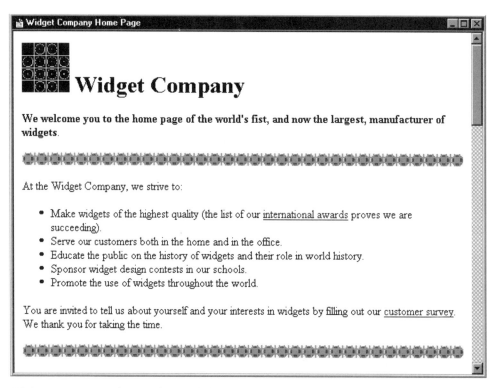

FIGURE 6.2: You can insert an image of a line instead of using an HTML horizontal line.

Adding Structure to Your Pages

Here's how you insert a clip art line image into the page:

1. Position the insertion point on the line where you want the line image to appear. Frequently that will be on a new blank line between the two sections you want to separate.
2. Choose Insert ➤ Image.
3. In the Image dialog box, choose the Clip Art tab, shown in Figure 6.3.
4. In the Category list, choose Lines.
5. You can now pick from a variety of line-like images by clicking the one you want; click OK when you're finished.

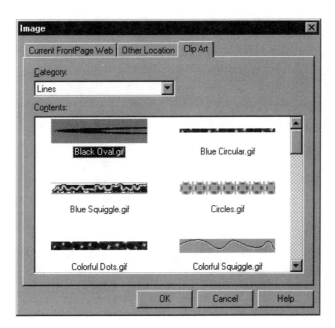

FIGURE 6.3: The Lines category in the Clip Art tab in the Image dialog box offers you a wide selection of line-like images.

The image that appears in the page is no different from any other image. You are free to change its properties, size, or position, or to delete it from the page. In fact, the only change you may need to make is to the image's width, so that it serves its purpose as a section divider. These issues are discussed in Chapter 9.

Creating a Hierarchy with Headings

A very common and quite efficient way to add structure to a Web page is through the use of headings. Just take a look at the table of contents of this book to see headings in action; a chapter is divided into several main headings, each of which may contain several subheadings. And those subheadings may contain yet other sub-subheadings. It's essentially the structure of an outline, only with lots of text and graphics between the headings.

A Web page can have up to six levels of headings, which you apply as a paragraph format. In other words, the heading style is applied to an entire paragraph, not just the text you might select. The HTML codes for the six different headings are conveniently named <H1>, <H2>, <H3>, and so on.

To make a heading, first click within the text you want as the heading, and then choose one of the six headings from the Change Style list on the Format toolbar, as shown here. You can also pick a heading from the list of paragraph styles with the Format ➤ Paragraph command.

If you look back at Figure 6.1, you'll see an example of three different headings. The Widget Company heading at the top of the page is level 1, the Table of Contents is level 2, and the International Awards heading is level 3. If you ignore the graphic at the top of the page and the items under the Table of Contents heading, the HTML code for the headings and the horizontal lines between them looks like this:

```
<H1>Widget Company</H1>
<HR>
<H2>Table of Contents</H2>
<HR>
<H3>International Awards</H3>
```

As with all HTML codes, there is no inherent style to the headings—different Web browsers might interpret the look of a heading in a different way. In general, a level 1 heading will be in a larger, bolder font than a lower-level heading and may have a blank line above and below it. Note that the way a heading appears in the FrontPage Editor just happens to be the same way it looks in Microsoft's Internet Explorer Web browser. What a nice coincidence! A sample of the six headings within that browser is shown here.

> **NOTE** The headings in this example are arranged in a two-column table, so they could be shown side by side. Tables are discussed in Chapter 11.

Although headings help organize a page, there is no inherent structure within the headings themselves. You are free to turn any text into a heading and use the various levels of headings in any order you prefer. But, it makes very good sense to use them as you would in an outline.

For example, the first heading you use on the page should usually be the highest level that will appear in that page, although you don't have to start with level 1. You may choose to start with level 2, because you know that most browsers display that heading in a smaller font than level 1. So in this case, you would never use a level 1 heading on this page, since you began by establishing level 2 as the highest level.

Organizing Data within Lists

A very practical way to organize groups of items on a page is to arrange them in a list. There are several built-in lists in HTML; the two most useful follow:

> **Bulleted:** Prefaces each item (paragraph) in the list with a bullet; the <UL> tag begins the list; also called an *unordered* list.
>
> **Numbered:** Numbers each item in the list; the <OL> tag begins the list; also called an *ordered* list. The browser applies the appropriate number to each line when it opens the page, so you can add or delete items from the list while you create the page without having to worry about updating the numbering.

You can create a list either before you enter its items or after (each item in a list is a separate paragraph).

Creating a List from Existing Text

Suppose you already have text in a page that you would like to turn into a bulleted list (the process is the same for a numbered list). The left side of Figure 6.4 shows the table of contents from Figure 6.1 before it was defined as a bulleted list.

To turn those lines into a bulleted list, simply select them all, such as by dragging over them with your mouse, and then click the Bulleted List button on the Editor's

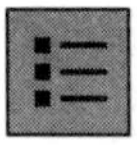

Format toolbar (or select Bulleted List from the Change Style list on the Format toolbar). The result is shown in the middle of Figure 6.4.

Because the list style affects entire paragraphs, you don't have to select all the text in the first or last lines of the list. In other words, the effect would be the same as long as you select at least one character in those lines.

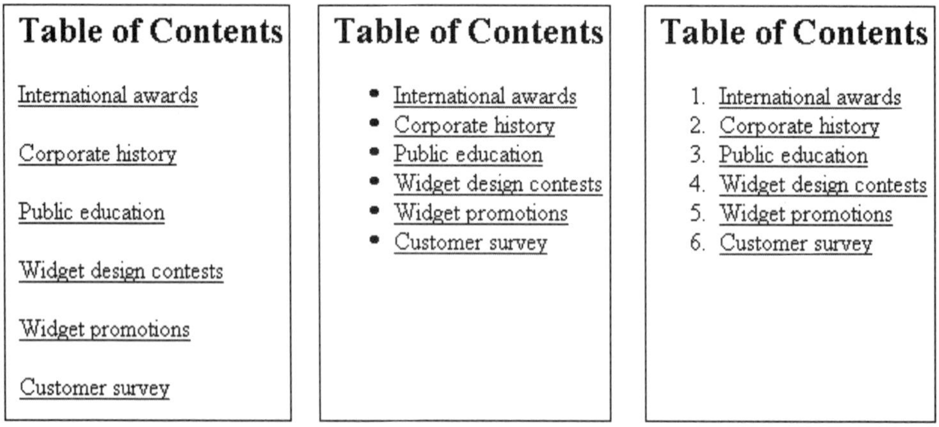

FIGURE 6.4: You can turn multiple paragraphs into a bulleted list.

NOTE As always with HTML, the way a browser formats the list, such as the amount of indentation and the style of the bullets, may vary from browser to browser.

While the text in this example is still selected, you can click the Numbered List button on the Format toolbar to change the text to that type of list. The result is shown on the right side of Figure 6.4. You can switch back and forth between the two list styles at any time. Later you'll learn how to change the look of bulleted or numbered lists.

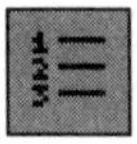

If you're interested, here's the HTML code for the bulleted list (to avoid confusion, the code for the hyperlinks is not shown, and indentations were inserted to make the code easier to decipher):

```
<H2>Table of Contents</H2>
<UL>
    <LI>International awards</LI>
```

```
        <LI>Corporate history</LI>
        <LI>Public education</LI>
        <LI>Widget design contests</LI>
        <LI>Widget promotions</LI>
        <LI>Customer survey</LI>
</UL>
```

The code for the numbered list would be same, except the `<OL>` and `</OL>` tags would appear in place of the `<UL>` and `</UL>` tags, respectively. Remember that HTML is not case-sensitive, so that uppercase and lowercase letters are interchangeable.

Creating a List As You Type

You can also create a list as you type the items into the list. Here's how to create the table of contents bulleted list shown in the center of Figure 6.4:

1. On a new blank line in the page, click the Bulleted List button. You'll see a bullet appear next to this line, which is now the first line in the list.
2. Type the text you want to appear on this line; in this case type **International awards**.
3. Press Enter to create the second line in the list, which will also be prefaced with a bullet.
4. Type the text for this line, **Corporate history**, and press Enter.
5. Continue with each new line in the list.
6. When you have typed the last item in the list, either press Enter *twice* or press Ctrl+Enter to finish the list. The new line this creates will be in the Normal style, outside of the list.

Working in a List

Let's look at some typical tasks you will perform in a bulleted or numbered list:

- To add an item within a list, place the insertion point at the beginning of a line in the list and press Enter.
- To add an item to the end of a list, place the insertion point at the end of the last item in the list and press Enter.
- To select one item in the list, point to its bullet or number and double-click.
- To select the entire list, point to the left of its bullets or numbers (in the area called the selection bar) and double-click.
- To delete an item, select it (as described above) and then press Del or choose Edit ➤ Clear.

- To change a list back to normal text, select the list (as described previously) and click the Decrease Indent button. You can also select the list, choose Format ➤ Bullets and Numbering, choose the Style tab, select None, and then choose OK. (The Bullets and Numbering command is discussed in the next section.)
- To change a list to another type of list, select the entire list and either click a list button on the toolbar or choose a list from the Bullets and Numbering dialog box (Format ➤ Bullets and Numbering).

Changing the Look of a Bulleted or Numbered List

The Bulleted List and Numbered List buttons on the toolbar create a list in the default style, but you can choose other types of bullets or numbering for these lists. The easiest way to see the effects of changing the list style is by first selecting an existing list, and then choosing Format ➤ Bullets and Numbering, or right-clicking on the list and choosing List Properties from the shortcut menu.

When you select an existing list and choose this command, the List Properties dialog box contains three tabs (all shown here):

Bulleted: Lets you choose the style of bullets that are used in the list, such as solid or hollow round bullets. The first choice, which shows no bullets, returns the list to normal text.

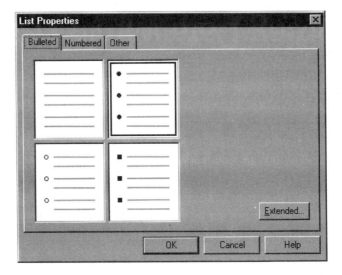

Numbered: Lets you choose the numbering style for a numbered list, such as Arabic or Roman numeral numbering or uppercase or lowercase lettering. The first choice, which shows no numbering, returns the list to normal text. In the option labeled Start At, you can specify the starting number for the list (the default is 1).

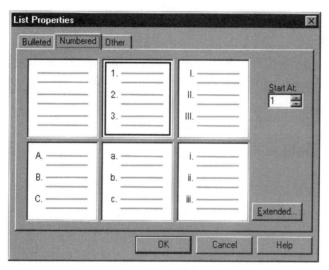

Other: Lets you choose a list style, such as Bulleted, Numbered, or Definition (see "Creating Other Types of Lists" later in this chapter). Choose None to turn a list back into normal text.

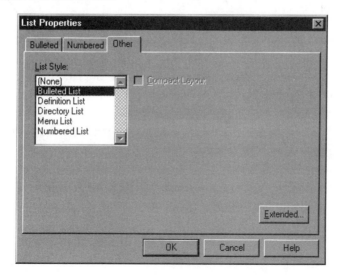

Changing the bullets or numbering from the default will add attributes to the HTML tag for the list. For example, if you select the Roman numeral numbering list that starts at number 5, the HTML `<OL>` tag would look like this:

```
<OL TYPE="I" START="5">
```

Creating a Nested List within a List

You can nest one list with another so that the second is a subordinate of the first. This allows you to create outlines, for example, or tables of contents that have their subheadings indented in their own lists. Shown here is the bulleted list from Figure 6.4, with a second list nested within it.

- International awards
- Corporate history
- Public education
    - Kidz Widget Magazine
    - Public television Widget Night
    - Widgets at Home pamphlet
- Widget hotline
- Widget design contests
- Widget promotions
- Customer survey

NOTE Although the Editor displays a different type of bullet in the nested list, not every browser will bother to do so.

Here is how you would create the nested list shown in the previous example:
1. At the end of the *Public education* line, press Enter to create a new item in the primary list.
2. With the insertion point still on the new line, click the Increase Indent button on the toolbar.
3. Now click the Bulleted List button to turn this new line into an item in a bulleted list (you could instead make it a numbered list by clicking the Numbered List button).

4. Enter the text for this line and then press Enter, which will create the next item in this nested bulleted list.
5. Continue to create new items until you're finished with the nested list. Then simply move the insertion point to another location in the page.

Creating Other Types of Lists

There are several other types of HTML lists that you can create in the Editor, although they seem to be used only rarely in Web sites. The menu and directory lists made early appearances in the HTML standard, but added little functionality to the basic unordered list and have essentially fallen into disuse. They look just like the bulleted list in the Editor, as well as in the most popular browsers. Instead of the `<OL>` tag, they use the `<MENU>` and `<DIR>` tags, respectively.

You can use the definition list to create a glossary of terms, such as the sample shown here. This type of list is a bit different from the ones we've discussed so far, because it actually consists of two different types of elements—a term and a definition.

> bookmark
> > Named text in a page that can be the target of a hyperlink.
>
> browser
> > A client-side program that can request files over the WWW or an intranet, and display HTML Web pages.
>
> CGI
> > The Common Gateway Interface is a standard for programs on a server that process requests or data from browsers.

Web browsers will usually display the defined term as normal text, with the definition for the term indented from it. Here's how to create a list of defined terms:

1. On the line where the first term to define will appear (either before or after you type that term), choose Defined Term from the Change Style list on the Format toolbar.
2. Press Enter; the Editor will assume that the new line will be a definition for the term on the line above.
3. Type the definition for that term and press Enter.
4. Now the Editor assumes that this new line will be a new term.
5. Continue to type terms and definitions, pressing Enter after each one. When you're finished with the list of terms and definitions, press Ctrl+Enter.

Here's the code for the definition list shown on the previous page:

```
<DL>
    <DT>bookmark</DT>
    <DD>Named text in a page that...</DD>
    <DT>browser</DT>
    <DD>A client-side program that...</DD>
    <DT>CGI</DT>
    <DD>The Common Gateway Interface is a...</DD>
</DL>
```

This chapter has shown you how to organize a page with the horizontal line, headings, and lists. The next chapter shows you how to change the formatting of the text within a page and the page itself.

Chapter 7

FORMATTING YOUR PAGES

FEATURING

- Selecting text before you format it
- Changing the font of text
- Changing paragraph styles
- Aligning paragraphs
- Indenting paragraphs
- Changing a page's title
- Setting the background color
- Specifying a background image
- Defining a background-definition page

This chapter deals with the way things look on a page and the way a page looks behind the text and images. You'll learn how to change the format of text, paragraphs, and the page itself.

Setting Character Properties

The first thing to remember about formatting your pages in HTML is that it is the *browser* that determines how your pages are displayed. You can play with the formatting of a page all you want, but once it's out on your Web site, all your design work and artistry may be lost on a one- or two-year-old browser that can't support the features you've included.

With that said, you are pretty safe formatting your pages in the FrontPage Editor, because most of its features are mainstream and part of the HTML specification. If a visitor to your Web site is using any browser that's newer than the first version, your page should come through basically as you intended.

Most of the formatting you can apply to characters (text) in a page will be found in the dialog box for the Format ➤ Font command. You will also find equivalent buttons on the Format toolbar. The properties, or attributes, associated with text include the familiar ones such as bold, italic, underline, subscript, and superscript.

You can also apply formatting to entire paragraphs and entire pages that produces similar effects as some of the character formatting discussed in this section. You'll read about these in the "Setting Paragraph Properties" and "Setting Page Properties" sections.

> **TIP**
> You can return selected text to its default style (for that paragraph) by pressing Ctrl+spacebar. This is a quick way to eliminate any changes you've applied to that text, such as a font, font size, or font style such as bold or italic.

Choosing the Text to Format

To change the format of existing text, first select it in any of the usual Windows ways:
- Drag over any text with your mouse.
- Click at the beginning of the text you want to select, hold down the Shift key, and click on the end of the selection.
- Hold down the Shift key and make the selection with one of the keyboard arrow keys.
- Double-click a word to select only that word.
- Point to the left of a paragraph (the mouse pointer will change to an arrow instead of an I-beam) and double-click to select the entire paragraph.

- To select the entire document, press Ctrl+Home to move to the top of the document, and while holding down the Shift key, press Ctrl+End.

Once you have selected the text, you can change its format by accessing its properties, discussed in the next section.

You can also set the format of text before you type it. Just change the properties *without* selecting any text, and any text you type after that will reflect the changes you made.

> **NOTE** Most of the character and paragraph formatting in this chapter will apply to a new paragraph when you press Enter. If you want to start a new paragraph at the end of the page without it inheriting the formatting, press ↓ from the last line of the paragraph, and you will see that a new paragraph is created below it in the default (normal) style.

Accessing Font Properties

Once you have selected the text whose format you want to change, you can display the Font dialog box in any of the following ways:

- Choose Format ➤ Font.
- Choose Edit ➤ Font Properties.
- Right-click on the selected text and choose Font Properties from the shortcut menu.
- Press Alt+Enter.

You can also change the formatting of selected text with the buttons and tools on the Format toolbar, shown below. For example, select text and click the Bold Text button.

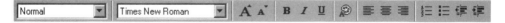

Changing Font Properties

The Font tab in the Font dialog box is shown in Figure 7.1 with its default settings (we'll look at the Special Styles tab in "Changing the Special Styles Properties"). Remember the default font settings here are actually a lack of any special formatting on the selected text so a browser will display the text in its own default style. A 12-point Times Roman font (or equivalent) is often the default font in a browser. But most

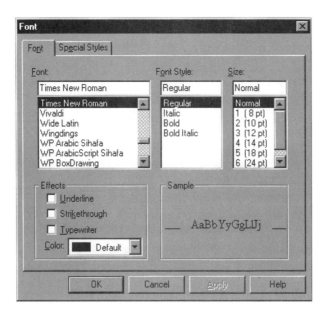

FIGURE 7.1:
You can change the look of text with the options in the Font dialog box.

browsers let you change their default font and also their screen magnification (making all fonts larger or smaller than their actual size).

To change the font properties for the selected text, make your selections in the dialog box, and watch their effect on the sample text in the dialog box. When you're finished, either click the Apply button to see the changes take effect in the page while keeping the dialog box open, or click OK to accept the changes and close the dialog box. Let's look at the font options.

> **NOTE** If you are creating webs in different languages, you can use the Tools ➤ Font Options command to specify the default fonts that should be used with different character sets.

Font

You can select a specific font from the list of all the fonts available to Windows on your computer. You can also choose a font from the Change Font list on the Format toolbar. Again, keep your eye on the Sample pane in the dialog box to see the effect of the font change on the sample text.

The font you choose will appear in the `FACE` attribute for the `<FONT>` tag in the HTML code, such as:

```
<FONT FACE="Arial">This is not the default font.</FONT>
```

Now comes the big caveat: Although you can apply any font available to you, that font must also be available to the browser that opens this page from your Web site. If the font you chose isn't on the browser's computer, the browser will display the text in its default font. The result may or may not be to your liking, but those are the breaks when you're publishing on the Web! To play it safe, stay away from the more obscure fonts that other computers aren't likely to have.

When you become more confident as an HTML author (or overconfident as the case may be), you can use the View ➤ HTML command and then include multiple font names in the `FACE` attribute. If a browser doesn't have the first font, it will try the second, and so on until it finds one it does have. Otherwise, it will use its default font. Here's how the previous code would look with alternative fonts included:

```
<FONT FACE="Arial,Helvetica,Humana">This is...</FONT>
```

Font Style

The choices in the Font Style list give you the expected options of Bold, Italic, and Bold Italic (you can also press Ctrl+B and Ctrl+I as shortcuts for those styles). The Regular choice removes any bold or italic formatting from the selected text. You can also use the Bold and Italic buttons on the Format toolbar to turn those text styles on or off for the selected text.

NOTE The HTML code for the text you make bold will be enclosed in the `<STRONG>` tag; italic text uses the `<EM>` tag (emphasis).

Font Size

To change the size of the font, select one of the seven sizes from the Size list. The other choice, Normal, specifies no size so that a browser will use its default font size, whatever that might be.

You can also change the font size from the Format toolbar with either the Increase Text Size or Decrease Text Size buttons. Click a button once to change to the next size.

The choices in the Size list range from 1 through 7. The Editor shows a point size in parentheses next to each of those numbers, but use that only as a guide. The font-size choices are really HTML-related, where each number represents a *relative* font size that is either bigger or smaller than the default font that a browser is using.

Size 3 is assumed to be the default size in any HTML page. If you choose a size bigger than that, the browser will display that text in a font larger than its default font. Specify a smaller number for a smaller font. The resulting HTML code will look like this,

```
<FONT SIZE="5">
```

which displays the text two sizes larger than the default text in a browser.

Font Effects

The Effects group of options in the Font dialog box (see Figure 7.1) lets you apply three different effects to the text: Underline, `<U>`, underlines the text, as you would expect; Strikethrough, `<STRIKE>`, draws a line through the text; Typewriter, `<TT>`, displays the text in a typewriter-style font (but read "The Formatted Paragraph Style" later in this chapter).

> **NOTE** Here's something to keep in mind before you underline text in a Web page—most browsers signify hyperlink text by underlining it. Therefore, most visitors to your Web site will likely assume any underlined text in a Web page is a hypertext link they can click to open another file on the site.

You can also change the color of text by choosing a color from the Color list in the Effects group of options. As always, the Default choice applies no specific color to the text; a browser will display that text in its own default color. Choose Custom to create your own color.

You can also use the Text Color button on the Format toolbar to change the color of text. It displays the Colors dialog box that contains a palette of colors from which you can choose. If you click the Define Custom Colors button in the Colors dialog box, you can even create your own custom colors that will appear in the Colors dialog box. Note that selecting the Custom color option in the Font dialog box displays this same Colors dialog box and customizing palette.

Changing the Special Styles Properties

The Font dialog box has another tab labeled Special Styles (shown in Figure 7.2). This tab offers you more choices for changing the look of text. These choices are relegated to a separate tab, because they often overlap other, more commonly used styles, or they are used so rarely you may want to avoid using them at all.

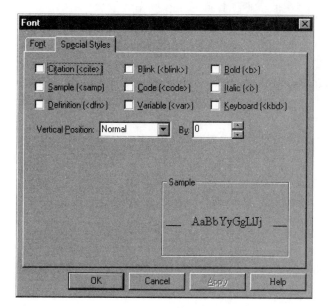

FIGURE 7.2:
The Special Styles tab in the Font dialog box

For example, when you click the Bold button on the Format toolbar or choose that style in the Font tab, you are applying the HTML code <STRONG> to the text. This has been the code for telling a browser to "do something to the text so it stands out." Most browsers have traditionally displayed that text in what we would call boldface. But it's up to the browser, and some browsers might display the text in a larger font, for example.

The Bold option in the Special Styles tab applies the bold tag, <B>. This is a newer HTML tag more specific in what it expects a browser to do. These days, most browsers will display text in either tag in the same way.

You'll find most browsers display the Keyboard, Code, and Sample options in the same style, as well as the Citation and Definition styles.

The Special Styles tab is also where you define subscript or superscript characters. For example, suppose you want to enter the formula 6.02 times 10 to the 23rd power.

Actually, we just created a superscript right here, but let's look at the formula to see how this works in the Editor:

1. Enter the formula in the page, **6.02*1023**, but don't worry about the superscript yet.
2. Select the text you want to make a superscript, in this case the 23.
3. Choose Format ➤ Font and choose the Special Styles tab.
4. In the Vertical Position list, choose Superscript.
5. In the By field, choose or enter **1**.
6. Click the Apply button to see the effect in the page.
7. If you want to increase the height of the superscript relative to its line of text, enter a larger number in the By field (note most browsers simply ignore any height change greater than 2, perhaps because that would be such an unusual layout).
8. Click OK when you're finished.

Shown below is the formula before making the superscript, with the superscript set to 1, and with the superscript set to 2.

$$6.02*1023 \qquad 6.02*10^{23} \qquad 6.02*10^{23}$$

You would use the same process to create a subscript but would choose the Subscript option in the Vertical Position list. These text formats use the `<SUP>` and `<SUB>` tags, respectively.

Setting Paragraph Properties

The FrontPage Editor has a variety of styles that affect entire paragraphs, not just some text within a paragraph. You've already seen some of them, such as the heading tags `<H1>` through `<H6>` and the list tags, where each item in the list is a separate paragraph.

First select the paragraphs whose style you want to change. If you only want to change the current paragraph, you don't need to select anything since the format will apply to the entire paragraph.

You can access the paragraph styles either in the Change Style list on the Format toolbar (shown here) or via the Format ➤ Paragraph command (shown in Figure 7.3). Note that the list of formats in the Paragraph Properties dialog box does not offer the list styles, such as Bulleted or Numbered. Turn back to Chapter 6 for directions on creating those types of lists.

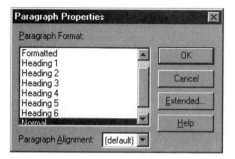

FIGURE 7.3:
You can change the look of paragraphs with the Paragraph Properties dialog box.

The opening and closing tags for each of these styles surround entire paragraphs. In fact, by definition these tags create paragraphs so you may not see the paragraph tag, `<P>`, when these paragraph-related format tags are present.

NOTE The Normal style removes any paragraph formatting and resets the paragraph back to its default style.

The Address style is usually represented by italicized text in a browser and may be indented, as well, in a few browsers. It is typically used for paragraphs that contain an address or other contact information, such as an e-mail address or URL.

When you create a new paragraph, you can choose whether it should have the same formatting as the preceding paragraph:

- To create a paragraph that has no text but is in the same style as the current paragraph, position the insertion point just after the last character in the paragraph and press Enter.
- To split a paragraph in two, position the insertion point where you want the split and press Enter.
- To create a new paragraph after the last paragraph in the page and that uses the default style, move to the last line of the paragraph and press ↓ to create a new line and a new paragraph.

The Formatted Paragraph Style

The Formatted style is a particularly useful one. A browser will display text in this style in a monospace (fixed-width) font, where each character takes up exactly the same amount of space. For example, a *W* would take up the same amount of space as an *i*. It is the one instance in HTML when multiple spaces or hard returns are displayed exactly as they appear in the code.

This style uses the `<PRE>` tag (for preformatted) and makes it possible for you to align text in columns or with indentations, having the characters fall exactly where you expect them to. The advent of the HTML table (see Chapter 11) obviated some of the need for the Formatted style, but the style is still quite important when you need to align text.

For example, Figure 7.4 shows a Web page in which the Formatted style was used. It was then quite easy to line up the form fields with one another just by pressing the spacebar.

Setting Paragraph Alignment

By default, paragraphs are aligned along the left side of the window (either the Editor's or a browser's). You can change the alignment of the current paragraph or

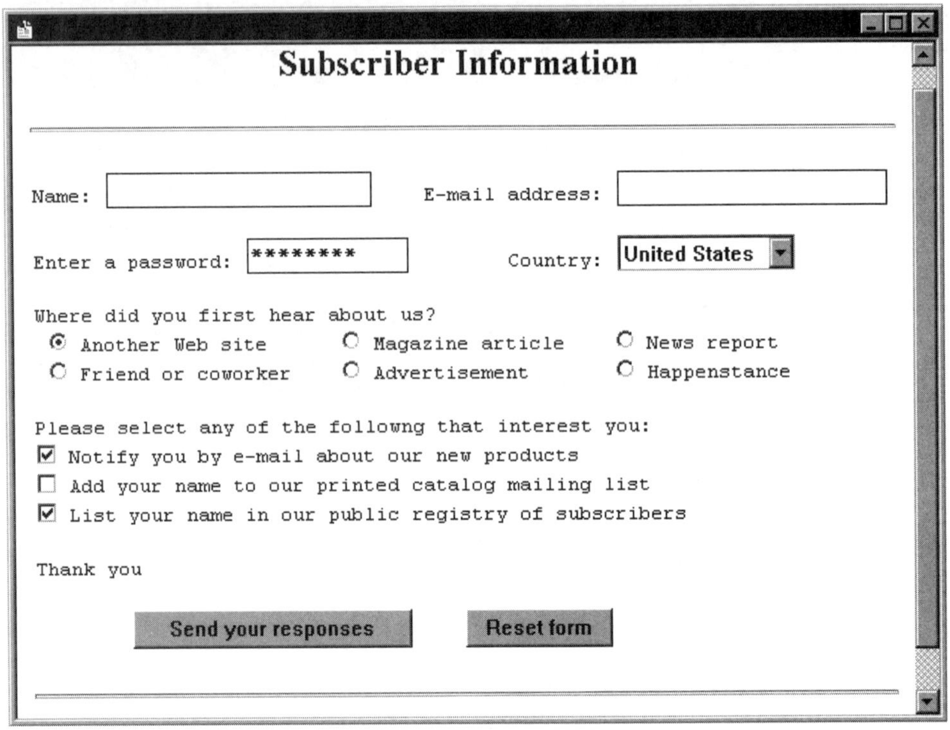

FIGURE 7.4: The Formatted style makes it easy to align the fields in this form page.

the selected paragraphs by clicking the appropriate button on the Format toolbar: Align Left, Center, or Align Right. You can also choose an alignment from the drop-down list in the Paragraph Properties dialog box.

> **NOTE** In the Paragraph Properties dialog box, the Default alignment removes any alignment setting from the paragraph and resets it back to its default alignment. In most cases this will have the same effect as choosing the Left alignment option.

In a regular paragraph, the alignment setting in the HTML code appears as an attribute to the paragraph tag, such as:

```
<P ALIGN="center">
```

Indenting Paragraphs

You can click the Increase Indent button on the Format toolbar to indent the current or selected paragraphs from both the left and right margins. The indent is the result of the <BLOCKQUOTE> tag, which is designed for quoted text that should stand out from the rest of the text. There may be a few browsers that will both indent and italicize the text, but indentation is the norm.

You can double the amount of indentation by clicking the Increase Indent button a second time, or go for more indentation with more clicks. To remove indentation one level at a time, click the Decrease Indent button. As described in Chapter 6, you can also use this button to change a selected bulleted or numbered list back to normal text.

Setting Page Properties

A Web page has its own set of properties you can access by choosing File ➤ Page Properties or by right-clicking anywhere on the page and choosing Page Properties from the shortcut menu. The Page Properties dialog box has four tabs: General, Background, Margins, and Custom. Each is described in the sections that follow.

Changing the Title and Other General Options

The General tab of the Page Properties dialog contains the following settings (see Figure 7.5):

Location: Shows the page's complete URL or file name as a matter of reference. To change a page's location, use the File ➤ Save As command or rename or move that file or the entire web in the Explorer.

Title: Displays and lets you revise the page's title. You usually create a title the first time you save a page (see "Saving a Page" in Chapter 5). You'll find the `<TITLE>` tag appearing within the `<HEAD>` tag near the top of the page.

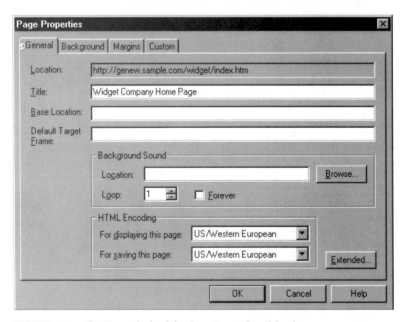

FIGURE 7.5: The General tab of the Page Properties dialog box

> **TIP**
>
> **Be descriptive with the title, as it is used frequently in the FrontPage Editor and the Explorer. The title is also used by Web searching and indexing programs to name your Web page. Web browsers will display the page's title in their title bar, and offer the title as the default name when you save the page's URL as a favorite or bookmarked location.**

Base Location: You can enter an absolute URL here, which will ensure that any hyperlinks on this page that use relative URLs will always point to the correct target (absolute, or complete, URLs are discussed in "Understanding Links" in Chapter 8). By declaring a base URL, you could move this page without moving all the targets of its relative URLs. The targets would be found using the base URL.

Default Target Frame: If this page will be displayed within a frame set, you can specify the name of the frame that should serve as the default frame for all hyperlinks in this page that do not otherwise specify a frame (frame sets are discussed in Chapter 13).

Background Sound: If you want to delight visitors to your page (or possibly annoy them), you can specify the name of a sound file, such as a WAV or MIDI file, that a browser will play when it opens this page. By default, the sound file will be played once, as specified in the Loop field in the Page Properties dialog box; increase the number to play the file more than once. Select the Forever check box, and the sound will play continuously while this page is open in a browser.

> **WARNING** Having a short, welcoming sound play when a page is opened can be a nice feature. Having an annoying sound file play more than once can be an absolute turn off. So use discretion with the background sound, which may mean that you never use the Forever option.

HTML Encoding: Lets you select the character set a browser should use when displaying or saving this page, which allows you to internationalize a page for other languages.

If you want to add HTML code to the page that is not offered by the Editor, press the Extended button. This was discussed in "Inserting Extended HTML Code" in Chapter 4.

Changing the Background Color

The options in the Background tab of the Page Properties dialog box let you set the look of the page's background (see Figure 7.6). Note that you can also access these

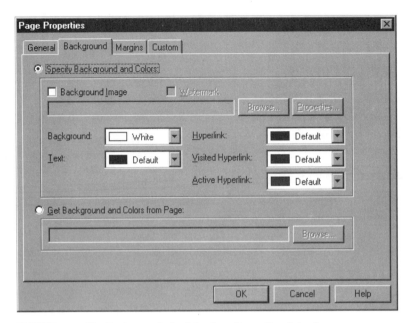

FIGURE 7.6: The Background tab of the Page Properties dialog box

settings via the Format ➤ Background command. The background settings are attributes of the page's <BODY> tag.

You can specify either a color or an image file that a browser will display as a page's background. The Editor also offers a trick that lets you change the background for many pages in a web in one operation; it's a real time-saver (see "Getting Background Options from Another Page" later in this chapter).

The Specify Background and Colors group of options is the default choice for the Background tab. In that group, you can change the color of the page's background and text. The defaults are black text on a white background, but you could, for example, change to white text on a blue background.

> **NOTE** You can also change the colors used for hyperlinks in the page with the three options: Hyperlink, Visited Hyperlink, and Active Hyperlink. However, it's easier to recognize hyperlinks when standard colors are used for them throughout your web. So you should probably avoid changing their colors for a page unless the default colors will conflict with the color you've chosen for that page's background.

Specifying a Background Image

You can specify an image file that will serve as the page's background instead of just a color. A browser will normally tile a small image to fill the background completely so there's no need to specify a large image. In fact, the smaller the image file, the faster it will load into a browser, which is always an important consideration. Often, a visitor to your Web site will skip over a page if it takes too long to load.

Another aspect of the image file is how well it serves as a background. For example, dropping a stunning M.C. Escher picture into the back of a page of text may make the page almost jump out of the screen at you, but it may also make the text mostly unreadable.

You'll find that most background images in use are small and textured and can be easily tiled together into a seamless background. They provide a muted and comfortable backdrop that will not dominate the page.

> **NOTE** When a background image is tiled to fill a page, a browser will scroll the background as you scroll the page. If you choose the Watermark option in the Background tab, those browsers that support this feature will leave the background image stationary while you scroll the page.

To specify an image for a page's background, select the Background Image option. You can use the Browse button to select an image from the Current FrontPage Web tab (such as in the web's `Images` folder) or from the Other Location tab. If you do choose an image file from outside of the web, you can later choose to have that file copied into the web, which ensures the image will always be available.

You can also choose an image from the Clip Art tab, which displays the FrontPage clip art collection, shown in Figure 7.7 (you'll read more about clip art in Chapter 9). Choose Backgrounds in the Category list, select one of the images, and then click OK. The name of that file will then appear in the Background tab of the Page Properties dialog box. When you're finished specifying page properties, you'll find the image you chose has been tiled to fill completely the page's background in the Editor, as it will also do in a browser.

Once you have specified a background image file, you can click the Properties button in the Page Properties dialog box to view or modify the properties of this image. For example, if you choose to make one color in a GIF image transparent, the page's

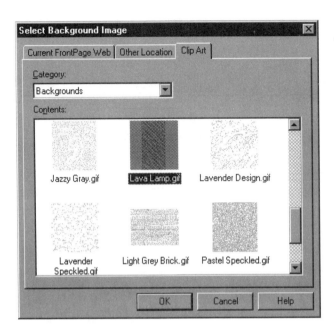

FIGURE 7.7:
The FrontPage clip art collection offers a variety of images that can serve as suitable page backgrounds.

background color will appear through that color. These and other image-editing issues are discussed in "Setting Image Properties" in Chapter 9.

Getting Background Options from Another Page

Imagine your Web site has dozens of pages for which you've tried to keep a consistent look. Most noticeable is the soft yellow background that shows through a pastel rendition of your company's logo that fills the background of each page. It's a real beauty.

Now imagine that someone has thoughtfully suggested that perhaps a soft, very light green would make a better background for these pages. Simple enough to try, if, that is, your Web site had only a page or two. Changing the look of many, many pages, however, is guaranteed to be a real chore.

Happily, FrontPage has a feature that can brush off this dilemma single-handedly, and earn FrontPage's keep in one operation. The trick is an option in the Background tab of the Page Properties dialog box, named Get Background and Colors from Page.

When you select this option, you simply specify a page in your web whose own Background settings will be used for the current page. There's nothing more to it. Each time the current page is opened in a browser or the FrontPage Editor, the settings for its Background options will be read from the other page. Therefore, if you simply change the background settings in that one page, you will effectively change those settings in all the pages that refer to it.

To really take advantage of the this feature, you should use it from the very beginning in building your web. If each new page you create refers to the same page (or one of several), it will be a snap to modify the colors and backgrounds of *all* the pages in your web just by modifying those in a style page. In fact, if you create a template on which to build your new pages, that template can reference a style page (see "Creating a Page from a Template" in Chapter 5).

If you look back at the web shown in Figure 3.2, you'll see the Colors page in the upper-right portion of the Hyperlink view in the Explorer. Although it's not fully apparent in this view, the Colors page serves as a background-definition page for the Widget Company Home Page.

> **TIP** The Colors page is only referenced by other pages in the web and is never opened directly into a browser. This is the type of page you should keep in the web's `_PRIVATE` folder, where the page will be out of the way but available when needed.

Setting Page Margins

You can use the options on the Margins tab of the Page Properties dialog box to specify a top or left margin for the page. By default, these are set to zero so that no margins are specified.

You can define the margin in pixels so the actual width of the blank area at the top or left side of the page in a browser will depend on the screen resolution for that computer. For this reason, and the fact not all browsers support the `MARGINS` attribute for the `<BODY>` tag, you should avoid setting margins for your pages.

Creating Meta Page Information

HTML offers the `<META>` tag as a way for a page's author to supply information about the page to a server that processes the page or a browser that opens the page. When included in a page, this tag appears within the page's `<HEAD>` tag. For example, an author can include a list of keywords in a `<META>` tag that the server will use to index that page for Web-wide searching. A browser might use the `<META>` tag to determine which character set should be used to display the page or at what intervals it should reload the page automatically.

In the Custom tab in the Page Properties dialog box, you (the page's author) can add, modify, or remove what FrontPage refers to as *variables*, which appear within the `<META>` tag for a page. It's unlikely you'll need to work with variables, but it's good to know where you can access them. In a sense, a variable within the `<META>` tag and an attribute within any other HTML tag perform similar functions. Each has a keyword and a corresponding value, and each provides information that goes with their tag.

NOTE Don't confuse these meta-variables with the FrontPage Explorer's configuration variables, which allow you to display information automatically in the pages in the web. You can read about web configuration variables in "Automating Text Entry with the Substitution WebBot" in Chapter 10.

By default, the Editor creates two variables for a page. The single system variable tells a browser or server what type of document this is and the character set that should be used for it. The user variable simply lets the world know which program generated this page.

Each variable consists of a name, such as Generator, and a value, such as Microsoft FrontPage 2.0. Any system variables you create will appear as part of the `HTTP-EQUIV` attribute for the `<META>` tag. The user variables you create appear as their own attributes of that tag.

This chapter has taught you how to change the appearance of your pages in the Editor by modifying the properties of text, paragraphs, and the page itself. Now we'll move on to the topic of hyperlinks, which is perhaps the most important aspect of any Web page you create.

Chapter 8

LINKING YOUR PAGES TO THE WORLD

FEATURING

- Learning about hyperlinks
- Creating a hyperlink
- Creating an internal hyperlink
- Linking to a bookmark
- Creating an external hyperlink
- Changing or deleting a hyperlink
- Creating bookmarks
- Creating an image map
- Keeping links up to date

This chapter describes probably the most important feature of any Web site you create—hyperlinks. You'll learn about the different kinds of hyperlinks you can place in a page, how to create hyperlinks from text and images, how to define the target of a link, how to create multiple links in one image, and how to let FrontPage keep your links up to date.

Understanding Links

The trick that puts the "Web" into the "World Wide Web" is the *hyperlink* (or *link* or *hotspot*), first discussed in Chapter 1. A hyperlink is either a graphic image or text (often a different color and underlined) in a Web page; you click the hyperlink in a browser to open the target resource referenced by that link. With hyperlinks, a Web author can create a document that links to several other documents anywhere on the Web.

There are several types of hyperlinks you can include in a page and many different ways to create them, but every hyperlink consists of two primary parts:

Hyperlink: The text or image in a page that you define as a hyperlink; clicking the hyperlink while using a browser opens the link's target resource.

Target: The URL, or address, of the file that opens when you click the hyperlink in a browser.

> **NOTE** The hyperlinks you create in your Office 97 documents consist of these same two components. When you include these documents in a FrontPage web, their hyperlinks will appear in the Explorer just like the hyperlinks in HTML pages.

Text or Image Hyperlinks

A text hyperlink is probably the most common type of hyperlink; it can be anywhere from one word to several lines long. However, remember that a hyperlink references another page, usually on a different but related topic. If the hyperlink's text is too long, maybe that's a hint of what should actually be on the target page.

You can see two examples of hyperlinks as displayed in Internet Explorer in Figure 8.1. On the top is a text hyperlink. Like most popular browsers, Internet Explorer employs several different ways to indicate text is a hyperlink. For instance, the link text is usually underlined and displayed in a different color, making it stand out on the page.

As you can see in the figure, when you move your mouse pointer over a link, the pointer changes to a hand and the name of the link's target appears on the status bar in the lower-left corner of the screen (the Editor does the same). This cue not only tells you this text is a hyperlink, but it also lets you know what URL you will access by clicking the link.

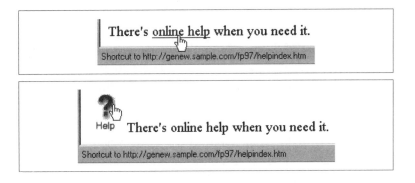

FIGURE 8.1:
Many browsers display the URL of a text or graphic hyperlink when you point to the link.

You can also define any image in a page as a hyperlink so clicking the image activates a link. An image not only livens up a page but can often purvey the proverbial 10,000 or so words.

The bottom of Figure 8.1 shows an image hyperlink. In this case, the text next to the image merely describes the link. As with a text link, when you point to an image hyperlink in Internet Explorer, the pointer changes to a hand and the status bar displays the hyperlink's target. In this example, the target URL is the same for both the text link on the top and the image link on the bottom.

You can bring an image into a page with the Insert ➤ Image command or by copying or dragging it from another program. You'll read more about images in Chapter 9, "Displaying Images in Your Pages."

> **TIP**
>
> As a Web author, you should consider that most browsers do not display a hyperlink image any differently than a regular image. Because not every person reading your page will be psychic, the context in which the image hyperlink appears in the page is very important. Descriptive text within or next to the image, as in Figure 8.1, can ensure the image's purpose as a hyperlink is understood.

Target Files and Bookmarks

You specify the target file of a hyperlink with its URL, such as

```
http://genew.sample.com/fp97/helpindex.htm
```

The file you name is what a browser will open when a reader activates the link, such as by clicking it.

The target can be any type of file. For example, the browser might open a Web page, a graphic image, a sound file, or a video file. The target could also be a program file that the target server will run, such as a CGI (Common Gateway Interface) script that might, for example, calculate the total number of accesses to the current Web site and then return the result to the browser. The target file can also be at one of several different locations. For example, the target file might be located on the browser's local hard disk, on an intranet site, or on a site anywhere on the World Wide Web.

When you specify a page as the target of a hyperlink, you can also include the name of a bookmark, or named location, within that page. The browser will display that location at the top of the reader's screen when the page is opened.

The HTML anchor tag, `<A>`, defines a link. It includes the source of the link (the text or image hyperlink) and the target file. Here is the code for the text link shown on the top of Figure 8.1:

```
There's <A HREF="helpindex.htm">online help</A> when you
need it.
```

Now look at the code for the image link shown on the bottom of Figure 8.1:

```
<A HREF="helpindex.htm"><IMG SRC="images/help.gif"
border="0" width="46" height="51"></A> There's online help
when you need it.
```

In each case, the target of the hyperlink is specified as an attribute of the `<A>` tag.

Absolute and Relative URLs

When you reference another file in a page, such as the target of a hyperlink, you can define the reference in two different ways. An *absolute* reference uses a complete URL to name the exact location of the file, starting with the protocol that should be used to access it. Here are three examples of absolute URLs:

```
http://www.widget.com/
http://www.widget.com/hist-toc.htm
http://www.widget.com/images/logo.gif
```

As always, if a URL does not include a specific file name, such as in the first example, the server at that location will send the default file, such as `INDEX.HTM`, or perhaps simply a listing of all the files in that folder.

A *relative* reference names the location of a file in relation to the location of the page that contains the hyperlink to it. For example, if a link in the `HIST-TOC.HTM` page, which is at the previous address, refers simply to

`history1-1.htm`

the implication is that this file resides in the same location as the source of the reference, `HIST-TOC.HTM`. In other words, a relative reference to the file

`images/logo.gif`

means the `Images` folder is a subfolder of the folder in which the source file, in this example `HIST-TOC.HTM`, already resides.

> **NOTE** In general, you should use a relative reference when the target of the hyperlink resides within the active FrontPage web (an internal reference). In many cases, you will use an absolute reference only when the target lies outside of the web (an external reference).

Because a relative URL is based on the source page's URL, you really can't create a relative hyperlink in a new, as yet unsaved, page in the Editor. For example, if you select a page from the Explorer's current web as the link's target, that reference will be absolute, because the new page you're working in is not yet a part of that web. Once you save the page, though, links you create to files in the same web will be relative links.

Because a relative reference always begins at the location of the source of the reference, it doesn't really matter where that source page resides. You could move the Web site to a new server, or to a new folder on a server, and all the relative references to files within that site should continue to work.

For example, if you rename the Widget Web site in the above example to Wudgett, you would have to spend hours and hours revising any absolute references to files on that site, such as

`http://www.wudgett.com/images/logo.gif`

But you could ignore any relative addresses to its files, such as

`images/logo.gif`

This relative URL still points to the `Images` folder within the source page's folder, which now happens to be `WUDGETT` instead of `WIDGET`. At all costs, avoid making absolute references to files when a relative one will do.

Creating a Hyperlink

As you have learned, you can create a hyperlink in the FrontPage Editor from either text or an image, and the target can be a file either within the active FrontPage web or outside of it. There are several ways to create a link, but here's the most common way:

1. In the Editor, select the text or image you want to serve as a hyperlink (either click on an image or use the Shift+drag method you would use to select text).
2. Choose Edit ➤ Hyperlink (Ctrl+K) or click the Create or Edit Hyperlink button on the toolbar.
   This displays the Create Hyperlink dialog box, where you specify the target of the link in one of its four tabs:

   Open Pages: Select the target from a list of all the pages currently open in the Editor.

   Current FrontPage Web: Select from any of the files in the active FrontPage web (the site that is open in the Explorer); this creates an internal link that will use a relative URL.

   Word Wide Web: Choose the type of hyperlink to create—such as HTTP, Mailto, or FTP—and the URL of the target; this will generally be a URL external to the active web.

   New Page: Enter a page title and URL to create a new Web page that will serve as the target for the link.

3. When you are finished defining the hyperlink, click the OK button.

If this was a text hyperlink, you would find the selected text is now underlined and displayed in blue (unless you have changed the default color for links, as described in Chapter 7). You can edit the text that serves as the link just as you would any other text in the page. When you move your mouse over the text or image hyperlink, you'll see the link's target on the left side of the status bar.

Once you understand how links work, you can take advantage of other methods to create links. For instance, you can do any of the following:

- Drag a file from the FrontPage Explorer into a page in the Editor to create a link to that file. If the target file is a Web page, its title will appear as the link text in the page as though you had typed the title at the line where you released the mouse button. For a page without a title, you'll see the file's name appear as the link text.

- Simply type the URL of the target file (it must begin with a protocol, such as HTTP), and the Editor will automatically define that text as a link to the URL you specified. If you want to link to a page you have open in a browser, copy the URL of the page from the browser's address field, paste it into the Editor, and then press the spacebar to signal the end of the link text.
- Drag a hyperlink from a page in your browser into a page in the Editor to create that same link in the Editor.

Linking to an Open Page

The Open Pages tab in the Create Hyperlink dialog box (Edit ➤ Hyperlink) lists the page title for each page open in the Editor (see Figure 8.2). The page you select in the Open Pages list will become the target of the hyperlink.

When you select one of the titles, its file name will appear near the bottom of the dialog box next to the Hyperlink Points To label. In Figure 8.2, the file `HISTORY1-2.HTM` is currently selected in the Open Pages list.

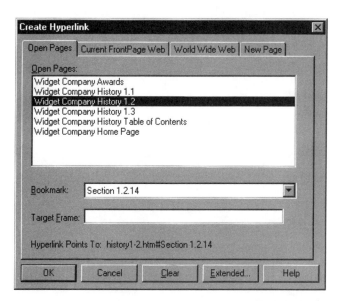

FIGURE 8.2: You can select one of the pages open in the Editor to serve as the target for a hyperlink.

Linking to a Bookmark

A bookmark is simply the FrontPage name for a specific, named location within one page that can serve as the target for a link (you'll read about creating bookmarks a little later in this chapter). You'll also hear the term *destination* or *named target* to describe this HTML feature. When you are defining a hyperlink, if the target page you select is either open in the Editor or part of the active web in the Explorer, you can select one of its bookmarks from the Bookmark drop-down list in the Open pages tab of the Create Hyperlink dialog box.

> **NOTE** To create a link to a bookmark in the current page (the page in which you're creating the link), just select that page in the Open Pages tab in the Create Hyperlink dialog box, and then choose a bookmark from the drop-down list.

In Figure 8.2, the bookmark named *Section 1.2.14* has been selected, and the bookmark has been appended to the file name in the Hyperlink Points To field. In HTML, a reference to a bookmark name is preceded by a pound sign (#); so the complete reference for this link is

```
history1-2.htm#Section 1.2.14
```

If this link were to a bookmark in the current page, you'd see only the pound sign and bookmark name, such as

```
#Section 1.2.14
```

When a reader later clicks on this link in a browser, the page `HISTORY1-2.HTM` will open, and the browser will display the bookmark named *Section 1.2.14* at the top of the screen.

So you don't lose touch with the underlying HTML code, here's how the anchor tag would look for this target file and bookmark:

```
<A HREF="history1-2.htm#Section 1.2.14">1.2.14—Widgets in
WWII</A>
```

The link text appears between the opening and closing anchor tags: <u>1.2.14— Widgets in WWII</u>.

Specifying a Target Frame

If the current page (the one containing the hyperlink you are defining) is part of a frame set, you can specify which frame will display the target file when it is opened. A *frame set* is a single page that displays other pages within *frames*, or windows, in that page. It allows your browser to display multiple pages, instead of having to close a page in order to open another one.

For example, if the current page is a table of contents that will be displayed in a frame on the left side of the frame set in a browser, you could specify that the right-hand frame will display the target page. You'll read about creating frame sets and naming frames in Chapter 13.

Linking to a Page in the Current FrontPage Web

You can link to any file in the web that's currently open in the Explorer by choosing the Current FrontPage Web tab in the Create Hyperlink dialog box (shown here). You

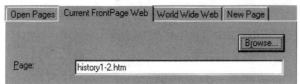

can either type the name of the target file in the Page field or click the Browse button to select from a list of all files in the site.

You can also specify a bookmark in the target page or the frame in which to display the page (these options were discussed in the previous section). Because the target file is in the same site as the source file that contains the link, the reference to the target will be a relative one.

Linking to a Page on the WWW

To create a link to a file not open in the Editor and not in your current FrontPage

web, choose the World Wide Web tab in the Create Hyperlink dialog box (shown here).

Select a protocol, such as HTTP, FTP, News, or File, from the Hyperlink Type drop-down list. This will preface the URL for the link and will be the protocol that accesses the file when the link is activated (clicked) in a browser. If you want to specify a different protocol or create a relative URL that does not include a protocol, choose Other.

Next, enter a URL for the file in the URL field. Don't include the protocol unless you selected the Other option from the Hyperlink Type list. You can also click the Browse button to find the file. This opens your default Windows browser, along with a message telling you to locate the URL you want. After selecting the URL, switch back to the Editor. The URL from the browser will appear in the URL field in the Editor's Create Hyperlink dialog box.

Linking to a New Page

You can create a link to a Web page that does not yet exist if you choose the New Page tab in the Create Hyperlink dialog box (see Figure 8.3). This is a convenient way to create pages as you create the links to them so you can continue to work in one page while creating links and their targets at the same time.

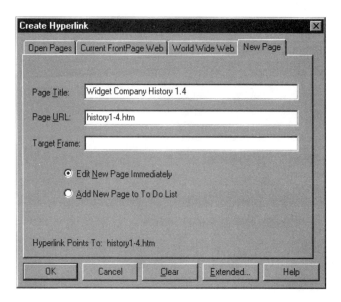

FIGURE 8.3: You can create a link to a page that does not yet exist in the New Page tab of the Create Hyperlink dialog box.

If you selected text in the page before choosing Edit ➤ Hyperlink, that text will appear in the Page Title field as a proposed title for the new page. The first eight characters of that text will appear in the Page URL field as a proposed file name for the new page.

Before you click OK to create the link, choose whether to have the new page displayed in the Editor (the Edit New Page Immediately option) so you can work on it right now or to have it left on disk where you can get to it later (the Add New Page To Do List option). If you choose the latter, the file will be created but not opened, and a task will be added to the To Do List to remind you that the page has been created.

With either choice, when you click OK, the New Page dialog box will appear, as though you had chosen the File ➤ New command. Select the type of page you want to create and click OK.

Revising, Deleting, and Following Hyperlinks

With FrontPage, you can change either component of a link—the text or image on which the hyperlink is defined (the source) or the hyperlink definition itself (the target's address). You can also delete the hyperlink definition while leaving the text or image you click to get there intact. And at the click of a button, you can navigate through the hyperlink's target pages in the Editor.

Revising a Hyperlink

You can change the text of a hyperlink (the text you click to activate the link) simply by editing it as you would any other text. As long as the text you revise is still underlined, you'll know it's still a link.

You can also change the image for an image hyperlink. Just right-click on the image and choose Image Properties from the shortcut menu. In the Image Properties dialog box, specify the new image in the Image Source field; you

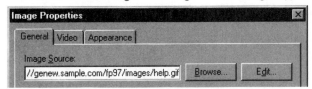

can click the Browse button to select an image from your FrontPage web or another location (shown above). The new image in the page will then serve as the image hyperlink.

To modify the hyperlink definition, select the image (click on it) or position the insertion point anywhere within the link text (you need not select any of the text), 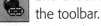 and choose Edit ➤ Hyperlink or click the Create or Edit Hyperlink button on the toolbar.

This action displays the Edit Hyperlink dialog box, which is essentially the same as the Create Hyperlink dialog box shown earlier in this chapter. You'll see the current link definition in the Hyperlink Points To field. You can specify a different target file, bookmark, or target frame for the link, and click OK when you're finished.

Deleting a Hyperlink

When you delete a text or image hyperlink from a page, you are not affecting the link's target file or bookmark. There are several ways to delete a link:

- Delete the image or all of the text for the link, and the link to the target file (but not the actual file) will be deleted as well. Keep that in mind when you're simply revising the text of a link, and be careful you don't accidentally delete all the text (if you do, remember Undo).
- To delete a hyperlink while not deleting the link text or link image from the page, select the link image or position the insertion point anywhere within the link text (you need not select any of the text), and then choose Edit ➤ Unlink.
- To remove the link definition from just some of the link text, select that text and choose Edit ➤ Unlink.
- When you're working in the Create Link or Edit Link dialog box, click the Clear button to delete the link definition.

Following Hyperlinks in the Editor

The FrontPage Editor lets you navigate through the links in a page in much the same way you do in a browser. If a hyperlink in the Editor's current page has a Web page as its target, you can open that page in the Editor by holding down the Ctrl key (the pointer will change to a right-pointing arrow) and clicking the link (or using the Tools ➤ Follow Hyperlink command). If the link also includes a bookmark, the Editor will display that location at the top of the screen when the page is opened.

When you follow a link to another page, especially one outside of the active FrontPage web and on another server, there's always a chance the server at that site will be running very slowly or be otherwise unresponsive. To cancel opening that page, press Esc or click the Stop button, just as you can do in your browser.

When you have opened several pages in the Editor, you can use the Back and Forward buttons on the toolbar to switch from one to another (or use the Back and Forward commands on the Tools menu).

Working with Bookmarks

In the previous sections you read about including a bookmark as the target for a hyperlink so when the target page is opened in a browser, the browser will display the bookmark location within that page. Without a bookmark reference, a browser will usually display the top of the page.

Defining a Bookmark

Creating a bookmark is essentially just naming a location in the page so you can then refer to that location by that name. Here's how to do it:

1. In the Editor, move the insertion point to the line where you want to create the new name.
2. Although you can create a name there without selecting any text, it's usually a good idea to select the text you want the name to define. That way, if you add more text to the paragraph, the bookmark will still be attached to the text you selected.
3. Choose Edit ➤ Bookmark, which displays the Bookmark dialog box (shown here).

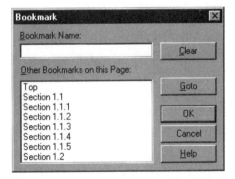

4. Enter the text for the new name in the Bookmark Name field. Note that if you selected some text before invoking the command, you'll find that text already in the field, which you can revise as necessary.
5. When you're finished, click OK.

NOTE The name you create for a bookmark should clearly describe the location you're naming so you or another author can easily find it in the list of bookmarks when you are creating a hyperlink to its page. Try to keep your bookmarks reasonably short, perhaps just a word or two in most cases.

The HTML tag for a bookmark is an attribute of the anchor tag. If you selected the text *Section 1.2—Production Cycles* and then created the bookmark name *Section 1.2*, here's how the code would look:

```
<A NAME="Section 1.2">Section 1.2 - Production Cycles</A>
```

In the FrontPage Editor, any text within the opening and closing anchor tags will be underlined with a dashed blue line, as long as the View ➤ Format Marks command is enabled (shown here). A browser, however, does not indicate any bookmarks within a page; it simply uses them as reference points when they are included in hyperlinks.

Section 1.2 - Production Cycles describes the cyclical nature of the Widget industry

Revising, Deleting, and Going to Bookmarks

Within the FrontPage Editor, you can jump to any bookmark in the page by selecting it in the Bookmark dialog box (Edit ➤ Bookmark) and pressing the Goto button. The dialog box will remain open, and because the insertion point is now on a bookmark, the Clear button will be enabled. Click that button to remove this bookmark from the page. Only the name will be removed; text in the page will not be affected.

To revise the name of a bookmark, click anywhere within the text defined as the bookmark, or use the Goto command to get there. In the Bookmark dialog box, you should see the name of that bookmark in the Bookmark Name field. Edit the name as needed and, when you're done, click OK.

> **WARNING** FrontPage does not keep track of all the bookmarks in your Web site. When you revise or delete a bookmark, FrontPage will *not* update the entire site for the change you made. You will have to revise "by hand" any links that referenced the bookmark.

Creating Clickable Image Maps

You've seen how you can create a clickable hyperlink from either text or an image. Now you'll see how to go one step further by creating an *image map*, which is a single image containing multiple hyperlinks. Each hyperlink is associated with a defined area of the image called a *hotspot*, which, when clicked, activates that link. In a browser, you see only the image; there is no indication it has clickable hotspots.

You've undoubtedly encountered image maps in many, many pages on the Web. They can be informative, attractive, and intuitive, and they can also transcend language, which is an important consideration on the World Wide Web.

A typical use of an image map is literally in the form of a map, where you can click on a city, state, or region to display information about that region. Creating an image map from a map of the United States works very well when you're defining the hotspots for the large, regularly shaped western states. But the plan doesn't work so well when you try to create hotspots on the smaller, irregularly shaped eastern states.

In such a case, you'd be better off with a regional map of the United States, where clicking in the east would then display a map of just that region of the country, and clicking in the west would display the western states (see Figure 8.4).

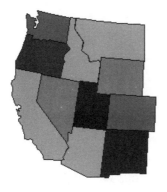

FIGURE 8.4: A geographic map can be a very practical way to implement an image map.

With those issues in mind, you should also be aware of the following when you incorporate an image map in a page:

- The context of the image map must be such that a reader of that page will have no doubt the image is, indeed, a place to click to open another resource. If the image isn't completely self-explanatory, then an appropriate title might do the trick.

- A large image can take a long time to download on a dial-up connection (about 3,200 characters, or bytes, per second at 28,800 bits per second); so use large image maps with some discretion.
- The image you use for the image map must be quite descriptive of the choices it contains. Although an image can easily convey 10,000 words, an image map just won't work if every visitor to that page sees a different 10,000.
- Hotspots in a image map must be easy to discern or readers will be clicking and going to pages they had no intention of visiting. The same problem would occur if the hotspots were too small or too numerous.
- You can't predict how clearly your image will appear in the browser of every visitor to your site or whether that image will appear at all (perhaps the visitor turned off the display of images to shorten connection time). To ensure a reader can access exactly the right link, it's good practice to include text hyperlinks, as well (as in Figure 8.4).

The process of defining an image map is really quite simple (each is described in the following sections):

1. First decide what type of image maps you want to use in your FrontPage web: server-side, client-side, or both.
2. Insert the image that will serve as the image map into a page.
3. Define a hotspot in the image for one of the hyperlinks.
4. Define the target of that hyperlink.
5. Define the other hotspots and hyperlink definitions for the rest of the image map.

Choosing the Type of Image Map

You can create one of two types of image maps in a FrontPage web. The difference between them is in the way the click of a mouse within the image map is handled:

- A *server-side* image map is the traditional type. When you click within an image map, the browser sends the coordinates of the click (relative to the image) to the server of that Web site. The server looks up those coordinates in a table of hotspots for that image map and processes the appropriate hyperlink target. Different servers may have different ways of storing the coordinates and targets for an image map.
- A *client-side* image map obviates any server interaction because the hotspot coordinates for the image map are included in the HTML definition that is sent to the browser. When you click within the client-side image map, the browser looks to see which target is associated with those coordinates and then opens that target.

A client-side image map not only reduces the processing burden on the server, but it also is guaranteed to work no matter which server is hosting the page that contains the image map. However, client-side image maps are a fairly recent invention, and not all browsers may yet support them.

With FrontPage, though, you can create image maps that use both the server-side and client-side definitions. If a browser to your web can support the client-side definition, it will do so. Others will use the server-side definition.

You set the image map type in the FrontPage Explorer for the entire active web.

1. Choose Tools ➤ Web Settings and then choose the Advanced tab in the Web Settings dialog box (see Figure 8.5).

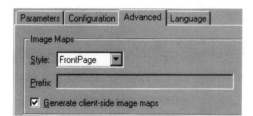

FIGURE 8.5:
You specify the image map type in the Advanced tab in the Web Settings dialog box.

2. To create client-side HTML code for each image map, select the Generate Client-Side Image Maps check box.
3. If you only want client-side image maps, choose None in the Style drop-down list.
4. If you want to create server-side HTML code, select a server from the Style drop-down list. Leave the client-side check box selected to generate both types of image map code, or deselect that check box if you only want server-side code.
5. Choose FrontPage from the server Style list if the server supports the FrontPage Server Extensions.
6. Otherwise, choose one of the other server types. In that case, you should also enter the path and name of the image-map handler (program) on that server that processes the coordinates when the map is clicked. For example, the default entry in the Prefix field for an NCSA-compatible server is `/cgi-bin/imagemap`.
   Revise this as needed for the actual location and name on the server that will be hosting this web.

Once you have chosen the type of image map, FrontPage will generate the appropriate code whenever you create an image map in a page in this web.

Defining the Hotspots

For this example, you can create an image map from any image in a page appropriate for the job at hand—large enough to contain the hotspots, not so large that it will take a long time to download to a browser, and meaningful to a reader. The image we'll be using here (see Figure 8.6) was conveniently captured from Sybex's Web site at

    http://www.sybex.com

This is a spacious image map that uses a desktop metaphor for its hyperlinks—a notepad and pen link to a feedback page, a couple of disks link to a download page, and a newspaper classified section links to a job listing page.

FIGURE 8.6: The Sybex home page uses an image map that offers hyperlinks to the main areas of the Web site.

Linking Your Pages to the World 163

> **NOTE** This image works well as an image map, because it is attractive and invites the reader to stay and browse through the site; its pictures (hyperlink buttons) are clearly defined and easy to locate in the image; each picture has a short text description next to it that pins down its purpose; and it has text hyperlinks below the picture for those browsers that can't handle images.

If you'd like to use this image for this exercise, go to the Sybex Web site and either copy the image to the Editor, or save the image to disk and then bring it into the Editor with the Insert ➤ Image command. For example, in Microsoft Internet Explorer, right-click on the image and choose Copy from the shortcut menu. In the Editor, choose Edit ➤ Paste.

Here's how to define the first hyperlink hotspot in this image, thereby making that image into an image map (with just one hyperlink so far). We'll start with the *About Sybex* picture in the center of the image.

1. Select the entire image by clicking on it; you'll see the selection handles appear on its corners and sides. If the Image toolbar (shown here) was not already displayed, it will appear now and its buttons will be enabled (not dimmed).
2. Click the Rectangle button on the Image toolbar so you can define a rectangular hotspot in the image.
3. Point to the lower-left corner of the laptop computer in the image, which is the widest edge of the laptop; notice that the pointer changes to a pencil.
4. Hold down the mouse button and drag toward the upper-right corner of the laptop's screen. As you drag, a rectangle will expand over the image, defining the area of the hotspot.
5. When the rectangle surrounds the laptop (as shown here), release the mouse button. This will display the Create Hyperlink dialog box, in which you define the target of this hyperlink.

Chapter Eight

> **NOTE**
>
> The hotspot you just defined extends slightly beyond the edges of the laptop and includes the text description, *About Sybex*, above it. This ensures a reader can click anywhere on the laptop or the description to activate the link.

6. At this point, you define the target of the hyperlink just as you would for a normal text or image hyperlink. For this example, you can either link to a file in your active web, or just enter a dummy target, such as **About Sybex.htm**. Click OK to complete the job of defining the first hotspot in the image map (if you entered a dummy name for a target, you'll be asked to verify that you want to create a link to a nonexistent target; choose Yes).

Let's define a second hyperlink in this image map. This one will be irregularly shaped, over the picture of the open book labeled *Updates* in Figure 8.6:

7. If the image is no longer selected, click on it to select it.
8. Click the Polygon button on the Image toolbar.
9. Click once on the lower-left corner of the *Updates* book in the image to begin the first line of the polygonal hotspot (this is simply a convenient beginning point).
10. Point to the lower-right corner of the *Updates* book; you'll see a line extend from the first point to the mouse pointer. Click once to end this line and establish the first edge of the hotspot. Try not to overlap the rectangular hotspot you already created, otherwise there could be confusion when a reader clicks in that area.
11. Continue from corner to corner, clicking on each one to extend the edges of this hotspot. As long as you don't overlap into another hotspot, try to extend this hotspot a little beyond the edges of the picture of the book so that a click that would otherwise be a "near miss" will still activate the link.
12. When you reach the beginning point, double-click to end the definition of this hotspot (as shown here).
13. Define the target for this hotspot, either to a file on your active web or to a dummy file such as **Updates.htm**.

14. Don't forget to save this page if you want to return to it later or test it in your browser.

Now this image map has two hotspots in it. You can continue to create others, as needed, using the appropriate button on the Image toolbar, either Rectangle, Polygon, or Circle (to create a circular hotspot, drag from the center of the circle outward).

Specifying a Default Hyperlink

You'll find that in many image maps, such as the one in the previous example, there will be some undefined regions not covered by a hotspot. This could present a problem when a reader clicks on the image, ostensibly on a hotspot, and then waits and waits for something to happen that never does, all because the reader clicked outside of any of the defined hotspots.

If you want to avoid this situation, you can define a default hyperlink for the image, in which you specify a target for all areas of the image outside of any hotspots for hyperlinks. This ensures no matter where a reader clicks on the image map, something will happen. For example, the default target for an image map might be a page that simply advises the reader to return to the previous page and try again.

To define a default hyperlink for an image map, right-click on the image and choose Image Properties from its shortcut menu. In the Appearances tab in the dialog box,

you'll find the Default Hyperlink options (shown here). Enter the target for the link in the Location field, just as you would for any other hyperlink. If the current page will be displayed within a frame set, you can use the Target Frame option to specify the frame that will display the target for this default hyperlink.

Viewing Hotspots

When you select an image map in the FrontPage Editor, each of its hotspots will be outlined. When the image map is not selected, or when you are viewing it in a browser, you won't notice anything different about the image; the hotspot outlines are invisible.

However, when you move your mouse pointer over a hotspot in a client-side image map (which contains the address of the target), the target of that link will be displayed in the status line in the Editor (and in most browsers, as well).

In some cases when you select an image map in the Editor, the image may hide the hotspot outlines or make them difficult to see. You can circumvent this problem by clicking the Highlight Hotspots button on the Image toolbar.

This hides the image completely while still outlining each of its hotspots so you can get a good idea of where each one lies in the image. You can't move or resize a hotspot in this view, but you can change the target of its hyperlink definition.

Revising Hotspots

Once you've created an image map, you can change any of its hotspots at any time in the Editor. You can delete a hotspot, change its shape, or change the target of that hyperlink.

To make any of these changes, first select the image. Then click the Select button on the Image toolbar and click anywhere within the hotspot you want to change to select it. You'll see selection handles appear around its edges.

> **WARNING** Remember, selecting an image is much the same as selecting text. If, for example, you select an image and then type a single character, you will replace the image with that character. So use caution when you are busily working on an image.

Once you've selected a hotspot, you can do any of the following:
- Select the next hotspot by pressing Tab.
- Delete the selected hotspot and its hyperlink from the image by pressing Del.
- Change the shape of the hotspot by dragging any of its selection handles.
- Move the hotspot by dragging it (but not from a selection handle) or by selecting it and using the arrow keys on your keyboard.
- Change the target definition by right-clicking within the hotspot and choosing Image Hotspot Properties from the shortcut menu. This displays the Edit Hyperlink dialog box where you can revise the target of the link (as discussed earlier in this chapter in "Revising a Hyperlink").

Fixing and Verifying Links in the Explorer

One of the most important Web-management jobs is maintaining all the hyperlinks in your pages. After all, without hyperlinks, a Web site really isn't a web at all:

- If you want to keep your Web site shipshape and running smoothly, you must ensure each hyperlink references the correct target. If you rename a file in your FrontPage web, for example, you must also revise the target name in any hyperlinks that reference that file.
- You must also ensure each hyperlink target's URL is still valid and works correctly. This is especially important for external links because you have no control over the location of their targets. The only way to perform this duty is by clicking on each link and seeing that its target is found. If it's not, then the link is broken and needs to be fixed (see the next section).

Because Web sites can have so many links, these jobs can be some of the most time-consuming aspects of managing a site—unless of course, you're using FrontPage.

Fixing Target Names Automatically

In "Renaming or Moving a File" in Chapter 3, you learned how to rename a file or move it to another folder in a FrontPage web. Doing so would normally leave any hyperlinks to this file essentially dead because they would still target the original name or location.

However, when you change a file's name or location in the FrontPage Explorer, the Explorer will automatically update any links to that file in the current web so they reference the new name or location.

When you rename a file, the Explorer will display the Rename dialog box, asking you if you want to update all the hyperlinks to this file. Choose Yes and those links will be revised to reference the new name, and you won't have to worry about a "dead" link. Choose No and the file will be renamed but the links will still reference the old name. You might do this when you are going to create a new file with that old name that will serve as the target of those hyperlinks.

When you move a file to another folder in the FrontPage web, just sit back and let the Explorer automatically update all links to that file, so they point to the new location. Again, this would be a very tedious job to perform by hand, but the Explorer does it in seconds while you take another sip of your coffee.

Verifying Links in the Explorer

The Explorer can also help you verify the links in your FrontPage web and find any that are broken (can no longer access their targets). You could check the links by actually browsing through the pages in your browser, clicking a link and verifying that it finds its target. You could certainly sip a lot of coffee while going through all the links, but that's about the only thing you'd get done.

To verify the hyperlinks in the active FrontPage web, go to the Explorer and choose Tools ➤ Verify Links. You will see the Verify Hyperlinks dialog box, which lists all external links in all the pages of the FrontPage web, as well as all broken internal links (shown in Figure 8.7). The color-coded bullet next to each link indicates the status of that link:

Green: The link has been checked and works correctly.

Red: The link has been checked but is broken.

Yellow: The link has not yet been checked, or you have edited it since it was last checked so you may want to check it again.

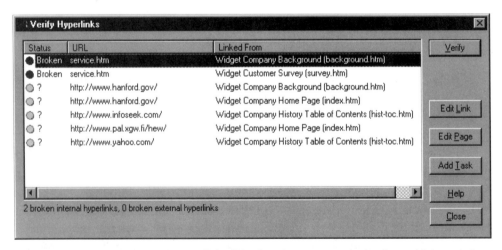

FIGURE 8.7: The Explorer's Verify Hyperlinks dialog box shows you any broken internal links and allows you to verify all external links.

In Figure 8.7, you can see there are two internal links to the file SERVICE.HTM that are broken (the source page of those links is displayed in the Linked From column in the dialog box). You know these two are internal links because only the file name is shown in the URL column, which means the file should be found in the same folder as the source file of that hyperlink.

> **NOTE** The primary cause of a broken internal link is the target file is "missing" (as far as the link is concerned). Perhaps someone deleted, moved, or renamed the file while outside of the control of the FrontPage Explorer, which would otherwise have updated the link for any of those changes. Another possibility is the target file exists but its name is misspelled in the hyperlink.

There are five external hyperlinks listed in Figure 8.7; you know they're external because their URLs are outside of the current FrontPage web. Their status at this point is still unchecked; the process of checking external URLs can be slow, and it's not done until you click the Verify button in the dialog box.

If any of the links don't look right, you can edit them right now before you proceed with verifying the external links, as discussed a little later. Otherwise, if you're ready to check all the external links, click the Verify button. The Explorer will access the target URL of each link as though you had clicked the link in a browser. Only the validity of the URL will be checked, however; the target page won't actually be opened. If a URL is valid, the bullet to its left in the list will turn green and the next link will be checked. You can press the Stop button at any time to cancel the validation process.

When you have checked all the external links, the valid links will have a green bullet and the word *OK* next to them, while the broken ones will have a red bullet and the word *Broken*. In this example, there is one broken external link (shown in Figure 8.8). Now you can decide how to handle the broken links.

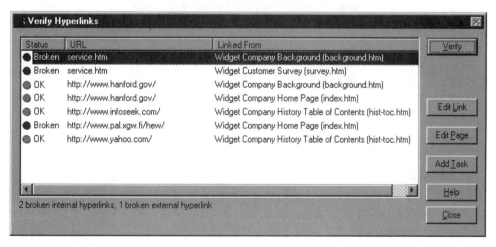

FIGURE 8.8: After you check the links, you can tell at a glance which ones are broken.

You have several ways to handle the broken links that are listed in the Verify Links dialog box:

- Leave things as they are and click Close; you can run the Tools ➤ Verify Hyperlinks command again at some other time.
- Select a broken link and click Edit Link to revise that link in the Edit Link dialog box (shown in Figure 8.9). You can enter a new URL, or click the Browse button, and select a page in your browser. Then choose whether to make the change to all the pages that contain that link or just to those you select. Click OK when you're finished.
- Select a broken link and click Edit Page to open that page in the Editor. The link in question will be selected and ready for you to choose Edit ➤ Hyperlink and fix the URL. Save the page when you're done and then return to the Explorer to continue with the broken links list.
- Select a link and choose Add Task, which will add a task in the FrontPage To Do List linked to this page, reminding you the broken hyperlink needs your attention.

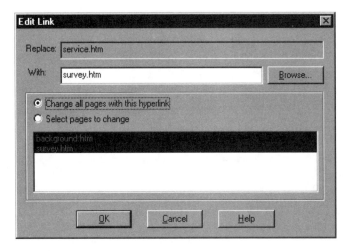

FIGURE 8.9:
You can revise a URL in the Edit Link dialog box.

This chapter has explained the ins and outs of hyperlinks in your FrontPage webs. You've seen how to create text and image hyperlinks, select the target and bookmark for a link, revise links, and verify the validity of the links in your web.

You'll learn how to work with graphic images in your pages in the next chapter and be introduced to an outstanding tool for creating Web-related images—Microsoft Image Composer.

Chapter 9

DISPLAYING IMAGES IN YOUR PAGES

FEATURING

- Working with GIF and JPEG images
- Inserting an image into a page
- Saving new images with the page
- Placing a video clip into a page
- Setting the properties of an image
- Making an interlaced image
- Making a color transparent
- Changing the size of an image
- Creating images in Microsoft Image Composer

This chapter will show you how adept FrontPage is at handling graphic images. You can bring an image into a page in the Editor, position it in the page, change its size, and more. With Microsoft Image Composer, part of the FrontPage package, you have hundreds of image-editing tools at your fingertips, as well as hundreds of photographic images and clip art.

The World of Image Formats

You can include images in your Web sites to convey information or to serve as clickable hyperlinks. Images are also valuable when they simply liven up an otherwise text-filled page. A bit of color can make a page more appealing and help distinguish one page from another.

An image within a Web page is called an *inline image*. Because HTML pages are always just plain text, an inline image is actually stored as a separate image file, which is then opened and displayed along with the page in a browser. Of course, you can also specify an image file as the target of a hyperlink so a browser will open and display only that image when you activate its hyperlink.

> **NOTE** The term *image* applies to just about any non-text object displayed in a Web page. It includes line drawings, photographs, charts, geometric shapes, and textures suitable for page backgrounds.

Image files on computers come in a wide variety of formats. Although you can actually create the same image in several different formats, two have become widely accepted standards among browsers on the World Wide Web: GIF and JPEG.

When you bring an image into a page in the FrontPage Editor, you can choose from a variety of file formats besides GIF and JPEG. However, because GIF and JPEG are the WWW standards, when you save a page that includes a new inline image, the Editor will offer to save the new image as either a GIF or a JPEG file.

The GIF Format

An image is compressed when it is saved in the Graphics Interchange Format (GIF), which CompuServe developed to shorten the time it takes to transfer images online. This format (which uses a `GIF` file name extension) supports up to 256 colors (or 8-bit color), often the maximum number of colors that most computers, except usually the newer ones, can display. Another advantage of having limited colors is that with or without compression, there will simply be fewer data to download.

When an image-editing program compresses an image as a GIF file, it leaves nothing behind—when you open a GIF image you'll see the original picture exactly as it was saved. This is called *lossless compression* and gives the best compression ratios when the image has many repeating patterns, such as broad fields of the same color or repetitive lines. If you want to scan your company's black and white logo into a computer file, the GIF format would probably be the one to choose.

The JPEG Format

The Joint Photographic Expert Group format (JPEG; the three-letter file name extension is `JPG`) can handle many more colors than the GIF format—up to 16.7 million colors (24-bit color). Like the GIF format, JPEG also compresses files. But in order to achieve a higher compression ratio, it uses a *lossy compression* method, which literally strips out and loses what it considers to be expendable bits of the image. When you later view that JPEG file, you'll see something with lower quality than the original image.

The trick, however, is that the sophisticated JPEG compression algorithm takes out bits that you may not really notice are missing. This is especially true in richly colored images such as photographs, where a significant reduction in file size has only a slight effect on the quality of the image.

When you save an image in the JPEG file format, you can specify the file-size to image-quality ratio. For example, you can choose a high-quality image with a larger file size, or you can choose a smaller file size with an image somewhat degraded. If you want to include a photograph of your company president on your Web site, the JPEG format would be the one to choose.

Inserting an Image into a Page

To bring an image file into a page in the Editor, first position the insertion point where you want the image to appear (although you can move the image later). Then use the Insert ➤ Image command, which displays the Image dialog box. Three tabs offer you three different sources from which to choose the image file:

Current FrontPage Web: Choose an image file from the active web in the Explorer (see Figure 9.1). In a typical FrontPage web, you'll store image files in the `Images` folder.

Other Location: Choose an image file either from a location on disk or from a URL. You can click the Browse button to select a file from disk in a standard

Windows files dialog box. To display only files of a certain type, such as Bitmap (BMP) or TIFF (TIF), select that type from the Files of Type drop-down list.

Clip Art: Choose an image from one of the categories, such as Animations or Buttons, in FrontPage's collection of clip art.

FIGURE 9.1:
When you insert an image into a page, you specify the location of the image file or choose a piece of clip art.

The image you select from any of these locations will be inserted into the page in the Editor.

Besides using the Insert ➤ Image command, you can bring an image into a page in the Editor in the usual Windows ways. For example, you can select the image in another program, choose Edit ➤ Copy, switch to the Editor, and then choose Edit ➤ Paste. Or, if the Editor and the other program are both displayed on the screen, you can simply drag the image into your page in the Editor. You can use the same procedure with images in the FrontPage Explorer and drag an image from the active web into a page in the Editor.

The HTML code the Editor uses for an image in a page specifies the name of the image and its size:

```
<IMG SRC="images/undercon.gif" WIDTH="40" HEIGHT="38">
```

You can read about changing the size of an image and other image properties later in this chapter in "Setting Image Properties."

Inserting a Video Clip

You can also include a moving image in a page in the Editor—a video clip with an `AVI` file name extension. The process is very much the same as inserting an image. Use the Insert ➤ Video command, and then select the video clip file from the active web or from a location on disk or a URL outside of that web.

The Editor will insert a box in the page for the clip. You won't see the video running within the Editor, but you can use the File ➤ Preview in Browser command to see how it will look in a browser.

> **WARNING** Video clips take up a lot of disk space, so even a few seconds of video can be several hundred thousand bytes. With that in mind, include a video only when its size is not a critical issue, such as when the video plays a key role in the web (but don't expect visitors to appreciate its importance if it takes 15 minutes or longer to download).

When you have inserted a video clip from outside of the active web, you will be given the opportunity to save the clip to that web when you save the page.

Saving New Images in a Page

You can insert a variety of image file formats into a page, but because the GIF and JPEG formats are standards on the WWW, the Editor will not save an image in any other format.

When you save a page with an image from outside of the active web, you will be asked if you want to save the image to the active web in the Explorer (see Figure 9.2). By saving the image to the active web, you are assured the image will always be available for the page (see also "Saving a Page" in Chapter 5).

> **NOTE** If your FrontPage web has an `Images` folder, you can include that folder with the file name when you save the image, as in the example in Figure 9.2.

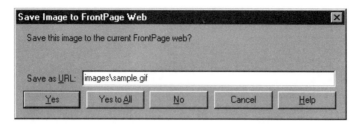

FIGURE 9.2: When you save a page in the Editor, you can also save images that you brought in from outside the active web.

When you save a page, you will also be asked to save any images you have made changes to in the Editor, even if the image originated in the active web. For example, you will have modified a GIF image if you make one of its colors transparent (see "Specifying the Type of Image" later in this chapter). When you save the page, you can choose to save that image under a new name. If you do, any other pages in the active web that included the original image will not be affected. It's up to you to decide whether to create a new image under a new name or to replace the existing one throughout the web.

Selecting an Image

Before you can view or change the properties of an image, you must first click on it to select it. You'll see the selection handles (small rectangles) appear at each corner of the image and in the middle of each side. Not only do these indicate the image is selected, but they also allow you to change the size of the image (see "Specifying Image Size" later in this chapter).

If the Editor's Image toolbar is not already displayed, selecting an image will display it (shown here). If you deselect the image by clicking elsewhere, the Image toolbar will be hidden again.

If you are going to be working with one or more images, you should use the View ➤ Image Toolbar command to display the Image toolbar all the time. This will prevent the page from "jumping" down or up whenever the toolbar is displayed or hidden. You can also position this or any other toolbar anywhere on the screen by pointing to any part of the toolbar outside of a button and dragging it.

As you learned in Chapter 8, you can use the first five buttons on the left side of the Image toolbar when you are creating or modifying an image map. The right-most button lets you make a color transparent in a GIF image (see "Specifying the Type of Image" later in this chapter).

> **NOTE:** Once you have selected an image, you can move it by simply dragging it to a new location (drag from within its border to avoid changing its size). You can also use the Edit ➤ Cut and Paste method. Use Edit ➤ Copy and Paste to make multiple copies of the image.

Setting Image Properties

Once you have inserted an image into a page in the Editor, you can adjust its look in several different ways. For example, in Chapter 6 you learned how to insert an image of a horizontal line from FrontPage's clip art. By adjusting its Size and Alignment properties, you can shorten the line and center it within the page.

Once you have selected an image, choose Edit ➤ Image Properties (Alt+Enter), or right-click on the image and choose Image Properties from its shortcut menu. This displays the Image Properties dialog box, which has three tabs:

General: Specify the source image file for this image, how to save the image (GIF or JPEG), and alternatives to the image when it is displayed in a browser. You can also specify a default hyperlink target if the image is serving as an image map (as discussed in "Creating Clickable Image Maps" in Chapter 8).

Video: Specify the source file for the video clip and how the video should be played when the page is opened in a browser.

Appearance: Specify the alignment of the image, its size, and the type of border that surrounds it.

Specifying the Image Source

You can specify the image source in the General tab of the Image Properties dialog box (see Figure 9.3). The Image Source option defines the source file for the image.

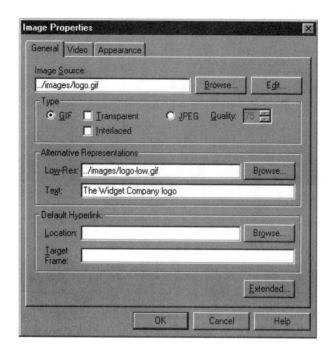

FIGURE 9.3:
You can adjust the settings for an image or video clip in the Image Properties dialog box.

If you want to use a different file for this image, either enter the name and location or click the Browse button and select the file from the Image dialog box (shown earlier in Figure 9.1). Selecting a different file will replace the current image in the page, and the other settings in the Image Properties dialog box will now apply to that new image. If the image you select is outside of the active web, when you save this page in the Editor you will be prompted to save this new image to the active web, discussed earlier in "Saving New Images in a Page."

Clicking the Edit button will open the image in the image-editing program associated with that type of image file (GIF or JPEG). In FrontPage, that would normally be Microsoft Image Composer.

Specifying the Type of Image

In the Type group of options in the Image Properties dialog box, choose whether this image should be saved in your web as a GIF or JPEG file. If the image is already a GIF or JPEG file, that option will be selected. If the image is any other file type, choose either the GIF or the JPEG option. Each of these formats was discussed earlier in this chapter in "The World of Image Formats."

Choosing the GIF Image Type

When the GIF option is selected, there are two GIF-related check boxes available:

Transparent: If the image already has a transparent color defined, this option lets you choose whether to display that color in the image or to keep it transparent.

Interlaced: Rearranges the order of the scan lines in the image file so the image seems to fill its allotted space faster in a browser.

A GIF image can have one transparent color, so any part of the image using that color will be transparent when the image is displayed. In a browser, for example, this means the background of the page can show through the transparent color. Here's how to make a color transparent:

1. In the Editor, select the image.
2. Click the Make Transparent button on the Image toolbar.
3. Point to the image, and you'll notice that the mouse pointer changes to a small pencil with an arrow. Now click on any portion of the color in the image that you want to make transparent.

That color becomes transparent in the image, and the page's background (or whatever is behind the image) shows through.

> **NOTE** A GIF image can have only one transparent color. If an image already has a transparent color defined, making another color transparent will return the first to its normal color.

Shown here are two copies of the same GIF image (FrontPage's UNDERCON.GIF) displayed on a white background (such as in the Editor or a browser). The image on the left has a gray border around it, which stands out on the white background. That border has been made transparent in the image on the right, so that it disappears from view.

Now back to the Image Properties dialog box. If you have made a color in a GIF image transparent, then the Transparent check box will already be selected. You can deselect it to display this color once again in the image, removing the transparent definition for that color.

When a browser opens a GIF image, the image is loaded line by line, from the top to the bottom. This happens so quickly in a small image that you will hardly notice how the image appears. But if the image is large or the network connection is slow, you will see the image grow from the top down. The effect can sometimes breed impatience as you watch the slow unveiling of the image.

When you save a GIF image in the Editor for which you have chosen the Interlaced option, the order of the scan lines in the image file will be rearranged into several alternating sets of lines. The result is when an interlaced image is sent to a Web browser, the picture will fill its space more quickly and seem to "come into focus" within that space, instead of appearing line by line.

Choosing the JPEG Image Type

When you select the JPEG option in the Image Properties dialog box, the image will be saved in that format in the active web when you save the page. You can specify the amount of compression to apply when the image is saved by adjusting the value in the Quality field. Remember the more a JPEG image is compressed, the lower the quality of the image.

The default value in the Quality field is 75 (the acceptable range is 0 to 100), which will compress the image with only a small loss in quality. Enter a lower number to compress the image more but further reduce the quality, or enter a higher number to improve the quality while also increasing the size of the image.

> **NOTE** If you're saving a large JPEG image in a page, you can experiment by lowering the Quality setting. Then see just how much the image is degraded when you later open it in the Editor, or a browser, and how small the resulting file was compressed.

Specifying an Alternative to the Image

The Image Properties dialog box lets you specify two alternatives to an image. If the image is large and takes a while to download to a browser, you can specify a second,

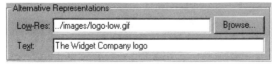

smaller image (smaller in file size) in the Low-Res option (low resolution). Most browsers will download and display this image first so the person viewing the page can see the image relatively quickly, even if it is a low-resolution version of the larger, primary image. The browser will then download the primary image, and once it has been completely downloaded, display it instead of the low-resolution version.

The second alternative is the Text option. Any text you enter here will be available to browsers to display either when the image is not available or when the browser cannot handle images. The text you enter should describe the image so the person viewing the page will have an idea of what was supposed to be shown.

For example, most browsers let you turn off the downloading and displaying of images in order to save time while online. Some browsers left in the world may not even be able to handle images at all. In those cases, the browser will display the alternative text for the image.

Specifying Video Properties

The Image Properties dialog box has a Video tab with options that affect a video clip image (see Figure 9.4).

The Video Source field displays the name of the video clip file displayed as the image. To specify a different file, either enter a new name or click the Browse button and select a file.

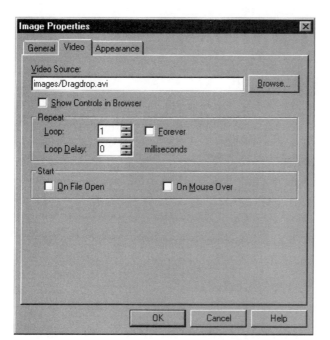

FIGURE 9.4:
The Video tab in the Image Properties dialog box

By default, a video clip is played only once when the page is opened in a browser (specified in the Loop field). That may be fine in some situations, but you are free to specify how many times the video should be played.

If you select the Show Controls in Browser check box, the browser will display standard video controls beneath the video clip window. The video controls that are shown here allow the reader to start or stop the video at any time.

You can also have the video play repeatedly by setting the options in the Repeat group in the Image Properties dialog box. Set the Loop field to the number of times you want the video to play. Specify the amount of time (in milliseconds) between plays in the Loop Delay field. For example, entering 500 will put a half-second pause between each playing of the video. If you want the video to run repeatedly without stopping, select the Forever check box (use with discretion).

Finally, the two check boxes in the Start group of options let you specify that the video will start when the page is opened in a browser (the On File Open check box) or when the reader moves the mouse over the video (the On Mouse Over check box).

> **NOTE** If you don't want the video to play at all for some reason, set the Loop option to zero and don't select either the On File Open option or the On Mouse Over option.

Specifying Image Alignment

To align an image within the width of the page, such as centered or right aligned, treat the image as you would any paragraph—select the image in the page or click within the paragraph in which it resides, and then click one of the alignment buttons on the Format toolbar.

You can set other image alignment options in the Appearance tab in the Image Properties dialog box (see Figure 9.5). You can also change the size of the image and choose to enclose it within a border.

The Layout group offers three choices for aligning the image with any text surrounding it:

> **Alignment:** Specify how the image should align with text to the right or left of it. The default is Bottom, so that the bottom of the image aligns with the bottom of the text. If you choose Middle, the text to the right or left of the image will

Displaying Images in Your Pages

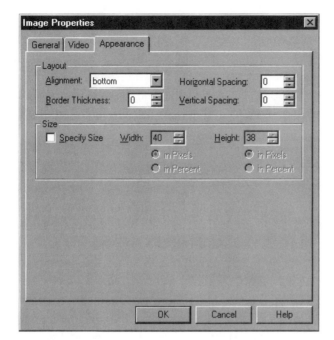

FIGURE 9.5:
The Appearance tab in the Image Properties dialog box

align with the center of the image. The choices Left and Right force the image to the left or right edge of the current line.

Horizontal Spacing: Specify the number of pixels of blank space that should separate the image from any text, image, or window edge to its left or right.

Vertical Spacing: Specify the number of pixels between the image and any text, image, or window edge above or below it.

To enclose the image in a border, specify its thickness in the Border Thickness field. The default is zero, so no border is displayed.

Specifying Image Size

By default, an image is displayed in its actual size, so an image that is 200 by 200 pixels will take up that amount of room on the screen. There are two ways to change the size of the image.

The easiest but less precise way is simply to select the image in the page and then drag one of its selection handles to expand or contract the image. If you drag a corner handle, the image's width and height will both change and the image's original proportions will be maintained.

If you drag a handle from the center of one of the sides, you can shrink or enlarge just that dimension of the image. For example, suppose you had inserted an image of a line into a page, as discussed in Chapter 6, and now you want to change its width without changing its height. Select the line and drag the selection handle in the center of one end of the line. Of course, if it's a very thin line to begin with, you may not even be able to see that selection handle. In that case, use the following method for sizing an image.

The more precise way to change the size of an image is with the Size options on the Appearance tab in the Image Properties dialog box:

1. First select the Specify Size check box, enabling the sizing options to its right.
2. Now choose how to define the image's width and height. To specify an exact size, select the In Pixels check box. To have the image sized in relation to the window in which it is displayed, choose In Percent.
3. Finally, enter a number in the Width and Height fields. If you have chosen In Percent, the largest number you can enter is 100.

Realize when you change the size of an image, you are also changing the way it looks. If you stretch an image in only one dimension, the image may end up looking pretty silly. If you enlarge an image to three or four times its original size, it may end up looking very "grainy."

Shown here are some examples of changing an image's size, in this case the

FrontPage image `UNDERCON.GIF`. The image on the left is in its actual size, 40 pixels wide by 38 pixels tall. The size of the second image has been doubled in both directions (80 by 76 pixels); the graininess is one effect of that enlargement. The width of the third image and the height of the fourth image have been doubled, and you can see the "fun house mirror" effect taking hold.

Donning Your Beret with Image Composer

Images can play a big role in the life of a Web site. The images you incorporate into a page can convey information, add snap and pizzazz, serve as clickable hyperlinks, act as image maps for multiple hyperlinks, and generally just make the site a more pleasant place to visit.

So far in this book, you've learned how to bring images into the FrontPage Editor in several different ways. Now here's an overview of not only another way to collect images, but a way to create them for your Web sites—Microsoft Image Composer. This is no small addition to the FrontPage package; it's a powerful image-editing program that can stand on its own.

> **NOTE** You'll find Image Composer is a wonderful tool with lots of features, but it also has a big appetite for your computer's processing power and RAM. Its minimum hardware requirements are a 486 processor with 16MB of RAM and a video card that can display at least 256 colors (but you'll get more work done if you have a faster processor and more RAM).

Starting Image Composer

You can start Microsoft Image Composer (which we'll abbreviate as MIC) in the usual Windows ways:
- You can run it from the Start menu to create or revise images, whether or not you're also working in FrontPage.
- In the FrontPage Explorer, choose Tools ➤ Show Image Editor, or click that button on the toolbar, to start MIC or switch to it if it is already running.
- In either the FrontPage Explorer or Editor, you can double-click on an image to open that image in MIC. When you're finished working on it, choose File ➤ Send to FrontPage, which will save the image back to the active web.

If you find double-clicking an image file in FrontPage does not open MIC and that image, you need to associate that type of image file with MIC. Use the Explorer's Tools ➤ Options and choose the Configure Editors tab in the Options dialog box, and proceed as discussed in "Specifying Web File Editors" in Chapter 3.

Working with Sprites in Compositions

In MIC, you can create your works of art by combining hand-drawn work, text, scanned images, or the hundreds of sample photographs and drawings that come with MIC.

Although just about all image-related programs let you combine various pieces, you'll see this process emphasized in MIC—both in the way the program is designed and in the way you build your images.

The image you create in MIC, or the final product you build from a variety of pieces, is called a *composition*. The basic component of every composition is the *sprite*. For example, a composition might contain three sprites: an image you brought in from disk, an image you copied from another program, and text you entered.

Each sprite has its own set of properties, such as size, color, fill pattern, font, and so on. To view or revise the properties, you must first select the sprite to make it the *current* sprite, such as:

- Click on a sprite to select it.
- Choose Edit ➤ Select All (Ctrl+A) to select all sprites.
- Point to any area outside of a sprite, drag over the sprites you want to select, and then release the mouse button.
- If a sprite is already selected, press Tab to select the next sprite.

Once you have selected a sprite, just about any action you take will affect only that sprite. You can also select multiple sprites so your actions will affect them all. To deselect all sprites, click outside of a sprite or choose Edit ➤ Clear Selection (Ctrl+T).

You'll find MIC shares the look and feel of the programs in both Microsoft FrontPage and Microsoft Office (see Figure 9.6). Its menus, shortcut menus, toolbars, and file-operation dialog boxes should look quite familiar, so you won't have any problem finding your way around the program.

You'll recognize the menus and toolbar at the top of MIC's window, and there's a status bar at the bottom that displays pertinent information about your composition and the program. On the left side of the screen is the *toolbox*; each of its buttons opens a set of image-editing tools displayed in the *tool palette* near the bottom of the window. In Figure 9.6, the Patterns and Fills tool palette is displayed. You can also access these tool palettes with the commands on the Tools menu.

The *Color Swatch* beneath the toolbox displays the current color, which is the one used the next time a color is applied to a sprite. To change the current color, click the Color Swatch and select a new color from the Color Picker dialog box. You'll read more about colors in MIC later in "Picking Colors for Your Web."

The white area beneath the toolbar and to the right of the toolbox is the *composition guide*, on which you create your composition. Think of it as the virtual page in MIC, which serves as the background for your image. You can change its size (the

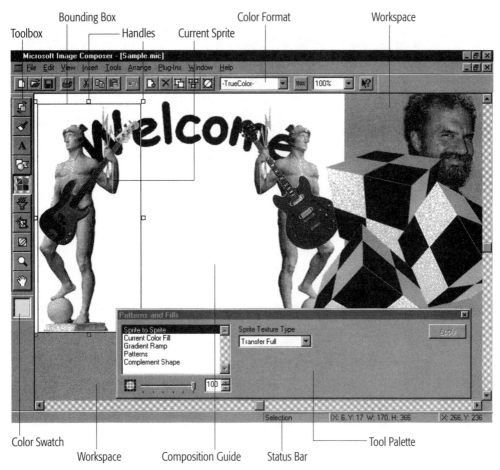

FIGURE 9.6: You create your image on the Image Composer's composition guide, and collect other sprites you might need for the image in the infinitely large workspace.

default is 640 by 480 pixels) and color (the default is white) to go with the image you're creating. Because its size is in pixels, you can specify exactly how large an image should be before any paint touches the electronic canvas.

The gray area around the composition guide is the *workspace*. Use it as a workbench where you can place sprites that you'll need in the image, or windows that display other views of your image. The size of the workspace is unlimited, so you'll never run out of room.

> **TIP** If you have scrolled the window to some far off realm of the workspace, you can use the View ➤ Go To Composition Guide (or press Home) to bring the composition guide back into view.

There are several sprites in Figure 9.6; some are on the composition guide, and

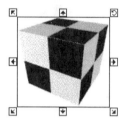

some lie on the workspace. When you select a sprite, such as by clicking on it or choosing Edit ➤ Select All, the sprite is surrounded by a rectangular *bounding box* (shown here). At each of the corners and in the center of each side of the bounding box are *handles*. Seven of them let you resize the sprite by dragging; the eighth (in the upper-right corner) allows you to rotate it.

All the sprites in MIC are arranged in a *stack*, where each sprite is assigned a position relative to the other sprites. For example, when you bring in or create a new sprite, it goes to the top of the stack. When you move this sprite, it will overlap any other sprites it encounters.

You can change a sprite's order in the stack by right-clicking on the sprite and choosing one of the stack-related commands. For example, if another sprite overlaps the current one, choose Bring Forward. This will place the current sprite one step higher in the stack; repeat the command until it is high enough in the stack to overlap the other sprite. Or choose Bring to Front to bring the selected sprite to the very front of the stack.

Saving the Workspace or Composition Guide

When you use the File ➤ Save command (Ctrl+S) in MIC, or click the Save button on the toolbar, the resulting file will be in Image Composer's default file format, named with an `MIC` file name extension.

The file will include everything on the workspace, including whatever is on the composition guide. When you later open that file in MIC, such as with the File ➤ Open command (Ctrl+O), all will be as you left it so you can continue with your work.

When you're ready to use your image in your FrontPage web (or for any other purpose), you must save the image in any of several popular image formats, such as GIF or JPEG. Use the File ➤ Save As command, and select a format from the Save as Type drop-down list. Then enter a file name and destination and click Save.

> **NOTE** When you save to any file format other than MIC, all the sprites on the composition guide will be saved as a single image (this is called *flattening* the composition). Any sprites not on the composition guide will not be included in the resulting image file, and any sprites overhanging the guide will be truncated at its edges. Note that only the resulting image file is flattened and no longer consists of individual sprites; your work in the Image Composer is not affected.

You can also save a selected sprite, no matter where it resides in MIC's window. Select the sprite and choose File ➤ Save Selection As, select a file format (MIC is not an option), and then specify the destination and file name.

Picking Colors for Your Web

Color is one of the most important considerations when you're creating images for display on the Web. In MIC, any color you use comes from a *palette* of colors. A palette can have millions of colors or only a few. Although your first impulse might be to plumb the depths of your artistic talent by using the largest palette possible, there are two important reasons to do exactly the opposite:

- No matter how many colors you include in an image, the colors actually displayed when viewed in a browser are very much dependent on the capabilities of the browser and the computer on which it is running.
- The more colors an image contains, the larger its file can become and the longer it will take to open on the Web.

In the world of computers and in MIC, the term *true color* refers to a palette of a little more than 16 million colors. It is called 24-bit color, because that is how much computer memory is required to display one pixel in any of the 16 million colors. All of your work in MIC is saved with 24-bit color, so you'll never lose any colors when you save your work in the MIC format.

In order to display all the colors in a true color image, your computer's video display must be able to handle the 24-bit color, and Windows must be set up to take advantage of its capabilities. To specify how many colors to display in Windows, choose Start ➤ Settings ➤ Control Panel, and double-click the Display icon. You'll find a list of available color palettes on the Settings tab in the Display Properties dialog box.

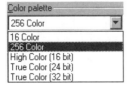

When displaying a true color image on an older computer that may not be able to handle it, that computer will simply approximate any of the 16-million possible colors by choosing a color from the 256 available colors.

> **NOTE** Going from 16 million to 256 colors isn't necessarily as bad as it sounds. The human eye cannot even distinguish between several adjacent colors in the true color palette. Many true color images degrade only slightly when displayed with 256 colors, while others, such as richly colored photographs, may suffer more.

Unless you are working on an intranet and know most visitors to your site have fast connections and computers that can handle true color images, you should probably limit the images you create to 256 colors. There's two ways to do that:

- When you save a composition in another file format, you can convert the image into a 256-color image by selecting Balanced Ramp or another 256-color palette from the Color Format list in the files dialog box. Remember, too, that a GIF file, one of the standards of the WWW, can handle no more than 256 colors (although JPEG can handle true color).
- When you create an image, choose colors from only a 256-color palette. This ensures the colors you see on your screen will be pretty much like the ones a browser displays on its screen.

You can choose a color or a color palette in MIC by clicking the Color Swatch (see Figure 9.6), which displays the Color Picker dialog box. Select the True Color tab to pick a color from a palette of 16-plus million colors (see Figure 9.7).

You can select a color from the palette simply by clicking that color, or by entering the exact RGB values in the fields for the Red, Green, and Blue sliders. Click OK to make that the current color in the Color Swatch.

If you choose the Custom Palette tab in the Color Picker dialog box, you can choose a different palette (all have 256 colors or fewer) from the Color Palette drop-down list (see Figure 9.8). MIC comes with several palettes; Balanced Ramp is appropriate for color images in your FrontPage webs. Once you pick a new palette, it is displayed when you click the Color Swatch.

Even if your computer has true color capabilities, you can view a true color composition in 8-bit color by selecting one of the custom palettes from the Color Format drop-down list on the toolbar. This allows you to see how the image will look when viewed as a 256-color image in your Web site.

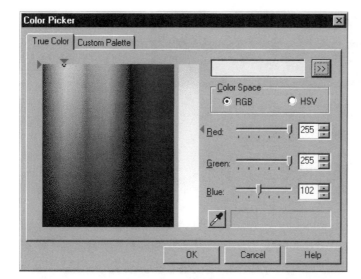

FIGURE 9.7:
The Color Picker displays the True Color palette, from which you can choose a color for the Color Swatch.

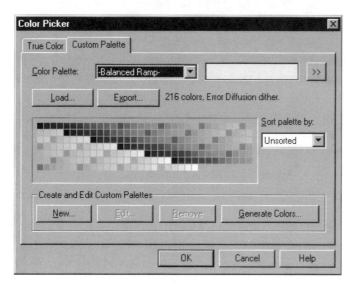

FIGURE 9.8:
The Custom Palette tab in the Color Picker lets you choose a color from a 256-color palette or choose a custom palette.

Creating a Sample Composition

For this example, you will begin the composition by creating a text sprite, to which you will apply a special MIC effect. You'll then fill the text in that sprite with an image to create an eye-catching treatment (see Figure 9.9).

You'll save the composition as a JPEG image file. Because that file format is designed for true color images, you can work with the True Color palette. When you're

FIGURE 9.9:
The finished image that was created in Microsoft Image Composer

finished, you'll have an image that you can use in a FrontPage web or in any other program that can display JPEG files.

Creating the Text Sprite

1. If MIC is already open, choose File ➤ New. Otherwise, first open MIC, such as by clicking the Show Image Editor button in the Explorer.
2. Set the size of the composition grid to the approximate size of the finished image; choose File ➤ Composition Properties.
3. In the Composition Properties dialog box, enter **400** in the Width field and **100** in the Height field. Then click OK. The composition grid will now be rectangular; if it's not fully visible in the workspace, press Home to align it in the upper-left corner of the window.
4. Choose Tools ➤ Text, or click the Text button in the toolbox (on the left side of the window). This opens the Text tool palette in the lower portion of the MIC window.
5. In the Text tool palette, enter **Widget** into the Text field.
6. Click the Select Font button in the Text tool palette and select a hefty font from whatever fonts you have available (the Bauhaus 93 TrueType font was chosen for the image in Figure 9.9).
7. Now select a large font size, such as **72**, and click OK to close the Font dialog box.
8. If you wanted to specify the color for this text, you would click the Color Swatch and choose a color. But you don't need to worry about the color for this example (as long as it's not white, which would hide the text on the white composition guide), so click the Apply button to create a new sprite in the workspace.
9. The text will be placed onto the composition guide as a new sprite (see Figure 9.10). The text that appears in that sprite can no longer be edited; if you want different text you'll have to create it with the Text tool palette.

Displaying Images in Your Pages

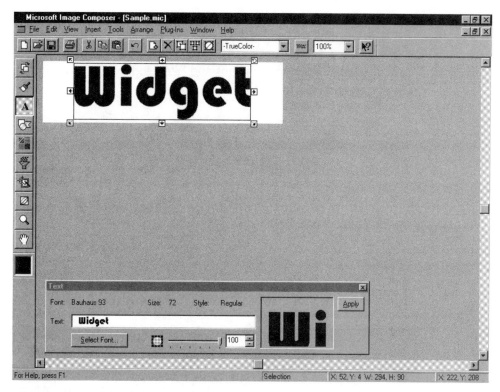

FIGURE 9.10: A new sprite on the composition guide

Adding an Effect to a Sprite

Now let's put some curves into the text you've just created.

1. Choose Tools ➤ Warps and Filters or click that button on the toolbox.

> **NOTE** Before you proceed, be sure the text you created is still selected. If it's not, click on it to make it the current sprite. You should always be sure the correct sprite is selected before you take any action that affects sprites.

2. In the Warps and Filters tool palette, choose Warp Transforms from the drop-down list.
3. Now choose Wave from the list of effects.

4. There are several settings for this effect, but we'll just use the default values; click the Defaults button.
5. Click the Apply button in the Warps and Filters tool palette to add a wave effect to the text, as shown here.

Changing the Size of a Sprite

Let's expand this sprite so it's the same size as the composition field, 400 pixels wide by 100 pixels tall:

1. Choose Tools ➤ Arrange, or click the Arrange button on the toolbox, to display the Arrange tool palette (shown here).

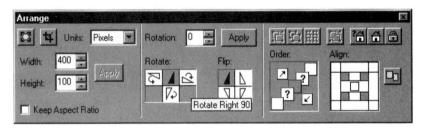

2. Deselect the Keep Aspect Ratio check box in the Arrange tool palette, because you'll be setting both the width and the height of this sprite and thereby changing its width-to-height aspect ratio.
3. Now enter **400** in the Width field and **100** in the Height field; set Units to Pixels. Then click Apply and the sprite will change to the new size.
4. At this point, it's probably a good idea to save this file as an MIC file. Choose File ➤ Save, specify a name and location, be sure the Save as Type option is set to Microsoft Image Composer, and then click Save.

NOTE Remember, the file you just created is strictly for use in MIC; it is not usable in a FrontPage web.

Displaying Images in Your Pages   197

Finding an Image in the Sprite Catalog

To bring in a photo from the collection of MIC sprites, you'll need to insert your FrontPage 97 CD into your CD-ROM drive.

1. To see thumbnail images of the available MIC sprites, choose Help ➤ Sample Sprites Catalog.
2. Choose the Index tab, select the Lightning entry, and then click Display. This displays a page of the sample sprite catalog, with thumbnail images giving you a good idea of what each sprite looks like. The image we want is the one named `LIGHTNIN.MIC`.
3. Click the Where to Find These Sprite Files button, and the Finding a Sprite File window will show you where this file is located on the FrontPage 97 CD (as shown here). You'll need to remember the location and file name when you insert this image into MIC.

4. Close this window and the Sample Sprites Catalog window.

Importing an Image

Now that you have found the image you want to import and know where to find it on disk, you can bring it into MIC.

1. In MIC, choose Insert ➤ From File or click the Insert Image File button on the toolbar.
2. In the dialog box, browse to the folder where the file is located, in this case the folder `Imgcomp\Mmfiles\Photos\Backgrnd\PhotoDsc`. In the Files of Type list, choose Microsoft Image Composer to display only those files.
3. Select the file `LIGHTNIN.MIC` and click OK to insert it into MIC.

> **TIP** If you're going to be viewing or inserting several images from disk, use Windows Explorer to find them and drag them into MIC. This can be much faster and easier than using the Insert ➤ From File command and working your way through the folders.

Changing a Sprite's Order in the Stack

When this photo of a lightning burst is brought into MIC, it is aligned with the upper-left corner of the composition guide and placed at the top of the sprite stack. Therefore, the Widget sprite you already created will be hidden from view. Here's how to bring that sprite back to the surface.

1. If your computer display is 640 by 480, you might want to lower the screen magnification so you can see all of the lightning sprite and more of the MIC workspace. Choose a value less than 100 from the Zoom Percent tool on the toolbar.
2. Even if you can't see the Widget sprite behind the lightning photo, you can press Tab to select it (if that selects the lightning photo, press Tab again). You'll see the bounding box appear within the lightning photo, although the sprite itself is still hidden.
3. To bring the Widget sprite to the top of the stack, choose Arrange ➤ Bring to Front (there's also a button for this in the Arrange tool palette). Now you'll see this sprite displayed over the lightning sprite. To use the lightning image as the fill (the pattern within the image) for the text in this sprite, you need to position this sprite over the area of the lightning sprite that you want to appear in the text.
4. Drag the Widget sprite over a suitable spot in the lightning, such as over the brighter part with the lightning bolts.

Transferring a Fill between Sprites

One of the many fun and interesting features in MIC is its ability to transfer the fill from one sprite to another, such as from the lightning to the text.

1. With the Widget sprite selected and positioned on top of the lightning sprite, choose Tools ➤ Patterns and Fills, or click that button on the toolbox, to display the Patterns and Fills tool palette.
2. Select Sprite to Sprite in the Patterns and Fills tool palette, and then choose Transfer Full in the Sprite Texture Type list.

3. Click the Apply button, and a dialog box will prompt you to click on the source sprite for the transfer. First click OK to close this message dialog box, then click anywhere in the lightning sprite, but outside of the Widget sprite.
4. In a "flash," the text will take on the fill of the lightning sprite. In doing so, it will completely blend into that sprite, effectively becoming invisible.
5. We're done with the lightning, so select that sprite (click on it outside of the Widget sprite) and either drag it away from the Widget sprite or press Del to remove it from MIC (just be sure the Widget sprite isn't selected when you press Del).

Saving Your Composition as an Image File

We're now almost ready to save this composition to disk in the JPEG format. If this composition had multiple sprites, you would need to position them all on the composition guide prior to saving the image. There's only one sprite in this example, however, so you can skip that step and use a shortcut to save it. No matter where the sprite is located on the workspace, the composition guide will automatically be used as the image's background.

1. Before saving the image, we should make the composition guide black, so it will serve as an appropriate background for this image. Choose File ➤ Composition Properties.
2. In the Composition Guide dialog box, enter a zero into each of the three color fields, Red, Green, and Blue. This RGB value represents black.
3. Click OK to close the dialog box, and you'll see the composition guide is now black.
4. Click on the Widget sprite to select it, and then choose File ➤ Save Selection As.
5. In the Save as Type drop-down list in the dialog box, choose JPEG. You can adjust the Compression value, or leave it at its default setting of 10 (the higher the number, the more the image file will be compressed and the more its quality will be degraded).
6. Enter a location and a name for the file (don't include the period and extension, that will be entered automatically), and then click Save.

The sprite and its black background will be saved to disk in the JPEG format. In the FrontPage Editor, you can use the Insert ➤ Image command to bring the image into a page, such as the one shown in Figure 9.11.

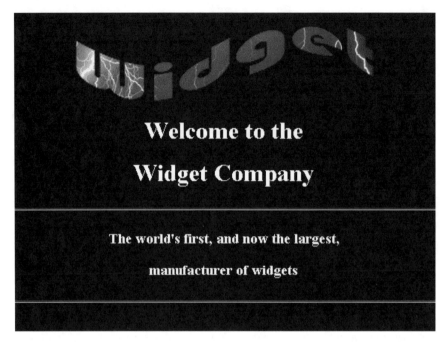

FIGURE 9.11: The JPEG image after being imported into a Web page in the FrontPage Editor

This ends our look at working with images in FrontPage. The tour of Microsoft Image Composer was really only the tip of the iceberg. Even after you've spent hours working with this program, you'll still uncover new tools and effects, as well as new ways to combine them in your compositions.

In the next chapter, you'll read about FrontPage WebBots. They can automate repetitive maintenance tasks in your pages and FrontPage webs, and they perform other tasks that would otherwise require the work of an experienced programmer.

Chapter 10

AUTOMATING YOUR WEB WITH WEBBOTS

FEATURING

- **Understanding WebBots**
- **Including a page in another page**
- **Understanding how WebBots are encoded**
- **Revising a WebBot**
- **Creating a comment**
- **Using variables and the Substitution WebBot**
- **Creating a table of contents**
- **Automatically entering the time or date in a page**

This chapter introduces you to the WebBot, the FrontPage solution to Web maintenance that automates many tasks on your Web site but requires none of the programming or script writing that would otherwise be needed. You can also insert other programmable objects into a page in the Editor, although that discussion is beyond the scope of this book. For more information about FrontPage and programmable objects such as Java applets, ActiveX controls, and browser plug-ins, see *Mastering Microsoft FrontPage 97*, also published by Sybex.

What's a WebBot?

A FrontPage *WebBot* is a page component that automatically creates the appropriate HTML code for its defined task. The word is derived from *robot*, which has been used in Web-related circles to describe automated routines. Some WebBots (or simply *Bots*) perform their jobs when you save your page in the Editor, while others get their jobs done when your site is running on a FrontPage-aware server.

When your site's host is a non-FrontPage–aware server, all the server-driven Bots will simply be ignored and, therefore, will not do their jobs. The server-driven Bots include Confirmation Field, Discussion, Registration, Save Results, and Search. The other Bots that work without the server will work in any page in the Editor.

> **NOTE** A programmer experienced in C, C++, or server-scripting languages, such as Perl or Tcl, can create custom WebBots with the FrontPage software developer's kit (SDK). It's available for free on Microsoft's Web site under `http://www.microsoft.com/frontpage/`.

You have already seen examples of several Bots in earlier chapters. Some of them you specifically inserted into the page with a Bot-related command; others were created automatically as part of another process. In Chapter 3, the sample web took advantage of the Include Bot, where the contents of the Included Header page were included automatically at the top of other pages in the web so that all shared the same information.

In Chapter 4, you learned you can add comments within a page in the Editor with the Insert ➤ Comment command. These comments are contained in the HTML code for the page within a WebBot that tells the Editor to display the comment in a different color (this is discussed in "Inserting a WebBot for Your Comments" later in this chapter).

Also in Chapter 4, you learned how to enter HTML code into a page that the Editor, but not a browser, would ignore. This process makes use of the HTML Markup Bot, which you create with the Insert ➤ HTML Markup command. Like comments, this Bot is inserted without actually using a Bot command. If you looked at the HTML code for the page, however, you'd see the code you entered is enclosed in FrontPage WebBot tags (see "How FrontPage Encodes a WebBot" later in this chapter).

The other WebBots you can insert into a page are described in the next section, "The FrontPage WebBots." You can incorporate WebBots into a page in several ways:

- In the Editor, use the Insert ➤ WebBot Component command or one of the other commands that uses a Bot behind the scenes, such as Insert ➤ Comment and Insert ➤ HTML Markup.
- In the Editor, WebBots are included automatically when you create a new page from several of the templates, including Confirmation Form, Search Page, and Table of Contents.
- In the Explorer, WebBots are an integral component of the FrontPage web you create with the Discussion Web Wizard; other web templates also utilize Bots in their pages.

NOTE The Common Gateway Interface (CGI) has been the traditional way to run automated tasks from Web pages. When you perform tasks with the FrontPage WebBots on a FrontPage-aware server, you avoid having to write CGI programs or scripts and avoid having to reference their somewhat arcane parameters.

A WebBot is generally treated as a separate object in a page in the Editor. For example, when you create a comment in a page with the Insert ➤ Comment command, the result is a block of text displayed in the page but not editable there. If you try to move the insertion point into that text, it will simply jump over it.

You'll know an object in a page is a WebBot when you point to it with your mouse, because the pointer will change to the WebBot pointer (shown to the left). You'll learn how to edit the contents of a Bot in "Revising a WebBot" later in this chapter.

The FrontPage WebBots

You will find the FrontPage WebBots (other than the ones created automatically when you invoke certain commands) in the dialog box for the Insert ➤ WebBot

Component command (shown here). You'll see how to insert a WebBot in the next section, "Including Another Web Page Automatically."

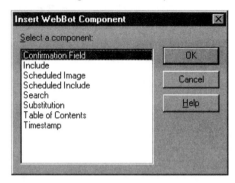

Later in this chapter you'll learn how to work with several of the FrontPage WebBots. Here is a description of each of the Bots in the Insert WebBot Component dialog box:

Confirmation Field: Displays the results of a specified field in a form, such as when a reader's input is displayed for confirmation in another page (FrontPage-aware server required).

Include: Displays another Web page within the current page; see the discussion in the next section.

Scheduled Image: Displays an image file you specify but only during the time period you specify. You can also specify an optional image that will be displayed before or after that time period. This Bot is active and checks the current time only when a change is made to the web under FrontPage control.

Scheduled Include: This is the same as the Scheduled Image WebBot, but you specify a page instead of an image. The result is the same as the Include WebBot but only within the specified time.

Search: Creates and displays a page search form with which a reader can search for specified words in your FrontPage web. Note the search does not go into the _Private folder (FrontPage-aware server required).

Substitution: Displays the current value for the FrontPage web configuration variable you choose, such as Page URL, Author, or Description. (Web variables and this Bot are discussed in "Automating Text Entry with the Substitution WebBot" later in this chapter.)

Table of Contents: Creates a table of contents of links to pages in the current web (see "Creating a Table of Contents" later in this chapter).

Timestamp: Displays the date and/or time of the most recent revision of the page in which this Bot resides (see "Stamping Your Page with the Date and Time" later in this chapter).

When you insert most Bots into a page in the Editor, you will see the complete result of each Bot, such as the current date or time with the Timestamp Bot. Others, such as Table of Contents, may only leave a placeholder in the page to indicate their presence. For example, with the Scheduled Include Bot, when the current date is not within the date range for the Bot, you will see *Expired Scheduled Include* displayed in its place. In a browser, however, you would see nothing at all.

A WebBot can sometimes produce an error, such as when you open a page in the Editor that contains an Include Bot but the file to be included no longer exists. In this case, the Bot will display an appropriate message in the page, such as

```
Error: Unable to include file: _private\header.htm
```

In the Explorer's left-hand pane in its Hyperlink view, you'll see a red triangle icon next to the name of the page containing the Include Bot, indicating there is an error

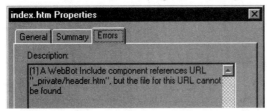

associated with it. If you right-click on that page and open its Properties dialog box, a new Errors tab will be available (shown here). It will display any error messages produced for that page, including those from WebBots.

Including Another Web Page Automatically

Now you'll learn about the Include WebBot and see how it lets you easily revise many pages in your FrontPage web in only one operation. In Chapter 3, you read about the Include Bot in the discussion of the Explorer. This Bot was used in the Widget Web site to display a common header in multiple pages without having to re-create the header in each page. When you insert another page into a page with the Include WebBot, there is no indication a Bot is displaying some of that page, which is precisely the whole idea.

When you select (click on) an Include WebBot, however, you'll know it is a WebBot (see Figure 10.1). In this example, the Include Bot has been selected in the page, so it

208 Chapter Ten

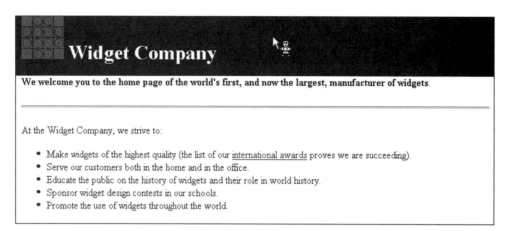

FIGURE 10.1: The home page in the Widget Web site takes advantage of the Include WebBot.

is highlighted. You can see the image and the Widget Company title are part of the Bot, and you can see the WebBot mouse pointer, too.

> **NOTE** Remember the Include Bot offers a double benefit. It gives you a way to display the same information in any pages that reference the same included page. You also get the added benefit of being able to revise the included page and have those changes appear in all the pages that include it. In a Web site with many pages, this can save you hours and hours of work.

Here's how to place an Include Bot in a page:

1. Position the insertion point where you want the included page to be displayed. In the Widget home page in Figure 10.1, the Bot was placed at the very top of the page.
2. Choose Insert ➤ WebBot Component.
3. In the Insert WebBot Component dialog box, select Include and then click OK.
4. In the dialog box, enter the URL of the page you want displayed in the current page (shown here). The page you want displayed must be in the active web; therefore, its URL will be relative. For example, in this case the other page is named HEADER.HTM and is located in the web's _Private folder.

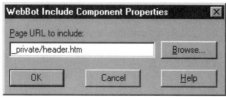

5. Finally, click OK to finish the Include Bot's definition.

The included page will be loaded into the current page and displayed as though it were actually a part of the current page. Although you can't spell-check or find and replace text in the included page (you'd have to open that page to do so), you'll find the bulk of its HTML code is, indeed, included in the current page, as described next.

How FrontPage Encodes a WebBot

When you insert an Include Bot into a page in the Editor, the actual contents (HTML code) of the included page are brought into the current page, so the included page really is part of the current page. Here's what the code looks like for the portion of the Widget home page (Figure 10.1) that begins with the Include Bot and ends with the first line of text in the current page:

```
<!--WEBBOT BOT="Include" STARTSPAN U-INCLUDE=
"_private/header.htm" TAG="BODY" -->

<H1><IMG SRC="images/logo.gif"
ALT="The Widget Company logo" WIDTH="68"
HEIGHT="68"> Widget Company</H1>

<!--WEBBOT BOT="Include" I-CHECKSUM="3701" ENDSPAN -->

<P><STRONG>We welcome you to the home page....
```

This probably looks confusing at first (remember that line breaks are ignored in HTML code), but it will make more sense if you notice the opening and closing tags for the Include Bot definition are each contained in the tag `<!--  -->`. This is actually a standard HTML comment tag, where the comments you enter appear within the pair of hyphens. A browser will always ignore this tag and not display whatever is contained in it.

FrontPage, on the other hand, always looks at comment tags when you open a page in the Editor. When you open the Widget home page in this example, the Editor will see the Include Bot definition's starting and ending tags (the standard comment tags). It fetches the named page, HEADER.HTM, and places all of its HTML code between the two Bot definition tags. The included HTML code in the previous sample begins with the `<H1>` tag and ends with `</H1>`.

When you save the page, all the included code will be part of the resulting file. When that page is opened in a browser, the comment tags (which contain the Bot definition) are ignored as always, while the code between them (the included page) is displayed in the usual way.

> **TIP** If you later modify the included page, such as by editing `HEADER.HTM` in the previous example, you don't have to worry about updating the pages including this page. The Explorer handles that automatically when you save the included page, which once again emphasizes the importance of using the Editor and the Explorer together.

Revising a WebBot

You can revise a WebBot at any time. For example, with the Include Bot in the previous example, you can change the name of the Web page it references. To revise a Bot, you can do any of the following:
- Double-click on it.
- Select the Bot and choose Edit ➤ WebBot Component Properties (Alt+Enter).
- Right-click on it and choose WebBot Component Properties from its shortcut menu.

This will display the same Properties dialog box in which you created the WebBot. Make the changes you want and click OK.

When you right-click on an Include Bot, you will also find an Open command on the shortcut menu. This allows you to open the included file in the Editor to make changes to it.

Inserting a WebBot for Your Comments

As you learned earlier in Chapter 4, you can place comments within your pages in the Editor with the Insert ➤ Comment command. As described earlier in this chapter, HTML has a special tag for entering comments, and a browser will ignore any text within that tag.

FrontPage adds its own twist to the comment by displaying it in the Editor in a different color (purple) with whatever formatting has been applied to its displayed text.

> **NOTE** Never put confidential information in your comments. Even though comments don't appear when the page is viewed in a browser, comments are still part of that page's HTML code. Visitors to your site will see your comments when they view the underlying code for the page, such as with a browser's View ➤ Source command.

To create a comment, position the insertion point where you want the comment to appear and choose Insert ➤ Comment. Enter the text of your comment in the Comment dialog box; press Enter to create a line break when the comment is displayed in the page. Click OK when you're finished, and your comment will appear within the page.

Here is the HTML code (shown on two lines) that FrontPage uses for a comment:

```
<!--WEBBOT BOT="PurpleText" PREVIEW=
"This is the text of the comment" -->
```

Again, this is a standard HTML tag, but FrontPage recognizes the WebBot in it and handles it appropriately in the Editor. There's also a newer comment tag, which you may find in other Web pages, but may not be supported by all browsers, that looks like this:

```
<COMMENT>This is the text of the comment</COMMENT>
```

Automating Text Entry with the Substitution WebBot

You can display text automatically anywhere you want in a page by taking advantage of two FrontPage features:
- In the Explorer, you can create *configuration variables* that consist of a name (the variable) and a value (the definition of the variable).

- In the Editor, you can insert a Substitution Bot that references any configuration variable and displays the text that defines that variable.

This is a very powerful technique for managing information in your FrontPage webs. Its benefits are similar to using the Include Bot: It's a convenient way to display the same information in many different pages, and you can change a configuration variable's definition and have that change reflected throughout the web automatically.

Referencing a Variable in a Page

There are several built-in configuration variables in every FrontPage web. Here's how to reference one of them; the process is also the same for variables you create:

1. In the Editor, place the insertion point where you want the variable displayed.
2. Choose Insert ➤ WebBot Component, choose Substitution in the dialog box, and then click OK.
3. In the WebBot Substitution Component Properties dialog box, select one of the variables from the drop-down list (shown here). The ones shown here are the built-in variables. For example, choose Author to display the name of whoever created the current page, or choose Modified By to display the name of the person who last worked on this page.

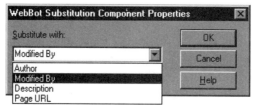

4. Click OK to return to the page.

The Substitution WebBot will be inserted into the page, and the current value (the text) of the variable you chose will be displayed.

For example, in a new page that has not yet been saved, you could create the following sentence that ends with the Page URL variable of the Substitution WebBot:

```
This page's URL is [Page URL].
```

That's how this variable is displayed when there is not yet a value for it. Once you save the page, thereby giving it a URL, the sentence might now look like this:

```
This page's URL is http://www.widget.com/somepage.htm.
```

The actual URL is displayed in place of the Substitution WebBot.

> **NOTE** The display of this variable is not updated until you save the current page. So in this case, you would have to save the page and either open it again or use the View ➤ Refresh command in order to see the latest value of the variable. However, if you were to later move this page in the Explorer, the new URL would be updated automatically in the variable in this page.

Creating a Configuration Variable

You can create your own configuration variables in the Explorer and then reference them in the pages in that web. In most cases, you'll create a variable only when that information needs to appear on more than one page, so you'll save a lot of time when you need to update the information—simply by changing that variable's definition. Here are some typical uses for variables:

Webmaster: Displays the name of whoever maintains the web; if a new person takes over the job, just enter the new name for this variable's definition.

Phone Voice: Displays a phone number to call for information; no matter where you might display this number in the web, you could easily revise it just by revising the variable.

Phone Fax: Displays a phone number for sending faxes.

Company Name: Displays the name of the company; although this won't change very often (if at all), by using a variable you're assured it is spelled consistently throughout the web.

Company Address: Displays the company's address.

Current: Displays the most recent stock price; just update the variable's definition when you want to update the displayed price.

> **NOTE** Displaying the value of a configuration variable with the Substitution Bot is very much like displaying another page with the Include Bot. The text (value) of a variable, however, can be only a single line long. Even so, it can be easier to update a variable in the Explorer than it would be to update every page in the Editor.

Chapter Ten

Let's create a configuration variable named *Phone Voice*, which will display a day and evening telephone number.

1. Open the web in the Explorer, and choose Tools ➤ Web Settings.
2. Select the Parameters tab in the FrontPage Web Settings dialog box (shown in Figure 10.2).
3. To create a new configuration variable, choose Add.
4. In the Add Name and Value dialog box, enter **Phone Voice** as the name of the variable in the Name field (shown in Figure 10.2).

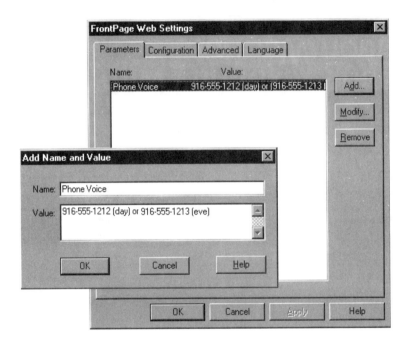

FIGURE 10.2: You can create or revise a configuration variable using the Parameters tab for the Tools ➤ Web Settings command.

5. In the Value field, enter the text you want to appear when this variable is inserted into a page, such as **916-555-1212 (day) or 916-555-1213 (eve)**. Text will wrap to the next line as needed; all the text you enter will be taken as a single line when it is displayed in the Editor.
6. When you're finished, click OK, which will return you to the FrontPage Web Settings dialog box.
7. Click Apply to incorporate the new variable into the web, or click OK to do that and also close the dialog box.

Once you have created a variable for a web, you can insert that variable into any page in that web using the Substitution Bot. You'll find the new variable name (*Phone Voice* in this case) on the list of variables in that Bot's dialog box.

Creating a Table of Contents

Just about every Web site includes some sort of table of contents, whether it's actually called that or not. The multiple pages of a Web site are just too easy to catalog within a single page of hyperlinks to exclude a table of contents from your site. Visitors to the site will find such a page a great convenience and even you, the Web author, will find that a table of contents gives you a practical way to organize the important "stepping stones" in your site.

FrontPage provides a WebBot for just such a need. If you insert it into a page, it will generate a complete table of contents of all the pages in your FrontPage web. Here's how to build it:

1. Position the insertion point where you want the table of contents to appear. It might be on the home page of your web or on a page appropriately titled *Table of Contents*.
2. Choose Insert ➤ WebBot Component, select Table of Contents, and then click OK.
3. This displays the WebBot Table of Contents Component Properties dialog box, where you define the scope and style of the table of contents (see Figure 10.3).
4. First, pick the page that will serve as the root of the table of contents. Normally this will be the home page, because the hyperlinks it contains should lead you through the chain of hyperlinks to just about every page in the web.
5. Next choose the heading style that will be used for each entry in the list. The choices are 1 through 6 (corresponding to the HTML tags <H1> through <H6>). Or choose None if you want each item displayed in the default text style.

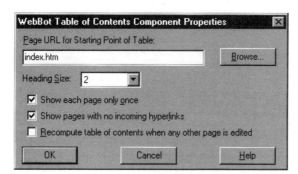

FIGURE 10.3: The Table of Contents WebBot lets you create a list of hyperlinks to all the pages in your web.

6. There may be multiple hyperlinks to many pages in the web. If you don't want to see those pages listed multiple times, choose the Show Each Page Only Once option.
7. The table of contents is built from the hyperlinks in the starting point page, but there may be pages in the web to which no other pages link. To display them as well, choose Show Pages with No Incoming Hyperlinks.

> **NOTE** The table of contents will list pages it finds in any other folders you may have created in this web. It will not, however, look for pages in any of the FrontPage program's folders in this web, including `_Private`.

8. The last choice, Recompute Table of Contents When Any Other Page is Edited, is deselected by default, so the table of contents will be rebuilt only when you open the page containing this WebBot. That should be fine in most cases, but if you're willing to put up with some delays and put some strain on your server, select this option and the table of contents will be updated whenever anyone makes a change to the web.
9. Finally, click OK and the Table of Contents Bot will be inserted into the current page, as shown below, when it was created in a page in the Widget Web.

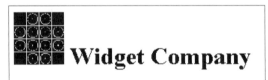

What you see in the table of contents page in the Editor doesn't really look like much, but save the page and then preview it in your Web browser. The result will look something like that shown in Figure 10.4 for the Widget Web. Each entry in the table of contents displays the title of a page and is a link to that page.

You can see there is a Widget Company History Table of Contents page in Figure 10.4. This isn't the WebBot table of contents page; it's another page in this web that contains hyperlinks to Widget history-related pages. These target pages are displayed as a nested list beneath it.

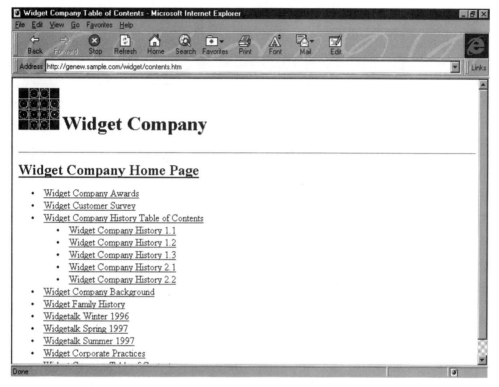

FIGURE 10.4: The Table of Contents WebBot builds a table of hyperlinks to the pages in the active web.

Stamping Your Page with the Date and Time

The Timestamp WebBot is a very convenient Bot that simply displays the date and/or time when the page was last revised. This information is frequently displayed on Web pages to remind you and other authors of when it was last worked on and also to let your readers know how current the information is. Would you trust pricing information displayed on a page last revised 10 months earlier?

The bottom of a page is often the place for this type of information; you might display a line that looks something like this:

```
This page was last updated on 10/11/97 at 10:15 AM.
```

Two instances of the Timestamp Bot are used, and here's how you create them in the Editor:

1. Type the first part of the sentence **This page was last updated on** and end it with a space.
2. Choose Insert ➤ WebBot Component, select Timestamp, and choose OK.
3. In the WebBot Timestamp Component Properties dialog box, select the option named Date This Page was Last Edited (shown here). This will set the date or time when someone actually opens this page in the Editor and then saves it back to disk. The other option, Date This Page was Last Automatically Updated, will also update the date or time whenever the page's HTML is updated by the server. For example, when you revise another page included in this page, this page's code will be updated along with the Timestamp.

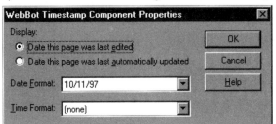

4. Select an appropriate date style from the Date Format drop-down list.
5. Select None in the Time Format drop-down list so this Bot will display only the date.
6. Choose OK to return to the page in the Editor, and you will see the current date displayed where you inserted this WebBot in the sentence.
7. Type the text that follows this Bot, starting with a space and continuing with **at** and another space.
8. Once again, choose the Timestamp WebBot, but this time set the Date Format option to None, and then choose an appropriate time style from the Time Format drop-down list.
9. Choose OK to close the dialog box, and you should see the current time displayed in your sentence.
10. Finish the sentence with a period.

Whenever you save this page, the current date and time will be saved along with it in the Timestamp Bots. When viewed in a browser, a reader will know exactly when the page was last worked on.

This chapter has shown you how to add dynamic features to your pages by inserting FrontPage WebBots. You'll see some other examples of form-related WebBots in Chapter 12 (these require a FrontPage-aware server). In the next chapter, you'll learn how to work with HTML tables to arrange data in neat rows and columns, and you'll learn how to organize those components on a page.

Chapter 11

ARRANGING DATA WITHIN TABLES

FEATURING

- **Understanding the layout of tables**
- **Creating a table**
- **Moving between the cells in a table**
- **Selecting parts of a table**
- **Adding a caption**
- **Changing table properties**
- **Changing cell properties**
- **Changing the size of a table**

This chapter explains the table, a very versatile HTML feature. You can easily arrange text or images in neatly ordered columns and rows in a table, but you can also use the structure of an "invisible" table (without its borders) to arrange broader areas of a page.

The Structure of a Table

The *table* is an HTML feature that helps you arrange information within rows and columns. If you've worked with tables in your spreadsheet program or in your word processor, you'll have a good idea of what the possibilities are with HTML tables.

A nice aspect of FrontPage is how easy tables are to create, modify, and fill with data. You simply specify how many rows and columns you want in the table, and you'll see the results immediately on the screen. And what you see in the Editor is pretty much what visitors to your site will see in their browsers.

The table is a very flexible feature you can use in countless ways. Sometimes it will look like a table, with border lines dividing its rows, columns, and cells. What you put in those cells is pretty much up to you; just about anything you create in a page in the Editor can be created in a cell in a table.

You can also take advantage of the structure of a table without displaying its borders. This serves as a convenient way to organize elements of a page without making them appear within the confines of an actual table. In many cases, when you see a page on the Web organized into columns, it may very well be within a borderless table.

Figure 11.1 shows a typical table you might find in a Web page; you'll build this table in the exercises beginning in the next section, "Creating a New Table."

Work Schedule for the Week of 9-Sep-97							
	Mon	Tue	Wed	Thu	Fri	Sat	Sun
Celeste	X	X	X			X	X
Gerald	X	X		X	X	X	
Gordon	X			X	X	X	X
Carol			X	X	X	X	X

(As of 6-Aug-97)

FIGURE 11.1: A table consists of rows, columns, and cells, as well as an optional border, caption, and header cells.

Here are some features to note in the table in Figure 11.1:
- The table has six rows and eight columns; at the junction of each row and column is a cell.
- The cells in the first row have been merged into a single cell.

Arranging Data within Tables

> **NOTE** By default, a column expands to meet the width of its contents, and a table will therefore be as wide as the longest entries in its cells. You can choose to specify an exact width for a table or for any of its columns. But if you don't, a table will not expand any wider than the window in which it is displayed; when it reaches that limit, text in cells will wrap to new lines to expand as needed.

- An optional border is displayed around the table and all its cells.
- There is a caption centered beneath the table.
- The cells with the names of the people and the days of the week have been formatted as header cells, so they stand out in the table.
- A color has been assigned to the background of those header cells.
- The days of the week and the contents of the cells beneath them have been centered.

The HTML coding for a table is pretty straightforward; you really only need three tags to build one (each has a closing tag, as well). The `<TABLE>` tag begins the table definition, the `<TR>` tag defines a new row in the table, and the `<TD>` tag defines a single cell within the table. Here is the code that builds a small table:

```
<TABLE BORDER="1">
  <TR>
    <TD>Cell A1</TD>   <TD>Cell B1</TD>
  </TR>
  <TR>
    <TD>Cell A2</TD>   <TD>Cell B2</TD>
  </TR>
  <TR>
    <TD>Cell A3</TD>   <TD>Cell B3</TD>
  </TR>
</TABLE>
```

The result (shown here) is a table with three rows and two columns; the text within the `<TD>` and `</TD>` tags is what appears in each cell. By default, a table has no borders, but a border one-pixel wide was specified in the `<TABLE>` tag for this one.

Cell A1	Cell B1
Cell A2	Cell B2
Cell A3	Cell B3

Creating a New Table

Now you'll see how fast it can be to define a new table in the Editor. You should follow along, because the example you build here will be used in several other exercises in this chapter.

Using the Insert Table Button

First we'll use the fast method of creating a table; then we'll look at the slightly slower method that lets you define the look and dimensions of the table.

1. Position the insertion point where you want the upper-left corner of the table to appear in the page. As always, don't worry too much about its position; you can move the table after you create it.
2. Point to the Insert Table button on the toolbar and then press and hold down the mouse button.
3. You'll see a table template appear beneath the button, which you can use to define the dimensions of the table. Slowly drag down and to the right to expand the number of rows and columns in the table. As you do, you'll see the current size appear beneath the template.
4. The table in Figure 11.1 has six rows and eight columns, so keep dragging until you've got that many highlighted in the template. Then release the mouse button and the new table will be created in the page.

Using the Insert Table Command

Now look at the other method for creating a table, which you'll probably use more often because you can define the look of the table as well as its dimensions.

1. Choose Edit ➤ Undo Insert to remove the table you just created.
2. With the insertion point located where you want the new table, choose Table ➤ Insert Table, which displays the Insert Table dialog box (see Figure 11.2).
3. Enter **6** in the Rows field and **8** in the Columns field.
4. By default, the Border Size option is set to zero so a new table has no border. To place a border around this table and around its cells, set the Border Size option to **1**, which will create a one-pixel wide border. Don't specify a width for this table; let it expand or contract to fit its longest entries.

Arranging Data within Tables

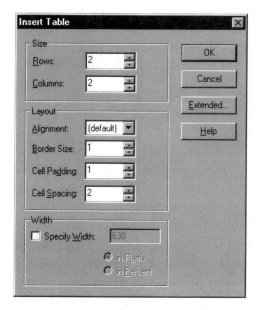

FIGURE 11.2:
You can define the size and look of a table in the Insert Table dialog box.

5. Click OK to finish the job.

The table will be created in the page and will have 48 cells surrounded by a border. Don't worry about its rather petite proportions at this point; the columns will expand as needed when you enter data into their cells, which you'll do in the next section.

Working within a Table

To move between the cells in a table:

- Use the arrow keys on your keyboard.
- Click within a cell with your mouse.

In the empty table you just created, enter the data from the table shown in Figure 11.1. As you do, the columns will expand (as shown in Figure 11.3) so that the table will look a little more like the one shown in Figure 11.1.

You can think of each cell in a table as somewhat of a mini-page. You can change a cell's background color, and just about anything you can put on a page can also be placed in a cell, including images, hyperlinks, and even another table!

That's right, you can nest a table within another table, as shown in Figure 11.4. In this example, four cells in the larger, surrounding table contain a two-row by two-column table. Each of the four cells in those smaller tables contains an image. Before you

Work Schedule for the Week of 9-Sep-97							
	Mon	Tue	Wed	Thu	Fri	Sat	Sun
Celeste	X	X	X			X	X
Gerald	X	X		X	X	X	
Gordon	X			X	X	X	X
Carol			X	X	X	X	X

FIGURE 11.3:
A table automatically changes the width of its columns to match the longest text entries or widest images in them.

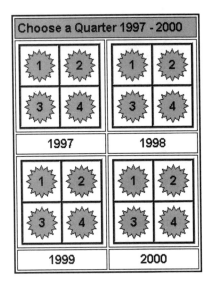

FIGURE 11.4:
You can create almost any layout by nesting tables within tables.

modify a cell or table in a group of nested tables, be sure you've selected the correct cell in the correct table.

Selecting Table Elements

To modify the look or shape of a table, you need to select one or more of its elements. To select a cell, row, column, or the entire table, move the insertion point to a cell and choose the appropriate command from the Table menu: Select Cell, Select Row, Select Column, or Select Table (from any cell).

You can also select various elements in the following ways:

Cell: Double-click on the cell's left border.

> **NOTE** Don't confuse selecting a cell, which highlights the entire cell, with selecting the contents of the cell. For example, if you select text in a cell, only the text will be highlighted. When in doubt, use the Table ➤ Select Cell command.

Row or Column: Move the mouse pointer to the far left border of the row (or top border of the column), and the mouse pointer will change to a solid arrow pointing across the row (or down the column), as shown here. Click to select the row or column.

Multiple Cells: Select one cell, row, or column, and then Shift+click on any others you want to select; they need not be adjacent to one another. You can also drag over adjacent cells, rows, or columns to select them. To deselect individual cells, Ctrl+click on each one.

Caption: Point to the left of the caption and double-click.

Table: Point to the left of the table to the area known as the selection bar, and the mouse pointer will change from an I-beam to the standard mouse arrow. Double-click the selection bar to select the table.

When you have created a table without a border, the Editor will display a dashed line in its place so you can see the limits of each cell. But you can hide those lines (and the other formatting marks in a page) with the View ➤ Format Marks command or by clicking the Hide/Show command on the toolbar. Invoke the command again to display the dashed lines.

Formatting a Table's Contents

You can add just about any type of formatting to the text or images within a cell. For example, you should make the title in the first row of the table a second-level heading. But before you do that, you need to merge all the cells in that row into a single cell that spans the width of the table. You'll learn more about merging and splitting cells in "Changing the Size of a Table" later in this chapter.

1. With the insertion point in any cell in the first row of the table, choose Table ➤ Select Row, which will select and highlight all the cells in this row.
2. Choose Table ➤ Merge Cells. The first row will now consist of a single cell; its width is determined either by its contents or the total width of all the columns below it, whichever is wider.
3. With the insertion point still in the first row, select Heading 2 from the Change Style drop-down list on the Editor's Format toolbar.

With the data in the table, the top row merged into one cell, and the title displayed in the Heading 2 format, the table (shown in Figure 11.5) looks a lot more like the one in Figure 11.1.

Work Schedule for the Week of 9-Sep-97							
	Mon	Tue	Wed	Thu	Fri	Sat	Sun
Celeste	X	X	X			X	X
Gerald	X	X		X	X	X	
Gordon	X			X	X	X	X
Carol			X	X	X	X	X

FIGURE 11.5:
The table after adding data to it and merging the cells in its first row

Adding and Aligning a Caption

You can add an optional caption to a table, which can appear either directly above the table or below it.

1. First click within any cell in the table so the commands on the Table menu will be enabled for that table.
2. Choose Table ➤ Insert Caption.
3. The insertion point will be centered just above the table, where you can enter the caption. You can switch the caption to the bottom of the table with a setting in the Table Properties dialog box, which you'll soon see.
4. Type the text for the caption, such as **(As of 6-Aug-97)**, as in Figure 11.1.
5. When you're done, click outside of the caption.

You can also have a normal line of text just above or below the table. But unlike a caption, the text would not stay centered on the table when the table expanded, contracted, or moved to another location.

To delete a caption, select it and press Del.

> **NOTE** You can apply text formatting, such as bold or italic, to a caption, but it does not accept paragraph formats, such as a heading. Although the Editor lets you set the horizontal alignment of the caption, it is not an accepted feature in HTML. In fact, you'll find no HTML alignment tag is actually entered; the caption will always be centered when viewed in a browser.

By default, a caption appears centered above the table, but you can choose to display it below the table (as was shown in Figure 11.1). To do so, click anywhere within the caption and choose Table ➤ Caption Properties. In the Caption Properties dialog box, choose Bottom of Table and then click OK.

Changing the Look of a Table

Once you've created a table, you can change the way it looks via the settings in its Table Properties dialog box (see Figure 11.6). Select any cells in the table and choose Table ➤ Table Properties, or right-click anywhere on the table and choose that command from the shortcut menu.

Most of the options in the Table Properties dialog box affect the formatting of the table. The Minimum Width group of options affects the overall dimensions of the table and are discussed in "Changing the Size of a Table" later in this chapter.

> **NOTE** When you have changed one or more of the settings in the Table Properties dialog box, you can click the Apply button to apply the new settings to the table without closing the dialog box. This lets you fine-tune the settings while you watch their effects on the table.

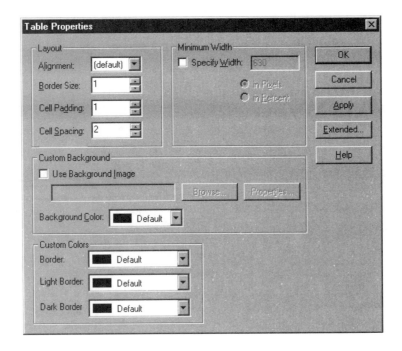

FIGURE 11.6:
The Table Properties dialog box lets you adjust the format and dimensions of a table.

Changing a Table's Alignment and Layout

The Layout group of options offers the following choices:

Alignment: Set the horizontal alignment of the table within the width of the page. Choose Left, Center, or Right, or choose Default to specify no alignment. In that case, most browsers will display the table left aligned.

> **NOTE** For the table you created earlier in this chapter, set its Alignment option to Center so it will be centered in the page.

Border Size: Set the width of the border (in pixels) that surrounds the table. This does not affect the width of the inner borders separating the cells; their widths can't be changed. By default, Border Size is set to zero, so no lines are displayed around or in the table.

Cell Padding: The amount of space (in pixels) that separates the contents of each cell from the cell's edges; the default is 1.

Cell Spacing: The amount of space (in pixels) between adjacent cells; the default is 2.

These last two options can be a little confusing until you see how they affect the cells in the table. Shown here are three copies of the same table. The one on the left has the default padding and spacing; the one in the middle has larger padding; and the one on the right has larger spacing.

Padding – 1
Spacing – 2

Padding – 8
Spacing – 2

Padding – 1
Spacing – 8

Setting a Table's Background and Border Colors

The Table Properties dialog box offers two groups of options that affect the table's background and borders. The Custom Background group of options gives you two ways to change the look of the table's background (these are similar to those that affect a page's background, as discussed in "Setting Page Properties" in Chapter 7):

Use Background Image: Choose an image file that will fill the table's background; either type a name or click the Browse button and select an image file.

Background Color: Choose a color for the table's background; the Default choice specifies no color for the table's background.

> **NOTE** If you choose both a color and an image for a table's background, the image will be displayed, not the color. However, the background color will show through a transparent color in a GIF image. Individual cells given a background color (discussed in the next section) will hide the table's background.

In the default mode, where no image is specified and the default color is used, the page's background will serve as the table's background. Remember when no color is specified in an HTML page, it is up to the browser viewing the page to apply an appropriate color. Most of today's browsers offer comparable representations of the standard features in a page, such as tables.

The Custom Colors group of options lets you change the color of all the borders in the table (although you can override the colors by changing the colors for selected cells). There are three options, all of which are set to Default, so no color is specified:

Border: If the Light Border and Dark Border options are set to Default, the color you choose here will affect all the lines in the border. In other words, if you set this option to Red, every cell and the entire table will be enclosed in a red border. On the other hand, if you set both of the other two options to a color other than Default, this option will be ignored.

Light Border: Choose a color for one of the pair of lines that make up the table's border. By setting light and dark colors, you can give the border a 3-D effect.

Dark Border: Chose a color for the second in the pair of border lines.

You can experiment with these options to see how the Editor applies color to the border. Note that Microsoft Internet Explorer supports the Light and Dark Border options, but other browsers may not. In that case, the browser would display the color in the Border option.

Changing the Look of Cells

The cells in a table have their own set of properties that affect how their contents are aligned, the color of their background and border, the width of their columns, and the number of columns or rows they span. We'll save the discussion of these last two items for the "Changing the Size of a Table" section later in this chapter.

To change the properties of a single cell, just click within that cell, making it the active cell, and choose Table ➤ Cell Properties (see Figure 11.7). Or right-click on the cell and choose Cell Properties from its shortcut menu.

To change the properties of more than one cell, you must first select them, as discussed earlier in this chapter in "Selecting Table Elements." For example, you can select several cells, an entire row, multiple rows, and so on.

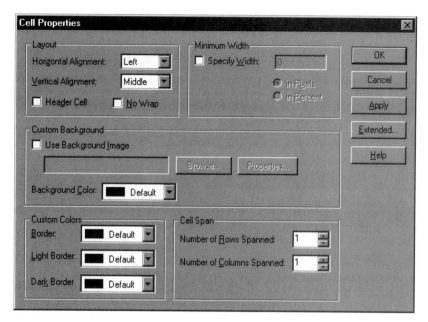

FIGURE 11.7: You can adjust the alignment and format of the cells in a table in the Cell Properties dialog box.

Changing a Cell's Alignment and Layout

Most browsers align the contents of a cell (whether it's text or an image) with the left edge of the cell (with the padding space in between) and center it vertically in the cell.

You can change these alignment settings with the Horizontal Alignment and Vertical Alignment options in the Cell Properties dialog box. The horizontal choices are Left, Center, and Right, and the vertical choices are Top, Middle, and Bottom.

By default, when text is longer than its cell is wide, the text will wrap to a new line, expanding the height of that cell and therefore its row. If you select the No Wrap option, a browser will not wrap text to a new line in that cell, most likely causing the width of the column to expand in order to display all the text (even if you have set the column's or table's width to something narrower).

Let's change the alignment of some cells in the table you built in the exercises earlier in this chapter (refer back to Figure 11.5). To center the contents in the cells that contain the days of the week and the cells below them:

1. Select the cell that contains *Mon*; for example, click within the cell and choose Table ➤ Select Cell.

2. Hold down the Shift key and drag over the other cells that contain the days of the week and all the cells below them. You will highlight a total of 35 cells. If you accidentally select a cell you don't want included in this operation, Ctrl+click on it.
3. For a shortcut, click the Center button on the Format toolbar and the job is done.
4. Or, choose Table ➤ Cell Properties, and in the Cell Properties dialog box (shown earlier in Figure 11.7), set the Horizontal Alignment option to Center and then click OK.

Now these cells should have their contents centered within them.

Creating Header Cells

You can define any cells in a table as *header cells* to give them emphasis, such as when the cells are row or column titles. In the table you've been working on in this chapter, the days of the week and the names in the left column should be defined as header cells, as they are in Figure 11.1.

1. Select the days of the week and the names cells (11 cells in all).
2. Choose Table ➤ Cell Properties.
3. In the Cell Properties dialog box, select the Header Cell option.
4. Click OK.

FrontPage and most browsers display the text in header cells in boldfaced type.

Setting a Cell's Background and Border Colors

In the Cell Properties dialog box, you can specify an image or a color for a cell's background and the colors for the border around the cell. The choices are the same as those for the background and border of an entire table, as discussed earlier in this chapter in "Setting a Table's Background and Border Colors."

When you set these options for a cell to anything but Default, the colors or image you specify will be displayed for those cells, overriding whatever is displayed for the table. Let's add some background color to some cells in the table we've been building:

1. If they are not already selected, select the cells that contain the days of the weeks and the names.
2. Choose Table ➤ Cell Properties.
3. Choose a color (other than Default) from the drop-down list for the Background Color (choose Silver for a light gray background).
4. Click OK.

Obviously, in the real world you would have enabled the Header Cells option and set the background color at the same time.

The last thing you need to do to the table is make all its columns the same width, which you'll do in the next section.

Changing the Size of a Table

A table and the columns it contains will widen or shrink as necessary to accommodate the longest entries in the cells. This may be fine in some cases, but many times this flexibility will result in a table whose columns are all a different size or a table too narrow or too wide to sit well in the page. All this tends to diminish the orderliness expected in a table.

Although it's not too obvious, the columns in Figure 11.1 are all different sizes. That is, each one's size is based on its longest entry. That's why the *Wed* column looks noticeably wider than the *Fri* column.

You're not restricted to ever-changing tables in HTML, you can specify a size for the entire table or for any of its columns.

Changing the Table's Width

You can set the width of a table when you create it with the Insert Table dialog box or revise it with the Table Properties dialog box. First select the Specify Width option in either dialog box (shown here).

You then have two ways to define the width of a table:

In Pixels: Enter the exact width of the table in pixels.

In Percent: Enter the width as a percentage (1 to 100) of the width of the browser's window when it is displaying the table, no matter how wide that window might be. For example, entering 100 makes the table as wide as the window; entering 50 makes the table half as wide as the window.

The method you choose will depend on how you want your table displayed. For example, when you set the width of the table you've been building in this chapter, you would probably not want to set it as a percent of the window size. If you did specify a percent, the table might look fine when it was displayed in a full-screen window at a screen resolution of 800 by 600, but what would happen if the browser's window were resized to half its original size, and the screen resolution was 640 by 480?

Setting the width as a percent is often the best solution when you want the entire table displayed no matter what size the browser's window might be. Such could be the case when you have a table on your home page displaying important information or hyperlinks for visitors to your site. By letting the table size with the window, its contents will always be visible.

In the case of the small sample table in this chapter, you can safely ignore the table's overall width and deal only with the widths of its columns, as discussed in the next section.

Changing a Column's Width

Instead of letting a cell change its width at will, you can specify a minimum width in the Cell Properties dialog box. The choices are similar to those you use to set the width of a table, as discussed in the previous section. You can specify the minimum width either in pixels or as a percentage of the *table's* width (not the window's width).

In the sample table, don't worry about drastic changes in the widths of columns that could affect the look of the table, you just want all seven columns (the days of the week) to be the same width. Here's how to do it:

1. Point to the top edge of the table above the *Mon* column so the pointer changes to the black arrow pointing down that column; then click to select all the cells in that column.
2. Hold down the mouse button and drag straight across the top edge of the table to select all the columns below.
3. Choose Table ➤ Cell Properties, and then select the Specify Width option.
4. Choose the In Pixels option, and enter a reasonable size for each column; try **50** at this point, and you can adjust it later if necessary.
5. Click OK to finish the job.

Since 50 pixels is larger than any of the entries in those seven columns, all the columns should now be the same minimum width. If you were using a larger font or had not abbreviated the days of the week, you would have to specify a wider minimum width.

Adding and Removing Cells

Once you've created a table, you are still free to add or remove cells. Note that a table need not be filled with cells; each row can have a different number of cells in it.

You can add either single cells or entire rows or columns. Before you add new cells to the table, first move the insertion point to a cell that will be adjacent to the new ones.

To add a single cell, choose Table ➤ Insert Cell; the new cell will be added to the *right* of the insertion point.

> **TIP** When you add a new row or column, keep in mind a new row will contain as many cells as there are in the row below it, and a new column will have as many cells as the column to its right.

To add a row or column, choose Table ➤ Insert Rows or Columns. In the dialog box that appears (shown here), choose whether to insert a new row or column, the number 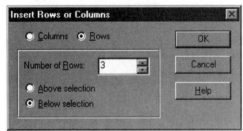 of new ones to insert, and where it should be placed in relation to the active cell (the one with the insertion point). For example, to add three new rows below the active cell, choose Rows, set the Number of Rows option to 3, choose Below Selection, and click OK.

To delete cells from a table, select one or more cells, or entire rows or columns, and either press Del or choose Edit ➤ Clear.

Merging and Splitting Cells

You can also change the layout of a table by combining multiple cells into one and by splitting one cell into multiple cells.

Earlier in this chapter in "Formatting a Table's Contents," you merged all the cells in the top row of the table into a single, table-wide cell. Here's the general method for merging cells.

Select the cells you want to make into a single cell (they must all be adjacent and form a rectangle), and then choose Table ➤ Merge Cells. The borders between those cells will dissolve. The resulting single cell will take up the same amount of room in the table, and the contents of the source cells will appear in that cell.

To split cells into multiple cells, select either a single cell or a rectangle of adjacent cells and choose Table ➤ Split Cells. In the Split Cells dialog box (shown here), choose whether you want to split the cells into columns or rows. A diagram in the dialog box reminds you what the effect will be. Set the number of new rows or columns you want to create and click OK.

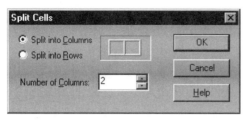

Changing Cell Span

Here's yet another way to change the cells in a table—although this method doesn't change the number of cells, it changes the size of the cells. You select the cells you want to change (they need not be adjacent to one another) and choose Table ➤ Cell Properties. You'll find the Cell Span group of options in the Cell Properties dialog box (shown here).

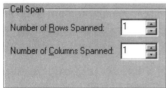

You can set either one or both of the two options to have the selected cells span the specified number of rows or columns. For example, if you select a single cell and set its Cell Span option to 2 rows, that cell will now expand downward into the row below, effectively doubling in size. The cell that had been below it, and all the cells to the right of that cell, will be pushed to the right so that the last cell in that row will now extend beyond what had been the right-hand edge of the table.

This chapter has shown you how to organize data into the regular columns and rows of a table and how you can use the flexible structure of an HTML table for more subtle organizational purposes, as well. In the next chapter, you'll see tables mentioned again as a way to help you organize HTML forms in your Web pages.

Chapter 12

LETTING THE READER INTERACT WITH FORMS

FEATURING

- **Learning the ins and outs of forms**
- **Selecting form controls**
- **Choosing a form handler**
- **Creating a form**
- **Adding fields to a form**
- **Adjusting the properties of form controls**
- **Setting data validation for text boxes**
- **Using a form**

This chapter introduces you to HTML forms, which allow visitors to your Web site to reverse the normal mode of Web browsing by sending their information to you. With forms, visitors can fill out surveys, request information, order products, and more. In this chapter, you'll see how easy it is to create forms in the Editor using any of the standard HTML form controls, such as text boxes, radio buttons, check boxes, and drop-down menus.

Working with Forms

An HTML *form* lets a visitor to your site enter information and send it to your server. You create a form on a page from a variety of *fields,* or *controls*, each of which lets the person reading the form either enter data, such as their name, or make a choice, such as selecting their country of residence from a drop-down menu.

A form looks and behaves very much like a typical dialog box in a Windows program. Figure 12.1 shows a form containing all the standard fields you can include in a form (you'll begin building this form in "Creating the Sample Form" later in this chapter).

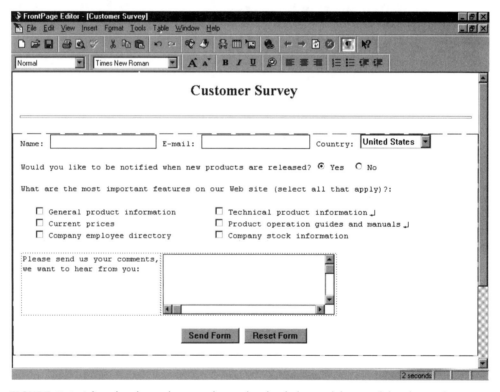

FIGURE 12.1: A form lets the reader enter data and make choices and then send that data to the server.

> **NOTE** You can place more than one form on a Web page. The Editor delineates a form with a dashed line around it, as you can see for the form in Figure 12.1. Any fields you add within that dashed line are part of that form. In Figure 12.1, only the heading and horizontal line at the top of the page are not part of the form.

Form-Building Basics

Creating forms is a snap in the WYSIWYG environment of the FrontPage Editor. You don't even have to build a form "from scratch," although the process is pretty simple. Instead, when you create a new page you can choose the Form Page Wizard, which will walk you through the form-building process while giving you a taste of the kind of decisions that go into creating a form page.

You can also create more specialized forms from these page templates: Confirmation Form, Feedback Form, Product or Event Registration, Survey Form, and User Registration.

> **NOTE** Once you understand how to create a form and define its properties, you can try the Form Page Wizard to create a form page. However, you'll probably find building a form so easy in the Editor that the Wizard isn't really needed.

To create your own forms, here are the main steps to follow:

1. Before you start creating a form, you should have a plan for what you will do with the data once your server receives it. For example, will it be appended to a database or perhaps added to an HTML page and displayed elsewhere on your Web site?
2. Insert the form fields you will need on a page in the Editor, such as text boxes, radio buttons, and check boxes, as well as any descriptive text or images you want.
3. Insert the push buttons (see the bottom of Figure 12.1) that allow users to send the data they have entered to your server or to reset all the controls in the form so the users can start over.

4. Anyone can open a form in a browser; it's just like any other page. In order to send its data back to the server, however, you as the author must specify a *form handler* as part of the form's properties. This determines how your server will handle the data that users send back to it. It's a critical part of the form-definition process.

If one page contains multiple forms, you must define the properties of each form independently of the others. Each form must also have its own button to submit the data it contains to the server. To define the properties of a control, see "Changing the Properties of a Control;" to define the properties of a form, see "Telling the Server How to Handle the Data."

NOTE In most cases, when all the data in the form is sent back to the server, the information entered into each control (called the control's *value*) is paired with the name of that control (a property you can modify). This *name-value pair* is how each datum is identified so the server can deal with the data appropriately.

Selecting Form Controls

The Editor lets you insert any of the standard HTML controls into a form. If you have not yet placed any form controls on a page, the first time you do so the Editor will create a new form. Thereafter, you can add more controls, descriptive text, images, and so on to that form. If you want to create another form on the page, move the insertion point outside of the dashed line that defines the form.

You choose a form control with the Insert ➤ Form Field command or by clicking a button on the Forms toolbar (shown here). Use View ➤ Forms Toolbar to display it.

Here are the fields you can include in a form:

One-Line Text Box: Enter a single line of text, such as a name, street address, or phone number (the Name and E-mail fields in Figure 12.1).

Scrolling Text Box: Enter multiple lines of text, such as several paragraphs of comments. The window for this field is a fixed size, but scroll bars are displayed to allow you to scroll through the text (the "comments" field in Figure 12.1).

Check Box: Click this field to select it (put a check in it); click it again to deselect it. Use check boxes to let a reader select items in the form and make multiple choices within a group of choices (the "Web site" options in Figure 12.1).

Radio Button: Click one, and only one, radio button in a group of them to make a single choice from that group (the Yes/No choice in Figure 12.1).

Drop-Down Menu: Select one or more items (depending on how the field was defined) from a drop-down list (the Country field in Figure 12.1).

Push Button: Click a button to activate it. Every form must have a button the reader can click to send the data from the form to the server. Forms can also have a button that resets all the fields in the form so the reader can start over (the Send Form and Reset Form buttons at the bottom of Figure 12.1). You can also insert buttons that perform any task for which you can write a script (a program normally run on the server).

Each of these controls has its own set of properties you can access by right-clicking on the field and choosing Form Field Properties from the shortcut menu. For example, you can define the width of a one-line text field, the width and number of lines for a scrolling text box, the items that appear in a drop-down menu, and whether a check box is checked or unchecked when the form is opened.

Aligning Fields in a Form

When you create a form, you may want to align the various text elements, images, and controls it contains. Two ways to do so involve little extra work.

One way to align a form's elements is to apply the Formatted paragraph style to the entire form (Format ➤ Paragraph). A monospaced font will be used, making it easy to align objects on the screen—just press the spacebar to move objects to the right. You can place the main items in the form on separate paragraphs (press Enter) or insert a line break (press Shift+Enter) between those items grouped together, such as the six check boxes in Figure 12.1.

The other way to align objects in a form is to create them within one or more tables. The table provides the structure, so you're not limited to the monospaced font of the Formatted paragraph style.

For example, the field descriptions could be in the left column of a table and the fields themselves in the right column. This method was used in Figure 12.1 for the scrolling text box near the bottom of the page and its description to the left. You can see the dotted table border around them, indicating the width of the table's border has been set to zero and will not be displayed in a browser. See Chapter 11 for more information about arranging data in tables.

Telling the Server How to Handle the Data

At some point after you create a new form in a page, you'll need to specify the form handler that will deal with the data when it is sent to the server. That is, when a person filling out the form clicks the submit button, a program (the form handler) gets the data from the form to the server.

Right-click anywhere within the form and choose Form Properties from the shortcut menu. This displays the Form Properties dialog box (shown in Figure 12.2).

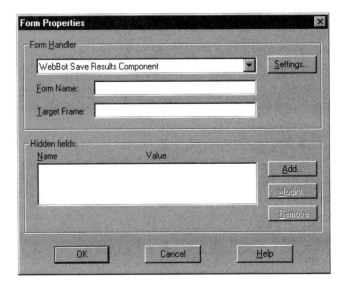

FIGURE 12.2: You specify how the form's data will be sent to the server in the Form Properties dialog box.

Choosing the Form Handler

In the Form Properties dialog box, select a form-handling method from the Form Handler list. Your choice will determine the other choices you need to make when you later click the Settings button. After you have selected a method, you have the following options:

> **Custom ISAPI, NSAPI, or CGI Script:** These acronyms represent three different types of programmable interfaces to a server. You specify (via the Settings button) the URL of the form-handling program on the server, the method used to send the data to the server, and the encoding method for the data transfer.
>
> **Internet Database Connector:** This handler uses a file you specify to define how the form's data will be added to a database on the server. You can create this file by choosing File ➤ New and selecting the Database Connector Wizard.
>
> **WebBot Discussion Component:** This handler adds the data from the form to a FrontPage discussion group web.
>
> **WebBot Registration Component:** This handler allows the user to register for server-provided services.
>
> **WebBot Save Results Component:** This handler saves the data in one of several different file formats on the server.

Let's look at the configuration settings for the WebBot Save Results Component. It's a common way to handle the data from a form in a FrontPage web.

Configuring the Save Results Form Handler

Choose WebBot Save Results Component in the Form Handler list in the Form Properties dialog box; then click the Settings button. This displays the dialog box, Settings for Saving Results of Form, for this form handler (shown in Figure 12.3).

In the Results tab, specify the following information for the WebBot Save Results Component:

> **File for Results:** Enter the name of the file where the form's data will be saved. Each time a user submits the form to the server (by clicking the Send Form button in Figure 12.1, for example), its data are appended to this file. If the file does not yet exist, it will be created the first time data is submitted from the form. Include the relative URL of the file if it is in the active web (the `_Private` folder might be a good place to store it). If the file is outside of the active FrontPage web, specify the path and file name.

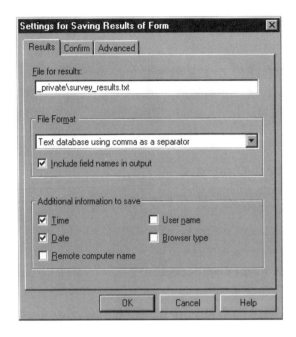

FIGURE 12.3:
The Results tab of the Settings for Saving Results of Form dialog box for the Save Results WebBot

File Format: Define the type of file by selecting one of the available file formats from the drop-down list. There are several HTML options that will save the data in a Web page (you should use an HTM or HTML file name extension in the previous option). There are also several plain text formats; one format, Text Database Using Comma as a Separator, creates a file where a comma is inserted between each datum. Many database and spreadsheet programs can read this type of file.

Include Field Names in Output: By default, this option is selected so the form's data is returned to the server as a name-value pair, where each field's name is paired with that field's data. You can deselect this option to send only the form's data.

Additional Information to Save: Select any of these check boxes to include the specified information along with the form's data when it is saved. For example, select the Time and Date options so you will know when each form's data was saved.

When a user sends in (submits) the data from a form, the WebBot Save Results Component returns a confirmation page to the user. It says "Thanks" and displays the information received from the form. By default, the WebBot uses its own layout for this page. You can specify a different page in the Confirm tab of the Settings for Saving Results of Form dialog box.

The page you specify might be nothing more than a message saying, "We received your data. Thanks!" But you can also include data in the confirmation page from selected fields in the form that was submitted. You do so by opening in the Editor the confirmation page you specified and inserting the Confirmation WebBot where you want to display a field (you'll need to have a list of the field names available to make this job easier). Save the page and the next time it is used to confirm the receipt of data from a form, the data in the specified field will replace each Confirmation WebBot.

Finally, the Advanced tab of the Settings for Saving Results of Form dialog box lets you specify a second file that receives the form's data. This lets you have two sets of data you might need for two different purposes. For example, one file might be saved as a comma-separated text file and eventually appended to a larger database, while the second file might be saved as an HTML page so it can easily be reviewed by the administrator of this FrontPage web.

You'll see how all this works later in this chapter in the section named "Filling Out the Form in a Browser."

Creating the Sample Form

To begin the process of building the form in Figure 12.1, follow these steps:
1. Start with a new blank page in the Editor, and display the Form Fields toolbar by choosing View ➤ Forms Toolbar.
2. Enter the text at the top of the page that will serve as a heading or title, **Customer Survey**. Center this text, apply the Heading 2 style to it, and insert a horizontal line below it.
3. Move the insertion point to the bottom of the page, just below the horizontal line you entered, and create the first form field. Choose Insert ➤ Form Field ➤ One-Line Text Box; you can instead click that button on the Form Fields toolbar.

This will create a new form in the page and insert the single-line text-entry field into it. You could modify the properties of this field now if you wanted, but let's wait until after the form has taken shape with the other controls.

> **NOTE** Once you've created a form, you can add controls to it at any time; the process is always the same as the one you just completed. To delete a field, click on it to select it and press Del.

Now add the descriptive text in front of this field.

4. Move the insertion point to the left of the text-entry field.
5. From the Change Style list on the Format toolbar, select Formatted to apply that style.
6. Enter **Name:**, which is the text that describes this field, and press the spacebar once so there is a space between the colon and the field.
7. Now move the insertion point to the right of the field, press the spacebar once, and type **E-mail:**, which will describe the next field.
8. Press the spacebar once and again click the One-Line Text Box button on the Form Fields toolbar to create the e-mail address field.
9. Move to the right of this field, press the spacebar, enter **Country:**, press the spacebar again, and then click the Drop-Down Menu button on the Forms toolbar.
10. Finish this line in the form by pressing Enter to start a new line; the form (defined by the dashed border) will expand as needed. To enter data outside of the form, just move the insertion point outside of its dashed border.
11. Because you'll be working on this form page throughout this chapter, you should save it to disk now with the File ➤ Save command, either as part of an existing FrontPage web or outside of a web.

Later on in "Changing the Properties of a Control," you'll learn how to adjust the properties of these form controls, which includes filling in the choices that will appear in the drop-down menu. For now, though, you created a new form, entered three fields into it, and entered descriptive text for those fields (as shown here).

Customer Survey

Name: [   ]   E-mail: [   ]   Country: [▼]

Adding Fields to a Form

The sample form is still in the somewhat rough draft stage, so there's no need to make things look perfect. You can change the various components in the form at any time. For now, let's add the rest of the fields and descriptive text:

1. On the blank line below the three fields you created in the previous section, enter the descriptive text from Figure 12.1 that begins with **Would you like to be notified**. Then press the spacebar, and click the button named Radio Button on the Forms toolbar.
2. At the right of the new radio button, type **Yes**, press the spacebar twice, and again insert a radio button. To the right of that button type **No**, then press Enter to start another line.

> **NOTE** Radio buttons should always appear in groups of two or more, because they let the reader make only one choice from several choices. You group radio buttons in a form not by placing them next to one another but by giving them all the same group name in their properties. This is discussed later in this chapter in "Changing the Properties of a Control."

3. On the new line, type the descriptive text that appears above the check boxes in Figure 12.1 beginning with **What are the most important**, and press Enter.
4. Click the Check Box button on the Forms toolbar to insert a check box. Then enter the descriptive text to its right.
5. Press the spacebar seven or eight times, create another check box, and enter the text to its right.
6. Press Shift+Enter to create a line break; you don't want the extra blank space that a new paragraph would create.
7. Repeat steps 4 through 6 until you have created the six check boxes and the text to their right, as shown in Figure 12.1.
8. After the last one, press Enter *twice* and then move the insertion point back up one line (the extra line will allow you to create more entries below the table you will create, but within the form).

Now you can create the table that will contain the scrolling text box and its descriptive text.

9. On the new line below the check boxes, choose Table ➤ Insert Table.
10. In the Insert Table dialog box, define the table with one row and two columns; choose Default for its Alignment option and zero for its Border Size option, then click OK.
11. In the left column of the new table, choose Formatted from the Change Style list on the toolbar to give the text the same look as the other text in the form. Then enter **Please send us your comments,** and press Shift+Enter.
12. Enter **we want to hear from you:** on the second line in that cell in the table.
13. Move the insertion point to the cell on the right and click the Scrolling Text Box button on the Forms toolbar. Don't worry about the size of the resulting control, you can adjust that later.
14. Move the insertion point down one line, which should place it below the table but still within the boundaries of the form.
15. Click the Center button on the Format toolbar, and then click the Push Button on the Forms toolbar. By default, a new push button is labeled Submit, but you can change that text if you want, as you'll see later.
16. Press the spacebar two or three times and click Push Button again. Another button will be inserted, which is also labeled Submit. We'll change this button later, too.
17. That's it, the form is halfway done, so this is a good time to save this page again with the File ➤ Save command.

The rest of the form-building process involves setting the properties of each field and of the form itself. Of course, you can massage the look of the form as much as you want, whether it's adding more fields, text, images, hyperlinks, or any other elements you can insert in a page.

Changing the Properties of a Control

Each control in a form has a set of properties defining its name, the way it looks, the type of data it will accept (validation), and so on. You can adjust the properties after you have entered all the fields for a form as you're doing here, or you can modify the

properties for each one as you create it. To open the properties dialog box for a control, you can do any of the following:
- Double-click on the control.
- Select the control (click on it) and then choose Edit ➤ Form Field Properties or press Alt+Enter.
- Right-click on the control and choose Form Field Properties from the shortcut menu.

In the sections that follow, you'll learn how to change the properties for each of the HTML form controls that you've used in the form-building exercise in this chapter.

One-Line Text Box Properties

In the sample form you've been building in this chapter, right-click on the first control in the form, the one-line text box (or on this control in another form if you don't have the sample form). This displays the Text Box Properties dialog box (see Figure 12.4), in which you can modify the control's properties.

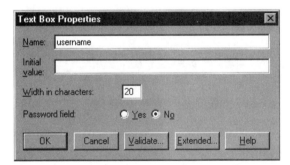

FIGURE 12.4:
The Text Box Properties dialog box for a form's one-line text field

The first item, Name, is found in all the other controls except the radio button (which is not individually named). When you place a control, it is given a short code-like name, such as *T1* for the first one-line text box in a form.

> **NOTE** It's a good idea to give each control a more descriptive name than the one FrontPage gives it automatically, because the control's name is usually paired with its data when the form is sent to the server. Whoever is in charge of the data-handling routines for the data on the server will need to identify each datum by the name of its control; therefore, a descriptive name will be a big help.

Here are the Text Box Properties options and how they should be adjusted for the first control in our sample form:

Name: Enter a name for the control to help identify the source of its data. Because this example is for a person's name, you could enter **username** (stick with one-word names unless you're sure your server can handle spaces in a name).

Initial Value: Enter the characters you want in this field when the form is opened. In this case, nothing should be entered. In other cases, a default entry can save the user some typing if the default is the typical response entered. A default entry can also serve as an example of what type of data should be entered.

Width in Characters: Specify the width of the text box in the form (you can also simply select the box in the form and drag one of its selection handles to change its size). It's easier to enter data when the field is wide enough to display all or most of the text you're entering. In this example, users will be entering their names into this field so the default width of 20 is about right. Note this is not a limitation on the number of characters that can be entered but on the number of characters the user will be able to see; you can limit the number of characters through validation (discussed in the next section).

Password Field: If this field will be used for entering a password in the form, choose Yes. Whatever a user types into this field will be displayed as asterisks to hide it from view.

Text Box Data Validation

You can limit the type of data accepted in a one-line text box or scrolling text box by applying data-validation rules to the field. You do so via the Text Box Validation dialog box (see Figure 12.5):

- Click the Validate button in the field's Text Box Properties dialog box.
- Right-click on the field and choose Form Field Validation.

Display Name

When a user submits the form's data to the server, the entry in each field will be checked against any data validation that has been applied to the field. If the data in a field falls outside of the validation criteria, an error message will be generated notifying

FIGURE 12.5:
You can specify the type of data accepted in a one-line or scrolling text box through data validation.

the user of the problem. Whether the browser or the server checks the data depends on the abilities of the browser.

If the browser supports Java, it will display any validation messages (as shown

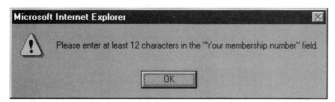

here) before the data is ever sent to the server. Otherwise, the browser will simply send the data to the server, and the server will check the data against the validation rules. It will generate a page with the appropriate error messages and send it back to the browser.

By default, each field mentioned in a validation message will be identified by the name you entered in the Name option in the field's Text Box Properties dialog box. In some cases, that name probably won't be very helpful to the user, such as when the field name is *T1* or *C3*. You can instead enter a name, such as *Your Membership Number*, in the Display Name field in the Text Box Validation dialog box, which will be used to name the field in the invalid-data message. This allows you, for example, to use exactly the same name or description that appears next to the field in the form.

> **NOTE:** The Display Name option will not be needed (and is not enabled) unless you have specified a Data Type other than No Constraints or have checked Required in the Data Length group of options to make this a required field.

Data Type

The Data Type option specifies the type of data allowed in the one-line or scrolling text box:

No Constraints: This default setting allows any type of data in the field.

Text: By default this option allows any characters to be entered into the field, but you can also apply other restrictions in the group of options named Text Format, Data Length, and Data Value.

Integer: This option requires a valid whole number be entered, either positive, zero, or negative.

Number: This option allows any valid number, with or without a decimal fraction.

Once you have selected the Data Type, you can then limit the acceptable entries for the field even further:

Text Format: When you have selected Text for the Data Type option, you can select the type of characters allowed in the field. For example, for a field in which a membership number will be entered, such as *123 45 6789*, you could select the Digits and Whitespace options. This would require only numbers be entered but would also allow the spaces between them.

Numeric Format: When you choose Integer or Number from the Data Type list, you can specify the Grouping character allowed within the entry to separate every three digits. Choose Comma, Period, or None. When you choose Number from the Data Type list, you can also specify the Decimal character that will be allowed, either Comma or Period.

Data Length: Choose the Required option to require an entry in this field, no matter what other options have been specified. Use the Min Length and Max Length fields to specify the minimum and maximum number of characters that will be allowed in the field.

Data Value: Enter a logical relationship between the entry in this form field and an amount you specify. For example, to require the entry be a positive whole number greater than zero but not greater than 100, choose Integer for the Data Type option, select the Required option, choose the Field Must Be option, select Greater Than, and enter 0 in the Value field. Then select the And Must Be option, choose Less Than or Equal To, and enter 100 in its Value field. If the user enters a negative number, a zero, or a number greater than 100, an appropriate error message will be generated (such as the one shown below).

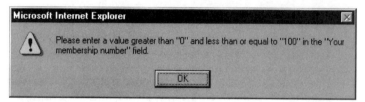

Drop-Down Menu

The Country field in the form in Figure 12.1 is a drop-down menu. The user can click the down arrow in that field and select a country name from a list of possible choices.

When you insert a drop-down menu into a form, it is empty and contains no choices. You fill the menu via the Drop-Down Menu Properties dialog box (shown in Figure 12.6).

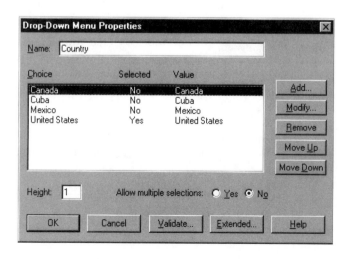

FIGURE 12.6: The Drop-Down Menu Properties dialog box for a drop-down menu form field

To add an item to the menu, click the Add button. In the Add Choice dialog box (shown here), enter what you want to appear as a choice on the menu. By default, the text you enter is exactly what will be sent to the server when a user has selected this item in the menu. Optionally, you can select the Specify Value check box and enter the characters that will be used as the actual value for this item in the menu. For example, you might want *United States* to appear in the list while using *USA* as the value that will be sent to the server.

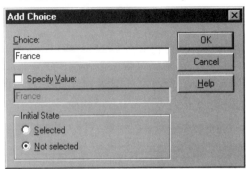

When you're adding an item to a drop-down menu, you can also specify whether the item is selected by default. For example, in Figure 12.6, the *United States* choice will be selected when the form is opened, which would be helpful if most of those filling out this form would make that selection.

By default, a user can select only one item from a drop-down menu; select Yes for the Allow Multiple Selections in the properties dialog box to let a user select more than one (using the Ctrl+click or Shift+click method).

Finally, you can select an item in the Choice list in the Drop-Down Menu Properties dialog box and then click the Move Up or Move Down button to change its position in the list; click the Remove button to remove it from the list; click the Modify button to revise its name, value, or selected status.

You can also set validation rules for a drop-down menu in its validation dialog box (shown here). The option named Disallow First Item lets you place a "dummy" item first on the list, which you can use as a short instruction, such as *Choose a country*. In that case, you would not want to mark any of the other items in the list as being selected when the form is opened so the first item would be displayed. If you have allowed multiple selections from the menu, you can also specify the minimum and maximum number of choices that will be allowed.

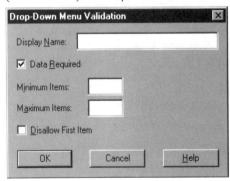

Radio Button

Radio buttons allow a user to make one choice from a group of choices and therefore should always appear in groups of two or more. In Figure 12.1, two radio buttons

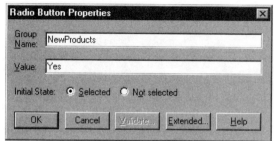

let the user choose either Yes or No. You define a group of radio buttons by giving each of them the same Group Name in its properties dialog box, as shown here. The name *NewProducts* was used for both of the radio buttons in Figure 12.1.

The value you assign to a radio button will be sent to the server if that button is selected by the user. In Figure 12.1, the value *Yes* was assigned to one button and *No* was assigned to the other.

You can also choose to have one of the buttons in a group selected, by default, when the form is opened. Again, offering a default choice can be a convenience to the person who's filling out the form.

If none of the buttons in a group is a default choice, you can require one be selected through that group's validation dialog box. Select the Data Required check box and, optionally, enter a name for the group of radio buttons in the Display Name field. In this case, applying validation to one radio button in a group applies it to all buttons in the group.

Check Box

The check box allows a user to select a single item by clicking on the box; clicking on the box again will deselect it. A check mark in the box indicates it's selected. In Figure 12.1, six check boxes let the user select one or more of those items.

The properties of a check box consist of its name and value and whether it will be selected or deselected when the form is opened. The default name for the first check box in a form is *C1*; the second will be named *C2*, and so on. You can assign a more descriptive name to a check box, but the default value of *On* might be sufficiently descriptive in most cases because a check box is either selected (on) or deselected (off).

Scrolling Text Box

The scrolling text box is essentially the same as a one-line text box, but it allows multiple lines of text. In Figure 12.1, a scrolling text box was used to accept comments from the person filling out the form.

> **NOTE** Some browsers will automatically wrap text when it reaches the right edge of the scrolling text box. Other browsers, however, will let the text extend to the right, so the user will have to press Enter to start a new line.

You can specify the width and height of a scrolling text box in its properties dialog box. As with the width of a one-line text box, these settings affect only the size of the field in the form; they do not limit the amount of text that can be entered into the field. You can apply validation rules to a scrolling text; the choices are the same as those for a one-line text box, as discussed in "Text Box Data Validation" earlier in this chapter.

Push Button

There is only one kind of push button control you can insert into a form, but it can serve multiple purposes. You inserted two of these buttons into the example form in this chapter (the Send Form and Reset Form buttons in Figure 12.1). After you modify each button's properties, clicking one button will send the form's data to the server using the form handler defined for this form. Clicking the other will reset the form controls to their default values (the values they contain when the form is opened).

The Push Button Properties dialog box (shown here) lets you change the text that appears on the face of the button and the task it will perform when clicked.

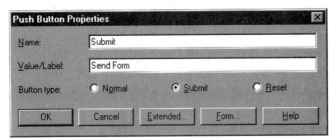

For the first button in the sample form, change its Value/Label setting to **Send Form**, and select the Submit option. For the second button, enter **Reset Form** for its Value/Label setting and select the Reset option. You could also change their Name options to something more descriptive, such as

Submit and Reset. When you have specified a Name/Value for a button, as in this case, it is that entry that will be sent to the server as the value for this control (the button).

Filling Out the Form in a Browser

You can open a page that contains a form in your browser in the same way that you open any other page. No server interaction is involved until you press the button that submits the form's data to the server.

The sample form is shown in a browser in Figure 12.7, with data entered into its various controls. At this point, a user could erase the data entered in the form by clicking the Reset Form button, which resets all the controls to their default values. If the user were ready to send the data to the server, a click of the Send Form button would do the job.

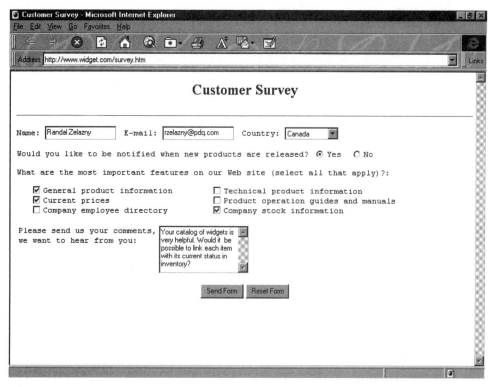

FIGURE 12.7: You open a form in a browser as you would any other page, and you can fill it out without any server interaction.

When you set up the properties for this form (see "Configuring the Save Results Form Handler" earlier in this chapter), you chose the WebBot Save Results Component as the form handler. It is this routine that sends the form's data to the server, sends a confirmation page back to the user, and saves the form's data in a file on the server.

The confirmation page created by the form handler from the form's data (the form in Figure 12.7) is sent back to the user (shown in Figure 12.8) to verify the data was received.

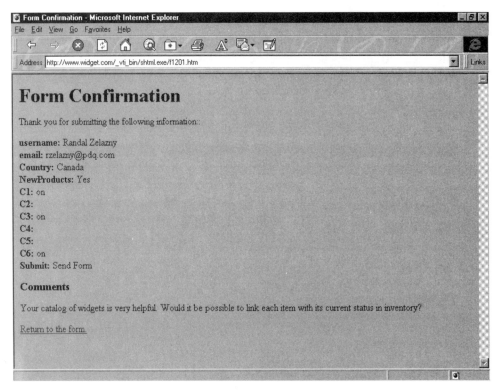

FIGURE 12.8: The server returns a confirmation page displaying the information received from the form.

The data from this form is stored on the server in the format specified in the Settings for Saving Results of Form dialog box for the form handler (see Figure 12.3). In that example, the file format for the results file was the one named Text Database Using Comma as a Separator; the file was named SURVEY_RESULTS.TXT and was stored in the web's _Private folder.

After the data from the form in Figure 12.7 was saved to that file, the result would be the text file shown in Figure 12.9. The first line in that file contains the names of all the controls in the form. A comma is used to delimit each name, and each is also enclosed in quotes.

The second line in that file is the data from the form (it wraps to a third line in Figure 12.9). Again, the data from each control is enclosed in quotes and followed by a comma to separate it from the next item. A control with no data in it, such as three of the check boxes, is signified only by a comma. In other words, there are just as many commas in this data from the form as there are in the first row of form control names.

> "username","email","Country","NewProducts","C1","C2","C3","C4","C5","C6","Comments","Submit","Date","Time"
> "Randal Zelazny","rzelazny@pdq.com","Canada","Yes","on",,"on",,,"on","Your catalog of widgets is very helpful. Would it be possible to link each item with its current status in inventory?","Send Form","6/3/97","9:41:43 PM"

FIGURE 12.9: The data from the form is saved to a text file; the first line contains the names of the form controls, and the second line contains the data from one form (that line wraps to a third line).

> **TIP**
> This is the type of file that most database and spreadsheet programs can read with ease. For example, when you open this file in Excel, you can choose to have each control name and its corresponding datum fall into the same column.

Notice the last two control names in the first line in Figure 12.9, the date and time, which go with the last two data items in the third line. These were not controls in the form but were selected as form handler options (see Figure 12.3) to time-stamp the form's data.

This results file contains data from just one form. Each time the form is filled out and submitted, another line of data will be added to the file. It will continue to grow until you either delete the file or move it to another location. The next time the form is filled out, the file will be created.

This chapter has shown you how to create forms that allow you to gather input from visitors to your site. In the next chapter, you'll learn how to create a frame set that lets you display multiple pages within a single page.

Chapter 13

GETTING FANCIER WITH FRAMES

FEATURING

- Framing pages in a frame set
- Using a frame set template
- Viewing a frame set in your browser
- Creating a custom frame set
- Adjusting the size or number of frames
- Assigning a name and default URL to a frame
- Specifying a target frame in a hyperlink
- Displaying a message in a marquee

This chapter will show you how to build a frame set, which is a Web page that displays more than one page within it. Each page is displayed within its own window, or frame. You'll also learn how to create a marquee—a scrolling message in a page.

Dividing a Page into Frames

One of the newer features of HTML allows you to create a Web page that displays multiple pages within it. Each page is displayed within a separate window, or *frame*. The page containing these frames is called a *frame set*; when a browser opens a frame set, it then opens and displays the page assigned to each frame. You can build all sorts of interesting and practical solutions with frames.

> **NOTE** There is no HTML <BODY> tag in a frame set page. Instead, that tag is replaced by the <FRAMESET> tag, which defines the layout of each frame and the URL of its contents.

A typical use for a frame set, which you'll build in this chapter, is shown in a browser in Figure 13.1. Perhaps without even realizing it, visitors to your frame set page will see three different pages in their browser:

- A frame in the top-left corner displays a banner and an image; this is the same page that was the target of the Include WebBot discussed in Chapter 10.
- A frame on the left side beneath the banner's frame displays a table of contents page, which is built from the Table of Contents WebBot discussed in Chapter 10.
- A frame on the right side displays a home page when the frame set is first opened. After that, when you click a hyperlink in the table of contents frame on the left, the target of the link is displayed in this frame on the right. Therefore, what you see in this frame will change as you click different links.

The frame set concept can be confusing at first, but it's actually quite simple to implement in the FrontPage Editor.

Creating a Frame Set from a Template

When you're creating or revising a frame set page in the FrontPage Editor, you always do so within the Frames Wizard. You can choose either a ready-built frame set template in the Wizard and fill its default pages with content (described in this section), or you

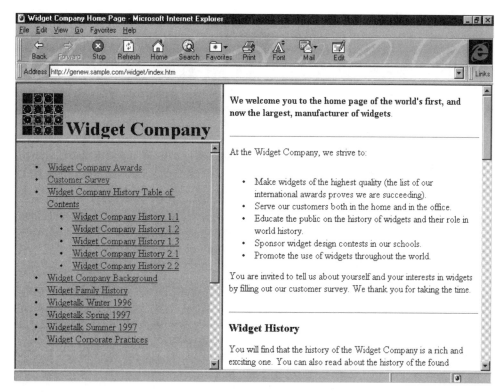

FIGURE 13.1: A frame set displays a banner and an image at the top, a table of contents on the left, and the target of each table of contents link on the right.

can let the Wizard take you through each step of defining the frame set (described in "Creating a Custom Frame Set" later in this chapter):

- The number of frames in the frame set
- The size of each frame
- The name of each frame, which can be used to specify a target frame for a hyperlink
- The page displayed in each frame when the browser opens the frame set page

Now you'll begin creating the frame set shown earlier in Figure 13.1.

Starting the Frames Wizard

When you are creating a new frame set, you can choose either to base it on a template or to define the layout of its frames yourself. Either way, you must start the Frames Wizard:

1. In the Editor, choose File ➤ New.

2. In the New Page dialog box, choose Frames Wizard and click OK. This displays the Choose Technique step of the Frames Wizard (shown in Figure 13.2).
3. Select the Pick a Template option and click Next (later in this chapter in "Creating a Custom Frame Set" you'll see how to design your own frame set).

FIGURE 13.2: The first step of the Frames Wizard lets you create a new frame set either from a template or by defining the frames yourself.

Choosing a Frame Set Template

This step of the Forms Wizard displays the Pick Template Layout dialog box (shown in Figure 13.3). Each of the frame set templates in the Layout list offers a different arrangement of frames in different sizes. When you click on each layout, a description of it appears below the list with a model of it on the left side of the Frames Wizard dialog box. Take the time now to select each one and see what it offers.

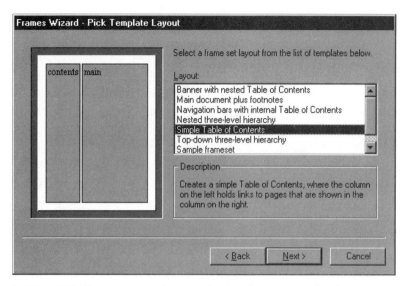

FIGURE 13.3: You can create a frame set by choosing an appropriate frame set template.

> **NOTE** When you create a frame set from a template, the default pages for each frame in the set are also created. Each of those pages contains comments that explain how the page is to be used in relation to the frame set. You can either replace those comments with your own material and continue to use them in the frame set, or you can modify the frame set to refer to other default pages of your choosing (see "Specifying a Name and URL for a Frame" later in this chapter).

There are several frame set templates that are almost, but not quite, perfect for the example in this chapter. That's not a problem, though, because it's easy to revise a frame set later on and make it just right. For now, start with the following:

1. Select the template named Simple Table of Contents, which is divided vertically into two frames.
2. Click the Next button.

Specifying an Alternate Page

The dialog box in this step of the Forms Wizard is named Choose Alternate Content (shown in Figure 13.4). This is an optional step, but one that is a courtesy to those whose browsers do no support frames (newer versions of most browsers can handle frames). This step is also a good way to ensure you don't "slam the door" on those visitors who can't view frames.

1. Click the Browse button and choose another page in the active web. When a browser is unable to display frames, it will open this page instead. Again, this is an optional step.
2. Click the Next button.

The page you specify will actually be loaded into the HTML code in the frame set page, between opening and closing `<NOFRAMES>` tags. A browser that can display frames will ignore this code, but a browser that cannot display frames will display this code only.

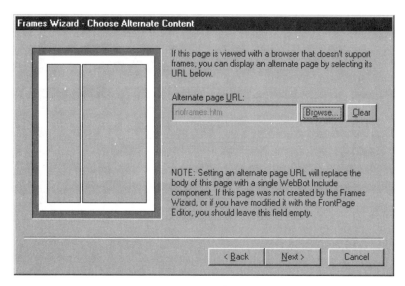

FIGURE 13.4: You can choose to display an alternate page for browsers that cannot display frames.

Saving the Frame Set

The last step of the Frames Wizard lets you save the frame set (see Figure 13.5).

1. In the Title field, enter an appropriate title for the frame set page.
2. In the URL field, enter a file name for this frame set (make a note of the name so you can open it in your browser later on). If you want this frame set to serve as the home page in the active web, you should give it the appropriate default home page name, such as INDEX.HTM. Of course, you would first want to rename the existing home page so the frame set would not overwrite it.
3. Then click Finish.

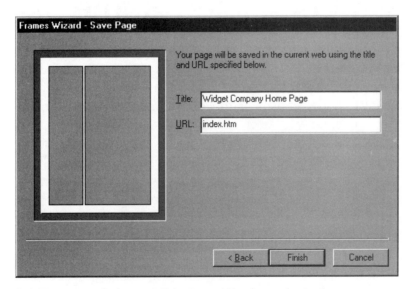

FIGURE 13.5: In the last step of the Frames Wizard, you give the frame set page a title and file name and save it to the active web.

> **NOTE** Besides the frame set page, which you named and saved in the Frames Wizard, two other pages are created for the Simple Table of Contents template. The file FRCONTEN.HTM is the default page for the frame on the left, and the file FRMAIN.HTM is the default page for the frame on the right.

Now for the big anticlimax—the Frames Wizard closes, and you're returned to the Editor but with no frame set to look at! That's because a frame set page is really just a collection of definitions. The text, images, and other content a browser displays in a frame set all come from the other pages whose names are part of the frame set definition. Again, the Frames Wizard is the only way you work on a frame set in the Editor.

The next section shows how you can view your finished frame set and see if it's working correctly. Later in this chapter, you'll learn how to add another frame to the frame set so it looks like the one in Figure 13.1, and you'll learn how to define different default URLs for its frames.

Viewing a Completed Frame Set

To see the result of creating this sample frame set from the Simple Table of Contents template, you need to open in your browser the frame set page you saved in the Frames Wizard. You can't use the Editor's Preview in Browser command because opening a frame set page in the Editor simply starts the Frames Wizard. Therefore, open your browser and then open this frame set page, such as by dragging this page from the Explorer into your browser. Figure 13.6 shows the functional frame set and its default pages that you created from a template.

At this point, the frame set is ready to be used if you want, but the contents of its frames are not. As mentioned earlier, you have two choices:

- Add content to each of the default pages. In the sample frame set, you could create a table of contents in the page `FRCONTEN.HTM`, and place everything for your home page (or any other page) within the page `FRMAIN.HTM`. The next time you open the frame set in a browser, you'll see your real table of contents on the left and your home page on the right, instead of seeing the Frames Wizard instructions displayed in Figure 13.6.
- Revise the frame set in the Frames Wizard and specify a different URL for each of its frames (see "Specifying a Name and URL for a Frame" later in this chapter). You would also need to define the default target frame for the table of contents page (this is discussed later in this chapter in "Specifying a Target Frame in a Link"). The next time you open the frame set in a browser, it will display the other pages; you could then delete the two default pages that were automatically created by the Forms Wizard.

Now you'll see how you can create a custom frame set instead of starting with a template. After that, you'll learn how to revise an existing frame set.

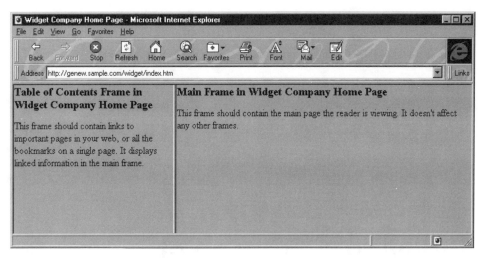

FIGURE 13.6: The result of creating a frame set from a template

Creating a Custom Frame Set

When you start the Forms Wizard in the Editor, you can define the structure of a frame set "from scratch" instead of choosing a template. You can bypass a ready-built template by following these steps (each is discussed in more length in following sections):

1. Choose File ➤ New in the Editor, select the Forms Wizard from the New Page dialog box, and then click OK.
2. In the first dialog box of the Frames Wizard, choose Make a Custom Grid and click Next.
3. This displays the Edit Frame Set Grid dialog box, in which you define the number of frames and their sizes, as discussed in "Changing the Number of Frames or Their Sizes" later in this chapter. Remember, you can revise the frame set at any time, so you're not locked into the choices you make.
4. Click the Next button, which takes you to the Edit Frame Attributes dialog box. Here you define the name for each frame and its *source URL* (the file displayed in the frame when the frame set is opened in a browser). You can also change several appearance options for each frame (see "Specifying a Name and URL for a Frame" and "Changing the Appearance of a Frame" later in this chapter).

5. When you click the Next button, you'll be taken to the Choose Alternate Content dialog box in the Forms Wizard. Now you're back on the same track you followed when you created a frame set from a template.

> **NOTE** At this point, the main difference between creating a custom frame set and using a template is that when you're finished and have saved the new frame set, no other files will be created automatically. It is up to you to specify the correct files for each frame's source URL.

Modifying a Frame Set

You can make changes to a frame set at any time by making new choices in the Frames Wizard dialog box that appears automatically when you try to open the page in the Editor. You'll have the opportunity to go through all the steps you would follow when creating a custom frame set, as discussed in the previous section.

This means that even when you have created a frame set from a template, as you did in the example earlier in this chapter, you can still return to that frame set and make changes to it that weren't available during the design process. This includes changing the number of frames it contains or their sizes and specifying a different default URL for any of its frames.

Changing the Number of Frames or Their Sizes

When you choose File ➤ Open in the Editor and select a frame set page, the Frames Wizard will automatically start by displaying the Edit Frame Set Grid dialog box (shown in Figure 13.7). This is the same one you see when you are creating a new frame set without a template, as discussed earlier in "Creating a Custom Frame Set."

The example frame set you created from a template had only two frames, which are displayed in the model on the left side of the dialog box in Figure 13.7. There are several ways to change the frame set at this step in the Frames Wizard:

- Change the number of rows and columns in the frame set to change the number of frames or their layout.
- Drag a border to change the size of the affected frames.
- Split a selected frame into four frames (which actually creates a *child* frame set within a *parent* one).

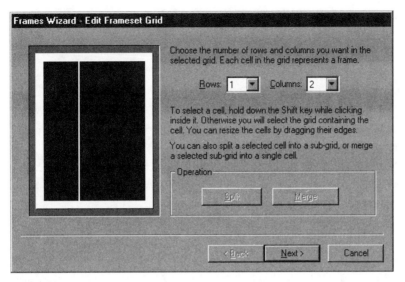

FIGURE 13.7: You can specify the number of frames and their sizes for the frame set you are either creating or revising.

- Change the number of rows or columns in a frame that was split.
- Merge a split frame back into a single frame (dissolve the child back into the parent frame set).

> **NOTE** FrontPage defines the size of each frame as a percentage of the window size (either the Editor's or a browser's), much as you can do with tables and horizontal lines. Therefore, the frames in a frame set will grow larger or smaller along with the window that displays them.

Before you can change the number of rows or columns in a frame set, you must select the entire model of the frame set (either a child or a parent) in the Frames Wizard dialog box. To do so, click any of its frames, but don't click on a border between the frames.

This will highlight all the frames in that frame set while also enabling the Rows and Columns options. You can then change those settings to divide the frame set into a different number of frames. The changes you make will appear immediately in the model.

If you want to change the size of the frames, simply drag the appropriate border to a new position in the frame set (the mouse pointer will change to a two-headed arrow when you point to a border).

You can split a frame into four child frames, but first you must select that frame by Shift+clicking on it. Once that frame is highlighted, click the Split button.

Let's add a third frame to the sample frame set, changing it from what was shown in Figure 13.6 to what was shown in Figure 13.1. There are several ways to add a third frame above the one on the left; after some experimentation, the method described here is a pretty straightforward one:

1. Open this frame set in the Editor; the Frames Wizard should look like the one shown in Figure 13.7.
2. Shift+click on the left-hand frame to select only that frame.
3. Click the Split button, which will divide this frame into four smaller ones, as shown in the Frames Wizard model on the left side of Figure 13.8. The Rows and Columns options in the dialog box are now each set to 2 for the selected portion of the frame set, which is the four new frames that occupy exactly the same space as the original frame.

> **NOTE** When you select multiple frames that are the result of a split, such as those in this example, you can click the Merge button to merge them back into a single frame.

4. With the four new frames still selected, change the Columns option to **1**, which will remove two of the frames from the selection and give you almost what you want—a full-height frame on the right and two frames on the left (see the middle example in Figure 13.8).

FIGURE 13.8: You can split and merge frames to find a frame set layout that works.

5. Now, to match Figure 13.1, you'll want the upper-left frame to be much smaller; point to the border between it and the lower frame and then drag that border up. When you're finished, the model should look something like the one shown on the right side of Figure 13.8.
6. If the frame set looks about right, click the Next button to go to the next step in modifying a frame set.

Specifying a Name and URL for a Frame

When you're revising a frame set, as in this example, or creating a new one without a template, you'll come to the Frame Wizard's Edit Frame Attributes dialog box (shown in Figure 13.9).

Here you can name each frame so you can specify it (by name) as the target frame for a hyperlink in this frame set. You'll find frame names are a lot like bookmarks, or named anchors, in a page (see "Working with Bookmarks" in Chapter 8). Both types of names are case-sensitive, so try to be consistent in your use of uppercase and lowercase letters.

You can also define several appearance options for each frame, and you can assign a source URL to each frame, which is the URL of the file that will be displayed in the frame when the frame set is first opened.

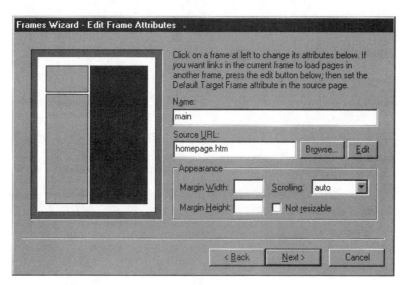

FIGURE 13.9: You name each frame and define the default target URL for it in the Edit Frame Attributes dialog box.

If you're creating a new frame set, both the name and URL options will be blank for each frame. In this case, you're revising a frame set built from a template so two of the frames already have these options defined. In Figure 13.9, the right-hand frame is selected (click on a frame to select it) and you can see the definitions for it:

Name: The name of the frame, *main* in this case, identifies this frame in the frame set. When you're creating a hyperlink in a page that will be displayed somewhere in this frame set, you can specify this frame name so the target of the link will be displayed in this frame (see "Specifying a Target Frame" in Chapter 8). Later in this chapter in the section named "Specifying a Target Frame in a Link," you'll see how to take advantage of this in the table of contents in the left-hand frame.

Source URL: The name of the file, HOMEPAGE.HTM in this case, that will be opened and displayed in this frame when the frame set is opened in a browser.

> **NOTE**
>
> In this example, the frame set was saved as INDEX.HTM so it will serve as the home page in its FrontPage web. Therefore, the page that had been the home page was renamed as HOMEPAGE.HTM. When the frame set INDEX.HTM is opened in a browser, this page, HOMEPAGE.HTM, will be displayed in the right-hand frame.

You created a third frame for this frame set, which is still undefined. Let's now give it a name and specify a source URL for it:

1. To modify the small frame that you added earlier, first select it by clicking on it in the Edit Frame Attributes dialog box (you don't need to Shift+click). Again, don't click on a border between frames or you might change the border's position.
2. In the Name option in the dialog box, enter an appropriate name for this frame. It's a good practice, and a simple one, to name a frame either by its contents or by its position in the frame set. In this case, you could enter the name **top**.
3. In the Source URL option, enter the URL of the file you want displayed in this frame when the frame set is opened.

> **NOTE:** In the case of the Widget Web sample, the page that contains the logo and company name, `HEADER.HTM`, was chosen for this frame. This is the same page that was included in other pages in the Widget Web via the Include WebBot file. Here it will be displayed separately in its own frame, where it will fulfill the same purpose.

In this new arrangement with the logo and company name displayed in their own frame, you would probably want to remove the Include WebBot that displays this same material from any pages that would be displayed in this frame set. Such was the case for the pages displayed in the left and right frames in Figure 12.1.

Changing the Appearance of a Frame

After you have named the third frame (the new one) in our sample frame set and defined its source URL, you can adjust two other Appearance options (look back at Figure 13.9):

Scrolling: By default, this option is set to Auto so when a frame is not large enough to display its contents in a browser, scroll bars will be displayed to allow the user to scroll through the frame. Choose Yes or No to have scroll bars always displayed or never displayed, respectively, no matter how the frame fits its contents.

Not Resizeable: The frames in a browser can be resized by the person behind the keyboard simply by dragging the frame borders. It can be a courtesy to allow a user to resize a frame, such as when that frame is displaying the page that needs the most attention. If you select the Not Resizeable option for a frame, that frame's borders will not be movable.

Margins: The two settings Margin Width and Margin Height define the margins (in pixels) between the frame's left and top edges and its contents. These are left blank in the Frames Wizard, by default, so the browser determines the default margin space.

Specifying a Target Frame in a Link

In the section named "Creating a Hyperlink" in Chapter 8, you learned when the page containing a hyperlink is displayed in a frame in a frame set, you can specify which frame will display the link's target file when it is opened. In the sample frame set you've been working on in this chapter, that's exactly what you want to do—click on a hyperlink in the left frame (the table of contents) and have the target of that link open in a specific frame—the right one.

In some cases, you might revise each hyperlink in the page so it pointed to the target frame name (*main* in our sample). That could be an awful lot of work, though, but fortunately there's a much better solution at hand.

In Chapter 7 in "Setting Page Properties," you learned about the Default Target Frame setting for a page. If a page will be displayed within a frame set, you can specify the name of the frame in which all target pages will appear when you click their hyperlinks. You can override this setting for any hyperlink by specifying another frame within that link. That sounds perfect for this frame set, and it's *almost* a one-step process:

1. Open the table of contents page that will be displayed in the left frame of our frame set (that's the frame named *contents*). For example, if you're working with the frame set created earlier in this chapter, open FRCONTEN.HTM. That is the page in which you would create the table of contents (via the WebBot), and that is the page you would now open in the Editor. Otherwise, open whatever page you specified as the Source URL for the left-hand frame.
2. In the Editor, right-click anywhere on the page and choose Page Properties from the shortcut menu.
3. In the General tab of the Page Properties dialog box, enter the name **main** in the Default Target Frame option (shown below).
4. Click the OK button to close the dialog box, and then save the page back to the Web.

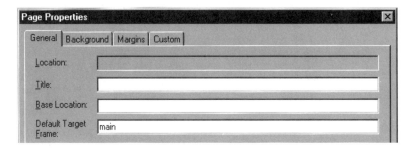

Now when a browser opens the frame set, a user can click on one of the hyperlinks in the table of contents, and the target of that link will be opened in the frame on the right, the one named *main*.

Delivering a Message with a Marquee

Microsoft Internet Explorer first introduced the *marquee*, which is an HTML implementation of the scrolling message you might find on the marquee of a movie theater, where it displays the current schedule, or above a stock brokerage firm, where it displays a live ticker tape.

> **NOTE** Although the marquee is not yet a part of the HTML standard, the popularity of Internet Explorer (which can display a marquee) may eventually make the marquee an official HTML element. If a browser cannot display a scrolling marquee, it will simply display the text that would have instead scrolled across the screen.

Now, you may be wondering why the discussion has turned from frames to marquees. The answer is quite simple—a marquee is a separate area on a page that displays its own text, much like a frame that displays its own page or image. Besides that similarity, there really wasn't another chapter in this book appropriate for this discussion, so here you are!

Figure 13.10 shows an example of a marquee in a page in the Editor. The marquee was added to the Widget home page, first shown in Chapter 1. Here the marquee displays a newsy and timely message that you might change every few days.

Of course, the only problem with the marquee in Figure 13.10 is that you can't see its most important feature—the message scrolling across the marquee from right to left, again and again. To see a marquee in action, you need to open its page in a browser; shown here is a series of looks at the same marquee in a browser.

Widget Company

Preview the 1998 widgets on this site....Today!

We welcome you to the home page of the world's first, and now the largest, manufacturer of widgets.

At the Widget Company, we strive to:

- Make widgets of the highest quality (the list of our international awards proves we are succeeding).
- Serve our customers both in the home and in the office.
- Educate the public on the history of widgets and their role in world history.

FIGURE 13.10: A marquee can be an effective way to catch the viewer's attention and display an important message.

It's easy to create a marquee in the Editor; it's very much like inserting a horizontal line. Here are the steps you can use to create the marquee in Figure 13.10:

1. Place the insertion point where you want the marquee to appear. As always, you can move the marquee later, if necessary.
2. Choose Insert ➤ Marquee, which displays the Marquee Properties dialog box (see Figure 13.11).

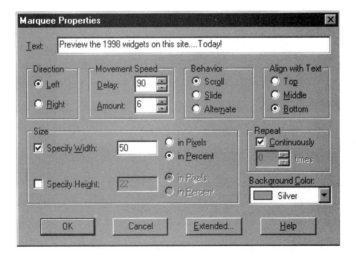

FIGURE 13.11: You can enter the text and define the size, shape, appearance, and behavior of a marquee in the Marquee Properties dialog box.

3. In the Text field, enter the text you want displayed in the marquee. In this example, that would be **Preview the 1998 widgets on this site....Today!** If you had selected text in the page before invoking the command, the text would appear in this field, and the marquee would replace the text in the page.

You could ignore all the other options at this time and click OK, which would create a functioning marquee in your page. But you can also make a few small modifications to it:

4. To change the color of the marquee's background, select a color in the Background Color option.
5. Select the Specify Width check box, enter **50** for the width, and select Percent. This will size the marquee so it is half the width of the window in which this page is displayed.

> **NOTE** You can also change the size of a marquee from within the page. Click on it and then drag one of its selection handles, just as you can do with an image or a horizontal line.

6. That's all you need in this dialog box, so click OK.

The marquee is now half the width of the window but is aligned with the left edge of the window. Its text is in the default size and style, but it should be a little bigger for this purpose. You can change both of these aspects right in the page, treating the marquee like other objects in a page.

7. Select the marquee not by clicking on it but by pointing to the left of it and clicking. This will highlight the marquee as though it were a line of text you had just selected.
8. Now click the Center button on the Format toolbar to center the marquee on the page.
9. Choose Heading 3 from the Change Style list on the Format toolbar so the marquee's message will appear in that heading style.
10. Save the page, and now you're ready to see the marquee in action.
11. Choose File ➤ Preview in Browser to preview this page and its marquee in your browser.

You'll see your message scroll across the marquee from right to left, endlessly repeating.

To modify the marquee, select it and use the Insert ➤ Marquee command to open its Marquee Properties dialog box (shown previously in Figure 13.11) and adjust its options. Experiment with the Behavior options, which affect the way the message moves across the marquee, and adjust the Movement Speed options to see how fast or how slow you can make it run without being distracting.

This chapter has shown you how to use the Frames Wizard to create a frame set, either from a template or from your own design, that displays multiple pages in its frames. You also learned about a new HTML innovation—marquees. In the next chapter, you'll look at the issues involved with administering your FrontPage web.

Chapter 14

ADMINISTERING WEB SITES

FEATURING

- **Testing your Web site**
- **Assigning permissions**
- **Running the FrontPage Personal Web Server**
- **Running the Microsoft Personal Web Server**
- **Registering users in the Microsoft Personal Web Server**
- **Running the FrontPage Server Administrator**
- **Upgrading to the Microsoft Personal Web Server**
- **Changing the default home page name**

This chapter turns to administrative tasks in your Web sites. It begins with some tips on testing your site for reliability and usability. You'll then learn how to limit access to your FrontPage webs by assigning access rights to users. Both the FrontPage and Microsoft Personal Web Servers are discussed, and you'll learn how to use both servers at the same time if you're upgrading from FrontPage 1.1 to FrontPage 97.

Testing and Refining Your Web Site

Before you present your finished Web site to the world, you'll want to be sure *everything* in it is working perfectly. There's nothing quite so anticlimactic as opening the curtains on your site and then having to close them immediately to make repairs.

With that in mind, you'll now see some of the ways you can ensure the dependability of your FrontPage webs. There have been many tips and snippets of testing and maintenance advice throughout this book. You'll find that just about all the advice relating to keeping a Web site healthy applies to all sites in general, not just FrontPage webs.

In fact, when you build and maintain a web under FrontPage, many testing and maintenance chores are either eliminated or vastly simplified. For example, if you rename a file in a non-FrontPage web, the job of finding and revising all the hyperlinks that target the renamed file is a major piece of housekeeping. In the FrontPage Explorer, it happens automatically.

Back up your FrontPage webs. This is the same advice you should heed for all your work on a computer, but it's just as critical with your Web publishing. Whether you're in the process of building your Web sites or already have them up and running, you'll likely be making changes to them on a daily or weekly basis.

Having a previous version of those files available can be a real lifesaver, such as when you hastily click OK when asked if you really want to delete that file. So be sure your FrontPage webs are included in your regular backups, or back them up separately by copying their root folder, such as `C:\FrontPage Webs` for the FrontPage PWS.

Test under a variety of browsers. The whole purpose of the typical Web site is to have its pages viewed in a Web browser. There are many different browsers on the market, all of which might produce different results when displaying the same page. Some browsers have more advanced features than others, and some are just plain old and outdated (when a browser is pushing a year old, its days seem numbered!).

So have at least several of the more popular browsers available for testing your FrontPage webs, and try to have both the newest and the previous version of each one. If you want to be really accommodating to visitors to your site, see how your Web pages look in an older browser—one that cannot display frames, for example. If you include newer HTML features in your pages, you may be leaving those old-timers out of the picture.

Administering Web Sites 289

> **TIP** On the other hand, Web browsers aren't exactly expensive or difficult to obtain; many are free and can be downloaded with the click of a button. Perhaps you can limit your testing to browsers no more than, say, a year old.

Use multiple testers. It's amazing how one person can discover something that many others have missed; the more people you can corral into being testers of your site, the better. Each person brings a different perspective, a different interest, and a different set of talents to the job. One person will tend to catch grammatical errors, while another might not notice them but will find an empty box that was supposed to display an image.

Test your sites with and without color. Although monochrome monitors are becoming rare, it's still a little early to assume everyone who visits your site will be using a color monitor. If your site is heavy with color graphics and, especially, backgrounds, you may want to develop an alternative for those who don't have color.

If you feel there are just too few people who would benefit from this to make the extra work worthwhile, at least take the time to see how your pages look when viewed on a monochrome monitor. If they're unreadable or just plain impossible, you might then consider at least a simple, pared-down alternate page, accessible through the next tip.

Offer a text-only page. There was a time when text-only browsers were common, but not any more. Nonetheless, some users may turn off the graphical image capabilities of their browsers so no images will be downloaded with a page. This can drastically decrease their connection time to the Web, which might save them money or simply make the Web tolerable when connection speeds are slow.

If your Web site has only a few images that aren't crucial to the site, you probably don't have to worry about those browsers that cannot display them. Otherwise, you can offer a text-only alternative page (or series of alternate pages for the site) that could be opened through a Text only link on the home page.

Test your pages at different screen resolutions. One of the more frustrating aspects of creating a Web page is trying to compromise on an "average" screen size. You can design your pages compactly so they nicely fill a monitor at a resolution of

640 by 480, but they might leave a lot of blank space on the right side when viewed at 800 by 600. If you design your pages for that higher resolution, a visitor working at a lower resolution might have to scroll the screen right and left to see the entire page.

One way to avoid some of this problem is to design your pages with a tall orientation rather than a wide one. Let the visitor scroll down through a page instead of having to scroll to the right and back again.

No matter how you design your pages, you should certainly test them at different screen resolutions. That's why the FrontPage Editor's File ➤ Preview in Browser command lets you specify a size for the browser. The command doesn't change your screen's resolution, it simply adjusts the size of the browser's window to show the equivalent amount of screen at the given resolution. Of course, this only works if your own screen is running at a resolution that's higher than the one you choose for the preview.

Test your sites at different connection speeds. You can test your Web sites on your local computer under one of the Personal Web Servers, but this just won't tell you what it will be like to access this site over a slow network connection, let alone over a dial-up connection at modem speeds.

So do yourself and visitors to your site a favor, and test your site over a slow, "real-world" connection. You might be shocked at how slowly that seemingly small image downloads at 28,800 bits per second (about 3,200 bytes, or characters, per second). When you've browsed through your site or others at modem speeds, you'll start to get a feel for how fast large pages or images are transferred.

Test your external hyperlinks. This was emphasized in Chapter 8: You must test the hyperlinks in your site on a regular basis to ensure they are not only still finding their target URLs, but the targets are still the files you expect them to be. The Explorer's Tools ➤ Verify Hyperlinks command can do the first part of this job by testing to see if a link actually has a valid target URL.

The second part is a little more difficult, however. There's really no automated way to confirm the target of a hyperlink is still relevant to you and your site. When a link goes outside of your Web site and your control, you're probably going to have to click that link and see what it returns. Having multiple testers go through your site on an ongoing basis is one way to find broken links; the next paragraph describes another way.

Provide a means for leaving comments. Browsing a Web site is often a read-only process, where visitors to a site get lots of information without returning any. It's important to give visitors the opportunity to let you know how things are going so they can report problems, leave comments, or ask questions.

In fact, on a busy site the visitors will actually be doing a lot more testing of the site than you ever will! Therefore, you should either have a form on a page for accepting their comments or simply include an e-mail hyperlink on your home page, such as *Please e-mail any questions or comments to webmaster@widget.com*.

To create an e-mail link in the Editor, choose the World Wide Web tab in the Create Hyperlink dialog box, choose Mailto from the Hyperlink Type list, and enter the complete e-mail address in the URL field. When visitors click that link, their e-mail program should open with a new message containing that address.

Watch out for orphans. As your Web site grows and changes, it's all too possible to end up with "orphan" pages no longer used anywhere in the site. No pages link to them and they aren't included in any pages. In the FrontPage Explorer, you can give the center of focus to a file in the Hyperlink view and see if any pages reference it. If none do, that might be an indication the file will never be used. You can either investigate how this file is supposed to be used, or you can put it on the To Do List for future reference.

Keeping Your Web Secure

There is always at least one person, an *administrator*, who has full access rights to FrontPage's root web (the folder in which all other FrontPage webs reside on that server). The administrator can create or delete FrontPage webs, create or delete files within a web, and assign access rights (permission) for those webs to others, either as users (browsers), authors, or other administrators.

Unless your server has been set up to restrict access to a FrontPage web, anyone can browse through the files in all FrontPage webs by default; although, they are not allowed to make changes to those files.

> **NOTE** The security restrictions and access rights for your FrontPage webs are very much dependent on the host server. This discussion assumes your server has the FrontPage Server Extensions installed or that you are using the FrontPage Personal Web Server or Microsoft Personal Web Server.

When you install FrontPage, you are asked for the name of a person who will serve as administrator. If the name you give is not already a registered user on your server, you will also be prompted for a password. The name you provide will then be an administrator of the FrontPage root web and, by definition, all FrontPage webs within it. This administrator can then restrict or assign access rights to others as needed.

Assigning Permissions

To change the permission settings for the active FrontPage web, choose Tools ➤ Permissions in the Explorer, which displays the Permissions dialog box. When you are running the FrontPage or Microsoft Personal Web Server (PWS), there are three tabs in this dialog box for defining the access rights to this web:

Settings: Choose to let the active web inherit all permission settings from the root web, or set unique permissions for the active web (you won't find this tab when the FrontPage root web is the active web).

Users: When you are setting unique permissions for a web, you can specify the users who will have access to this web.

Computers: Under the FrontPage PWS when you are setting unique permissions for a web, you can specify the IP (Internet Protocol) addresses of those computers that will be given access to this web.

Groups: Under the Microsoft PWS when you are setting unique permissions for a web, you can specify a group of users who will all have the same access to this web. You cannot create new groups in FrontPage, you must do so in the Microsoft PWS administration tool (see "Registering Users in the Microsoft Personal Web Server" later in this chapter).

> **NOTE** If your server is still using the older FrontPage Server Extensions 1.1, you should not attempt to change access rights with the Tools ➤ Permissions command. You should update the Extensions to the newest version.

There are three levels of access rights you can assign to an individual, a computer, or a group for each FrontPage web on a server.

Administrator: As mentioned earlier, an administrator can do just about anything in the way of editing or viewing webs and their files and can also grant or revoke access rights to a web.

Author: An author can view or make changes to the files in a web but cannot create or delete entire webs or change permission settings. Therefore, if you have logged in with only author permissions, you will not be able to invoke the Tools ➤ Permissions command in the Explorer.

Browser: In this context, a browser is a user who has browsing rights (read-only) in a web and cannot make any changes to it (cannot open a web in the Explorer, for example). In most cases, a person with browsing rights will be accessing that web in a Web browser.

> **NOTE** The access rights of an author include all the browsing rights of a browser, and the rights of an administrator include all the rights of an author.

Assigning Unique Permissions for a Web

Each new FrontPage web inherits the permission settings of the root web by default, so anyone who has access rights in the root web will have those same rights in a new web within the root. To assign unique permissions for a web, open that web in the Explorer and choose Tools ➤ Permissions, and then choose the Settings tab in that web's Permissions dialog box (shown in Figure 14.1). Remember that this tab is not available for the FrontPage root web.

The two options in the Settings tab let you specify how the permissions will be set for this web. By default, the Use Same Permissions as Root Web option is selected so whatever permissions have been set for the root web will also apply to this web. In this case, because there are no permissions to be assigned for this web, you will not be able to make changes in the other two tabs in the Permissions dialog box.

To apply different permission settings to this web, you must select the Use Unique Permissions for This Web option, which will allow you to make changes in the other two tabs in the dialog box.

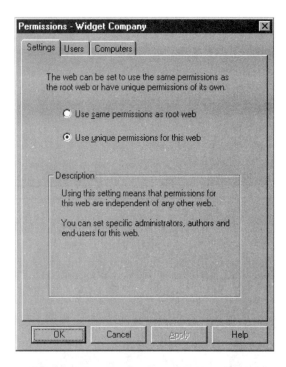

FIGURE 14.1:
You can choose to assign unique access rights for the active web in the Settings tab of the Permissions dialog box.

> **NOTE** To have changes you make in the Permissions dialog box take effect, you must click either the Apply or OK button. The first will leave the dialog box open; the second will close it. When you have clicked Apply, clicking Cancel will not undo any changes you made; it will simply close the dialog box.

At this point, if you make no other changes in the Permissions dialog box, the access rights in this web will still be the same as those in the root web. You use the other two tabs in the dialog box to restrict access to the site further or specify permission settings for other users.

Assigning Permissions to Users

When you have chosen the Use Unique Permissions for This Web option in the Settings tab of the Permissions dialog box, you can then assign access rights for the web in the Users tab (shown in Figure 14.2).

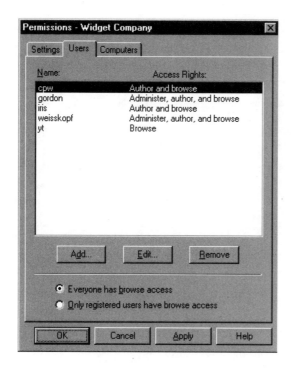

FIGURE 14.2:
You specify the type of access that users will have to the active web in the Users tab of the Permissions dialog box.

If you do not want to restrict browsing rights in this web, select the Everyone Has Browse Access option near the bottom of the dialog box. That way, anyone can view pages and other files in this web (this is the default setting).

If you want to limit browsing only to those you specify, select the option named Only Registered Users Have Browse Access. Now when anyone tries to open a file on this site, their browser will display a dialog box prompting them for their name and password (as shown here). Only those users whose names appear in the list in the Permissions dialog box will be able to browse this web (assuming they remember their passwords).

To add a new user to the list of registered users for the active web, click the Add button in the Users tab in the Permissions dialog box.

The left side of Figure 14.3 shows the Add Users dialog box when the FrontPage PWS is the active server. The right side of Figure 14.3 shows this dialog box under the

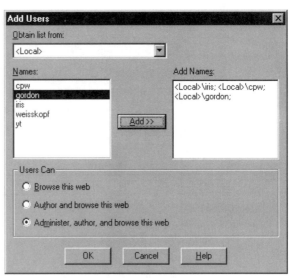

FIGURE 14.3: You assign a user access rights to a web in the Add Users dialog box.

Microsoft PWS, which will be discussed shortly. You (or the user) enter a username, a password, and the password again in the Confirm Password option for verification.

Then select the type of access for this user, either as a browser, an author, or an administrator. Remember, an author's access rights include the rights to browse the web, and an administrator's rights include all the rights of an author. Click OK to close the dialog box, and you'll see the new username in the list in the Users tab of the Permissions dialog box (see Figure 14.2).

When assigning access rights under the Microsoft PWS, you can choose only those names or groups that are already registered with that server (see "Registering Users in the Microsoft Personal Web Server" later in this chapter).

When you click the Add button in the Users tab in the Permissions dialog box, you'll see the Add Users dialog box (shown on the right side of Figure 14.3). Under this server, you select a user in the Names list on the left, choose one of the three access levels, and then click the Add button to place that user's name in the Add Names list on the right. When you're finished adding names, click OK.

> **NOTE** Assigning access rights to groups under the Microsoft PWS is exactly the same as doing so for individual users. Just select the Groups tab in the Permissions dialog box and click the Add button.

When you start the FrontPage Explorer under the FrontPage PWS and then try to open a web, create a new web, delete a web, or perform some other web-wide operation, you will be prompted for your username and password. Whether you are allowed to complete the operation in the Explorer depends on your access rights:

- A user with browser-level access rights in a web will not be allowed to perform any of these operations—the username and password will not be accepted.
- A user with author-level access rights will be allowed to open a web in the Explorer and make changes to it either in the Explorer or the Editor. However, when you open a web with the rights of an author, you will be prompted for a name and password when you invoke a command that only an administrator is allowed to perform. For example, if you choose File ➤ Delete FrontPage Web, your name and password will be rejected because you do not have the rights of an administrator.
- A user with administrator-level rights can do all of the above, plus create and delete webs and assign access rights to the web. Once you open a web in which you have administrator access rights, you will not be prompted again for your name and password while working in that web.

To change the access level of a user, an administrator can select a name in the list in the Users tab in the Permissions dialog box and click the Edit button. Then choose one of the three permission settings for this user and click OK. To remove a user from the list, thereby excluding that user from working on this web, an administrator can select a name in the list and click the Remove button.

Assigning Permissions to IP Addresses

Another way to assign access rights to a web when you are running the Explorer under the FrontPage Personal Web Server is by specifying computer IP addresses instead of usernames and passwords (other servers may not support this). You do so in the Computers tab in the Permission dialog box (shown in Figure 14.4).

An IP (Internet Protocol) address is the numeric address assigned to a computer on a TCP/IP network such as the Internet. It consists of four numbers (each less than 256) separated by periods.

> **NOTE** When you're running FrontPage and a Personal Web Server on a computer that is not networked, the default IP address for the root web on that "local" computer is 127.0.0.1.

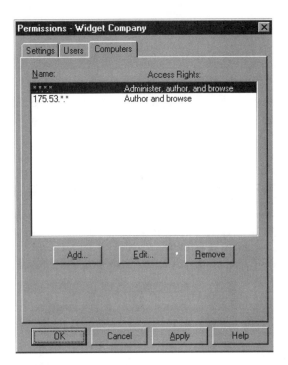

FIGURE 14.4:
You assign access rights to computer IP addresses in the Computers tab of the Permissions dialog box.

You can assign access rights to individual IP addresses, much as you can with individual usernames. You can also specify a *range* of addresses so any IP address that falls within that range will have the given access rights. In the Computers tab of the Permissions dialog box, click the Add button. This displays the Add Computer dialog box (shown in Figure 14.5) in which you specify the IP address and the associated access rights.

Enter the four-number IP address in the four IP Mask fields in the Add Computer dialog box (don't include the periods). Then select the level of access rights for this computer.

To specify a range of IP addresses, enter a single asterisk in any of the four IP Mask fields. The asterisk is a wildcard that represents any number in that field so that the IP address *.*.*.* gives all computers the specified access rights. If you specify the address 175.53.*.*, then all computers whose IP address begins with 175.53 will be given the same access rights.

As with the usernames in the Users tab, you delete an IP address or revise its settings by selecting that address in the list and clicking the Remove or Edit button, respectively.

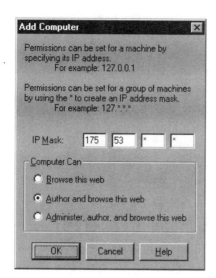

FIGURE 14.5:
You assign access rights to a computer's IP address in the Add Computer dialog box.

Working with the Personal Web Servers

If you already had FrontPage 1.1 installed on your computer when you installed FrontPage 97, you probably have both the FrontPage Personal Web Server (PWS) and the Microsoft PWS on your computer. If this is the first time you've installed FrontPage, then you may have only the Microsoft PWS installed.

You can run FrontPage 97 with either PWS, although you may at some point want to migrate to the more robust Microsoft PWS, which is a subset of Microsoft's popular Internet Information Server (IIS).

You can also run FrontPage 97 while *both* servers are running. You would need to do this if you have existing FrontPage webs that you want to continue to run under the FrontPage PWS, but you also want to create new sites under the Microsoft PWS. In the Explorer, you can easily open a web from either server. You would also need to run both servers when you want to upgrade your existing FrontPage 1.1 webs to FrontPage 97 and the Microsoft PWS. These issues are discussed later in this chapter in "Migrating to the Microsoft Personal Web Server."

Running the FrontPage Personal Web Server

If you have just the FrontPage PWS installed, when you start the Explorer and then open a web, that server will start automatically. It will remain open until you specifically close it—it does not close when you close the Explorer.

To close the FrontPage PWS, right-click on its icon on the Windows taskbar and choose Close. You can also switch to the FrontPage PWS window and choose File ➤ Exit from its menu. That's about all you can do there, however, as there are no commands or settings to adjust. You make most server adjustments within the Explorer, such as assigning access rights to a FrontPage web.

Running the Microsoft Personal Web Server

If you have installed the Microsoft PWS, it starts each time you start Windows 95 by default; so, it will be available to the FrontPage Explorer at all times. When it's running, you'll see an icon for it on the right side of the Windows taskbar, as shown here.

Like the FrontPage PWS, you really won't see any interaction with the Microsoft PWS while you're working in FrontPage. Setting permissions is a little different in each server, as you saw earlier, but otherwise the server is pretty transparent.

You can stop or start the Microsoft PWS at any time via its Properties dialog box, where you can also adjust a few settings and access its administration utility:

- Right-click on its icon on the taskbar and choose Properties.
- From the Windows Start menu, choose Settings ➤ Control Panel and then open the Personal Web Server.

The General tab of the Microsoft Personal Web Server Properties dialog box (shown in Figure 14.6) shows you the Internet address of your computer and the URL of the root web's home page. If you click either the Display Home Page or the More Details button, your Web browser will start and open the appropriate pages for the Microsoft PWS.

On the Startup tab in this dialog box, you can stop the server by clicking the Stop button. When stopped, a Start button will be enabled. You can also choose whether the Microsoft PWS will start each time Windows starts, and whether its icon will appear on the taskbar when it is running.

> **NOTE**
>
> Taking care of administration duties in the Microsoft PWS is outside the scope of this book. If you're in charge of administering all aspects of the server, you might want to read Sybex's *Mastering Microsoft FrontPage 97*.

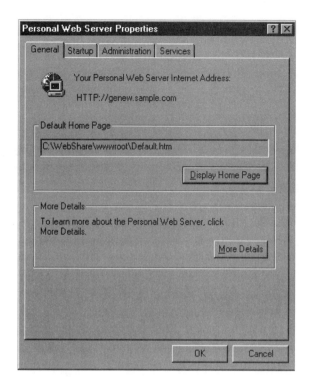

FIGURE 14.6:
The dialog box where you can adjust the settings for the Microsoft Personal Web Server

On the Administration tab, you can click the Administration button to change user access rights on the server (discussed in the next section), the folders (directories) that the server uses, its default home page name, and more. Again, this opens appropriate pages in your Web browser, where you perform administration duties via Web pages (one convenience of this PWS). Later in this chapter in "Changing the Name of the Home Page," you'll see how to change the default home page name.

Finally, on the Services tab, you can enable or disable HTTP and FTP on the server, and adjust related properties.

Registering Users in the Microsoft Personal Web Server

Earlier in this chapter in "Assigning Permissions to Users," you saw how to assign access rights to users of your FrontPage webs. When you're running your webs under the Microsoft PWS, you can assign access rights in the Explorer only to those users who are already registered with the server. You can't register a new user from within the Explorer; you do so with the Microsoft PWS administration utility in your Web browser.

Open the Microsoft PWS Properties dialog box (as described in the previous section) and choose the Administration tab; then click the Administration button. Your Web browser will start and open the first administration page (shown in Figure 14.7)

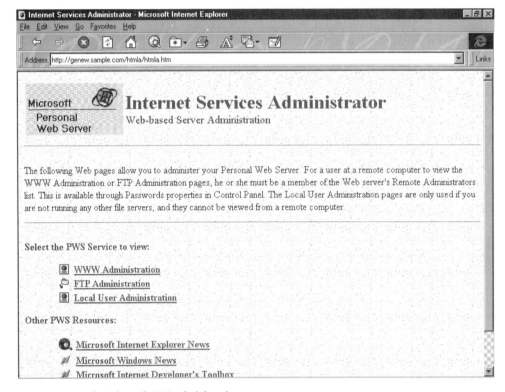

FIGURE 14.7: The Microsoft PWS administration page

> **TIP** This opening page is stored within the Microsoft PWS folder. You can add this page to your browser's list of "favorites" or "bookmarks" so you can later return to it right from your browser.

In our discussion here, you would click the Local User Administration hyperlink, which opens the Local User Administrator page (shown in Figure 14.8).

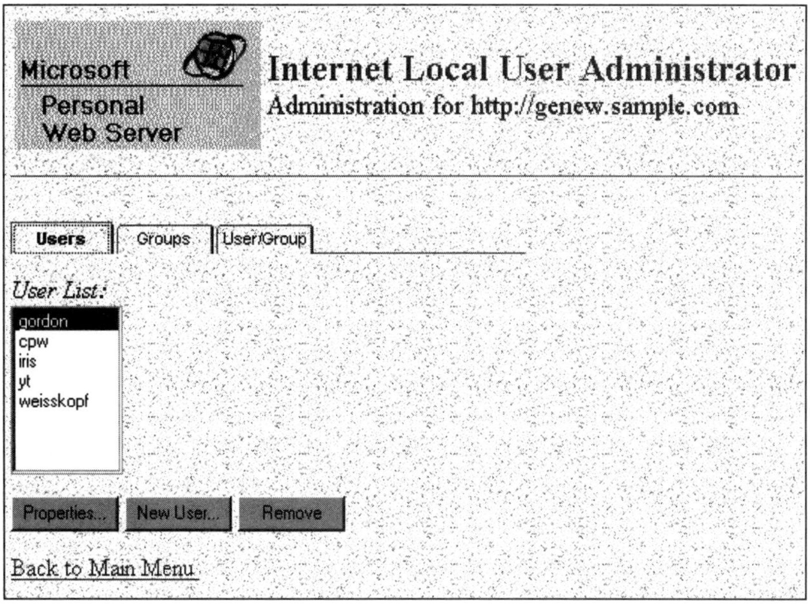

FIGURE 14.8: The New Users page (tab) in the Local User Administrator page

There are three tabs in this page:

> **Users:** Add or remove a user, or revise the name or password of a user.
>
> **Groups:** Add or remove a group, or revise the properties of a group; a group is much like a virtual user, in that all the users within a group have the same access rights.
>
> **User/Group:** Add or remove a user from a group.

To add a new user in the Users tab of the Internet Local User Administrator page, click the New User button, enter a username and password, and then click Add. You can change a user's password by selecting a name in the list and clicking the Properties button. To remove a user, select a name and click the Remove button.

To add a new group, click the Groups tab, click the New Group button, enter a group name, and then click Add. To see who belongs to a group, select it in the list and click the Properties button. To remove a group, select a group name and click the Remove button.

To add a user to a group, click the User/Group tab. Select a name in the User List and a group in the Group List, and then click the Add User to Group button. You can remove a user from a group by selecting a name and a group and clicking the Remove User from Group button.

When you're finished, you can choose the Back to Main Menu link at the bottom of the page to return to the Microsoft PWS administration page. Or, simply close your browser if you no longer need it—the changes you made took effect as soon as you made them.

When you choose the Tools ➤ Permission command back in the FrontPage Explorer, you can assign web access rights to any of the users or groups that were displayed in the Local User Administrator page.

Running the FrontPage Server Administrator

There are several server-related tasks you perform in the FrontPage Server Administrator (see Figure 14.9), a program that is part of the FrontPage package. You run it from the Windows Start menu on the same computer that runs the server for your FrontPage webs. If you don't find it on the Start menu, double-click the program FPSRVWIN.EXE in your FrontPage program folder.

The primary function of the FrontPage Server Administrator is to let you install or remove the FrontPage Server Extensions from a *port*, or input/output channel, on this computer. In the screen shown in Figure 14.9, the Administrator shows there are two different ports being used by servers on this computer.

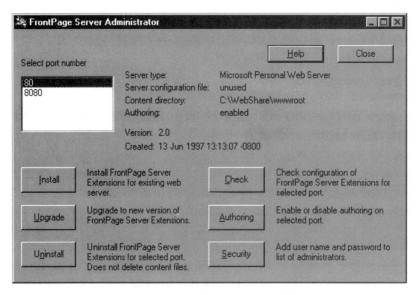

FIGURE 14.9: You perform server-related maintenance tasks in the FrontPage Server Administrator.

You can select a port in the list and see its current settings. For example, you can see in Figure 14.9 that the Microsoft PWS is installed on port 80 (which is normally the default port used for a Web server) and that its content directory (folder) is `C:\WebShare\wwwroot`.

Selecting port 8080 shows the FrontPage PWS is using that port (shown in Figure 14.10).

> **NOTE** This is all helpful information, but you may never need to change these settings once you have your server(s) and FrontPage up and running. This is especially true if your FrontPage webs are ultimately being hosted by a server on another computer. In that case, you will only be concerned with the server(s) you use for building your FrontPage webs.

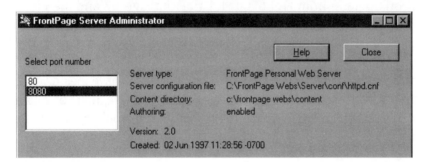

FIGURE 14.10: The settings for port 8080 in the FrontPage Server Administrator

When you have installed a Web server on this computer, you can use the Server Administrator to install the FrontPage Server Extensions on that server. Be sure this server is running smoothly *before* you install the Server Extensions.

Click the Install button and select that server's name from the Configure Server Type dialog box (shown here). Click the OK button, which will display the Confirm Dialog, where you can verify that the correct server and port were found. Click OK and the process will begin. For some servers, such as the FrontPage PWS, you will be prompted for the name of the server's configuration file. When the job is done, that server will now be FrontPage-aware and ready to handle all your FrontPage webs.

You can also remove the FrontPage Server Extensions from a server. First, you should shut down that server so it is no longer running on this computer. Then select a port in the Server Administrator and click the Uninstall button. The FrontPage-related server software will be removed from your FrontPage webs on that server, but none of your FrontPage web content will be affected.

Migrating to the Microsoft Personal Web Server

If you are upgrading to FrontPage 97 from FrontPage 1.1, you may also want at some point to upgrade from the FrontPage PWS to the Microsoft PWS. You certainly don't have to, but you'll find the newer PWS, which was derived from Microsoft's Internet Information Server (IIS), is more integrated with Windows and offers features that aren't found in the FrontPage PWS.

When you upgrade from FrontPage 1.1 to FrontPage 97 and then install the Microsoft PWS, that server will be installed to its own port. In a typical installation, preference will be given to the Microsoft PWS and it will be given port 80. The FrontPage PWS will then have port 8080.

You'll find that both the Microsoft and the FrontPage PWS have their own root web folder—they do not share the same FrontPage webs. Therefore, none of your existing webs will be available to the Microsoft PWS. That's not a problem, though, because you can run either one server or the other, or both servers at the same time.

> **NOTE**
> You can find more detailed instructions for upgrading to the Microsoft PWS in the file `\Pws\Upgrade\Upgrade.htm` on your FrontPage CD. It's a Web page so you can simply open it in your browser.

To use both servers, all you have to remember is that to access a FrontPage web on a server that's connected to any port other than 80, you must include the port number in the server's name. For example, when you use the File ➤ Open FrontPage Web command in the Explorer, suppose you normally specify the Web server in this way:

```
http://genew.sample.com
```

You would then specify your FrontPage PWS in this way:

```
http://genew.sample.com:8080
```

The same is true when you specify the URL of a server in your Web browser—include the colon and port number after the server name, such as:

```
http://genew.sample.com:8080/widget/contents.htm
```

To bring an existing FrontPage web into the root web of the Microsoft PWS, you first open the web in the FrontPage Explorer from the FrontPage PWS; remember to include the port number in the name if this is the server that is not using port 80.

Then use the File ➤ Publish FrontPage Web command, and copy the web to your Microsoft PWS server, as discussed in "Publishing a Web to a Server" in Chapter 2. You'll end up with the same web now running under the Microsoft PWS.

When the FrontPage PWS is not connected to port 80, that server may not start automatically when needed by the Explorer. In that case, you can start it manually from the Windows Explorer by double-clicking the file `VHTTPD32.EXE`, which you should find in the folder `C:\FrontPage Webs\Server\`. If you will be doing this again, you may want to create a menu shortcut to this file on your Window Start menu.

Changing the Name of the Home Page

The home page in a Web site is the page the server sends to a browser that opens the site without specifying a file by name. If that home page doesn't exist, both Personal Web Servers (and many other servers) will send back a directory listing, or directory index, of the site you requested. By default, the home page in a web hosted by the FrontPage PWS is named `INDEX.HTM`. In the Microsoft PWS, it's `DEFAULT.HTM`.

> **NOTE** Both of these servers ignore the case of a file name you request, while other servers are absolutely rigid about uppercase and lowercase letters.

The name for the home page can vary with other servers. If the need arises, you can change the default home page name used by FrontPage and the Personal Web Servers. For example, you might want to change the name if you're creating your FrontPage webs under a PWS, but they will ultimately be hosted on a non-FrontPage server that uses a different home page name (if it were a FrontPage-aware server, the home page name would be updated automatically when you publish your webs to it).

When you then create a new FrontPage web, the home page will have that new name (existing home pages will not be renamed—you'll have to do that in the Explorer).

Changing the Home Page Name with the Microsoft PWS

Here's how to change the default home page name for the Microsoft PWS:

1. While the Microsoft PWS is running, start its Internet Services Administrator, as discussed earlier in "Running the Microsoft Personal Web Server."
2. Choose the WWW Administration hyperlink, and then choose the Directories tab. The page opened displays a table of the directories (folders) used by the Microsoft PWS.
3. At the bottom of the page is a Default Document option (shown here), where you can enter a new home page name. Then click OK, and the job is done.

Almost done, that is, as you'll need to rename the home pages in any existing FrontPage webs under this server so they match the new name. You can do that easily in the Explorer.

Changing the Home Page Name for the FrontPage PWS

The process of changing the default home page name for the FrontPage PWS is a little more involved, although it is not difficult. You'll need a text editor for this job, such as Windows Notepad, in order to edit the FrontPage PWS server resource configuration file, `SRM.CNF`. If you installed FrontPage with its default settings, you should find this file at the following location:

```
C:\FrontPage Webs\Server\Conf\srm.cnf
```

Edit this file with care, as the FrontPage PWS may not run correctly if you accidentally make some errant changes.

1. In Notepad, open `SRM.CNF`.
2. You should be able to find the following line of text in this file:

    ```
    # DirectoryIndex index.htm
    ```

    The pound sign makes this line a comment in the file so FrontPage ignores it (all the entries in this file that are already FrontPage defaults appear as comments).

3. If you can't find this text in the file, simply create it on a new line anywhere within the file.
4. Remove the pound sign so the line will be read as an actual configuration setting instead of a comment.
5. Then revise the home page file name as needed. For example, you might change it so this line reads

    ```
    DirectoryIndex default.html
    ```

    This not only has a different file name, but it also uses a four-character file name extension.
6. With that done, save `SRM.CNF` back to disk and exit Notepad.
7. If the FrontPage PWS was running, you'll need to close it and start it again for the change to take effect.

In this case, when you access a FrontPage web under this server, the home page will be the file named `DEFAULT.HTML`. Again, you'll have to rename the home pages in any existing Webs to match the new name.

This concludes the discussion of Web site management in the FrontPage Explorer and its Personal Web Servers, and this is also the last chapter in this book. Your head is undoubtedly brimming over with ideas for creating sites, pages, hyperlinks, tables, images, frame sets, image maps, and all the other myriad Web and HTML features you can produce in FrontPage. Good luck with all your projects on the Web!

Appendix A

INSTALLING AND STARTING FRONTPAGE

- **Learning about RAM and disk space requirements**
- **Installing FrontPage**
- **Installing FrontPage's Bonus Pack software**
- **Starting FrontPage**
- **Getting help**

Installing FrontPage and its Bonus Pack software does not take long, but it does involve several choices and considerations. If you have already installed FrontPage and have it up and running under a Web server, then you may not need to read this appendix. For further help with FrontPage, be sure to check out Microsoft's Web site:

```
http://www.microsoft.com/frontpage/
```

Running the Setup Program

When you insert the FrontPage 97 CD into your computer's CD-ROM drive, the setup program should start automatically. If for some reason it does not start, you can double-click the program `SETUP.EXE` on the CD.

The setup program displays its opening screen, where you click a button to install FrontPage or one of the programs in its Bonus Pack of extras (shown in Figure A.1).

FIGURE A.1: You can install the FrontPage components in its setup program.

NOTE Most of these programs require a computer with at least a 486 processor and 8MB of RAM, although more RAM is recommended for them all, and it is *required* for Image Composer.

Let's take a quick look at these programs and their RAM and disk space requirements when running under Windows 95:

FrontPage 97: Create and manage Web sites and their pages with the Explorer, Editor, To Do List, and the FrontPage Personal Web Server (8MB RAM or 16MB when running the Microsoft Personal Web Server; 30MB disk space).

Image Composer: Create images for your Web sites or other uses; it offers a huge collection of photographs and clip art, as well as a dazzling array of image-editing tools and effects. In order to access its collection of images while working on a Web page, you'll need to insert the FrontPage CD when prompted (16MB RAM; 17MB disk space).

Microsoft Personal Web Server: Allows you to develop your FrontPage webs under Web server control and host your sites while they are actually up and running for public access. This Web server was developed from the Microsoft Internet Information Server (IIS) and is more robust and integrated with Windows 95 than the FrontPage Personal Web Server is (16MB RAM when used with FrontPage; 1MB of disk space).

Internet Explorer: Browse the Web with Microsoft's Web browser (8MB RAM; 11MB disk space).

Web Publishing Wizard: Helps you upload your FrontPage webs to another server when that server does not have the FrontPage Server Extensions installed and is not FrontPage-aware (8MB RAM; 1MB disk space; also requires Microsoft Internet Explorer 3 already be installed).

Each of these components is a separate program you can install at any time, although when you install FrontPage you will be asked if you also want to install Microsoft Personal Web Server, which you should do.

> **NOTE** When installing the Microsoft Personal Web Server, have your Windows 95 CD or disk available, because you may be asked to insert it so certain files can be copied.

Appendix A

When you already have FrontPage 1.1 installed on your computer, you can either install FrontPage 97 in the same folder and overwrite version 1.1, or you can install FrontPage 97 in its own folder and leave FrontPage 1.1 untouched and still available. You may not need to keep version 1.1, however, because your existing FrontPage webs should work fine in FrontPage 97.

Here are the steps you follow to install FrontPage:

1. From the FrontPage setup program, click the FrontPage 97 Installation button.
2. If you do not already have a Web server available on this computer, you will be asked if you want to install the Microsoft Personal Web Server (PWS). You'll need a FrontPage-aware Web server such as this one in order to use FrontPage to its fullest; choose OK if you have no other server available.

The next few steps are the same ones you would follow if you chose to install the Microsoft PWS from the FrontPage setup screen (shown previously in Figure A.1).

3. If requested, insert your Windows 95 CD or disk so the necessary files can be copied from it; then click OK.
4. In order to complete the installation of the Microsoft PWS, you will be prompted to restart your computer. If you want to complete the installation now, you should choose Yes.
5. After your computer restarts, you will be prompted to insert the FrontPage 97 CD back into the CD-ROM drive. Do so and click OK.
6. You will then be back at the FrontPage installation screen, and the Microsoft PWS will be flagged as already installed.
7. Once again, click the FrontPage 97 Installation button.
8. This time a message should tell you it needs to disable the Microsoft PWS during installation. Unless you are already using the server for other tasks, choose OK to close it.
9. Now continue with the FrontPage installation. After you have entered a registration name, you will be shown the default destination directory (folder) for FrontPage, `C:\Program Files\Microsoft FrontPage`. Either choose Next to accept this default, or click Browse to choose another folder and then choose Next.
10. The next step lets you choose a Typical or Custom install. Choose Custom so you can install the FrontPage Personal Web Server (PWS).
11. Choose Next, and if you have chosen to install the FrontPage PWS, you will be alerted there is already a server (the Microsoft PWS) on port 80 (the default port for Web servers), and that the FrontPage PWS will be installed on port 8080. Choose Next.

> **NOTE** This was the original Personal Web Server that came with previous versions of FrontPage, and you may find it useful to have on your computer with FrontPage (it's not a large program, and it won't interfere with your computer). Otherwise, you can choose Typical to install only FrontPage (client software) and its Server Extensions.

12. You will then be shown a list of the Web servers that are installed on this computer. If you installed the Microsoft PWS, you should see it listed. You can deselect any servers on which you do *not* want to install the FrontPage Server Extensions. You should definitely install them on the Microsoft PWS, however, so be sure that name is selected and then choose Next. The Server Extensions make a Web server FrontPage-aware and allow FrontPage to work with it hand-in-hand.
13. Next you will see a summary screen that shows you the procedures performed during installation (see Figure A.2). You can choose Back if you want to change any of the installation options.
14. If all looks correct, choose Next and the files will be copied to your disk.

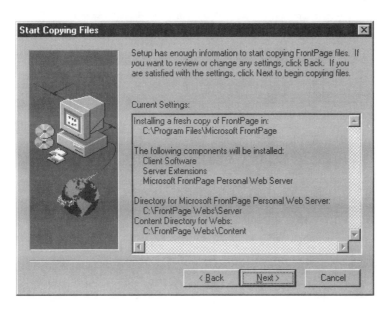

FIGURE A.2: Before the FrontPage files are copied to your disk, you will see a summary of the steps that will be performed.

15. When finished, if you chose to install the FrontPage PWS, you will be prompted to supply a name and password that will be used by you or the person who will be creating and administering webs under that server (the name cannot contain spaces).
16. When you click OK, the FrontPage Server Extensions will be installed on that server.
17. Then, if you have also installed the Microsoft PWS, you will be prompted for the account name that will be used for creating and administering Webs under that server. Again, don't include spaces in the name.
18. Finally, you will be asked if it's OK to stop and restart the Microsoft PWS. Unless you're using that server for another purpose, choose OK.
19. When finished, you can either start the FrontPage Explorer, or you can deselect that option and then click the Finish button to exit the installation routine.

At this point, FrontPage, its Server Extensions, and one or both of the Personal Web Servers will be installed on your computer.

Starting FrontPage

You will normally work with FrontPage by starting its Explorer—choose Programs ➤ Microsoft FrontPage from the Windows Start menu. This opens the FrontPage Explorer, where you can create a new FrontPage web, open an existing one, or start the Editor to create or revise Web pages.

> **NOTE** In the FrontPage Explorer, if you try to open or create a web and get an error message to the effect that there is no server on port 80, you may need to restart the Microsoft PWS or the Web server handling that port. See "Running the Microsoft Personal Web Server" in Chapter 14 for more information.

Keep in mind you should use the FrontPage Explorer and Editor in concert, along with a Web server, such as the FrontPage or Microsoft PWS, that is running the FrontPage Server Extensions. You can then work on any FrontPage web and make changes as needed. When you modify a Web page in the FrontPage Editor, the changes you make, such as the addition of new links, will be tracked by the Explorer and the site will be updated accordingly.

So become accustomed to starting the Explorer, opening a FrontPage web, and *then* working on its pages in the Editor as needed. You should close the Editor *before* you close the Explorer so the final changes you make in the Editor will be recorded by the Explorer.

Getting Help

You'll find plenty of help available in FrontPage, which you can access in several ways:
- Choose a topic from the Help menu.
- Press F1 to bring up a context-sensitive Help screen that will describe your current location in the program.
- Click the Help button on the toolbar and then click a command on the menu for which you would like some help.
- If you're connected to the World Wide Web, choose Help ➤ Microsoft on the Web. This will open your Web browser and connect with Microsoft's Web site, where you can choose from a variety of FrontPage topics.

You should definitely set aside some time to run through the FrontPage tutorial in the user manual. It walks you through the process of building a small Web site from the Learning FrontPage template. It is a very step-by-step process that will introduce you to many of the tools in FrontPage and give you a feeling for the way the individual resources interact and contribute to a Web site.

Appendix B

GLOSSARY OF TERMS

absolute URL A complete address on the Internet's World Wide Web that points precisely to one file. In terms of street addresses, it's the equivalent to an exact address that includes a country, city, street, house number, and the name of the person (see also *relative URL* and *URL*).

active web Also called the "current web." The Web site currently open in the FrontPage Explorer. When you save a new page in the Editor, it will be saved to the active web unless you specify a different location.

ActiveX control A programmable object that can be placed in a Web page and executed after someone opens the page in a browser. For example, an ActiveX control in a page would allow you to enter an interest rate and principal amount in two form fields and then calculate a loan payment, all without having to invoke a program on the server.

administrator One who has full access rights to a Web site and can modify the pages and files in a site, create new files or delete existing ones, and assign access rights to others. In the FrontPage Explorer, you can define access rights to the active web with the Tools ➤ Permissions command.

anchor The source (the text or image) of a hyperlink in a page, as defined in the HTML anchor tag, `<A>` (see also *bookmark*).

applet A compiled Java program (normally with a `CLASS` file name extension) that you can reference in a Web page to produce effects that would otherwise be difficult or impossible to create in HTML. Instead of the server executing the program, the browser's computer executes it.

attribute A parameter added to an HTML tag that affects the way the tag is interpreted in a browser. For example, the paragraph tag, `<P>`, can take the `ALIGN` attribute, which defines its alignment. When you center a paragraph in the FrontPage Editor, the resulting HTML code looks like this: `<P ALIGN="CENTER">`.

binary The inner machine language of virtually all computers. It consistis of only two characters, 0 and 1, as opposed to the usual numbering system that has 10 characters, 0 through 9. In terms of computer files, only a computer can read a binary file, while people can read a text or ASCII file that consists of plain text.

bit The smallest piece of information that a computer can handle, represented by either the number 0 or 1. Transmission speeds are often stated in the number of bits per second, so a 28.8 modem can theoretically handle 28,800 bits per second.

bitmap An image, such as a picture or a character in a bitmapped font, created from many tiny dots (or pixels on a computer screen). Each dot's color and position defines the image. The two most common types of bitmapped image file formats used in Web sites are GIF and JPEG (see also *GIF*, *JPEG*, and *TIFF*).

bookmark The FrontPage designation for a named location within a page that you can specify as the target of a hyperlink by preceding its name with a pound sign; also known as a "destination," "named target," or "named anchor."

browser A viewer or reader program that can request files over the World Wide Web or an intranet and display HTML Web pages.

byte A collection of eight bits that can represent a single character, such as a letter, punctuation mark, or symbol.

C, C++ Programming languages (pronounced "see" and "see plus plus") widely used by professional developers to create programs for just about any computer. They first came from the world of the Unix operating system, as did many computer servers, so they are used extensively among programmers of Web-related software, such as Web servers and server extensions.

CD-ROM A CD (*compact disk*)-ROM (*read-only memory*) is a data-storage disk that can store hundreds of megabytes of data but, unlike a floppy disk, can only be written to when it is manufactured.

CGI The Common Gateway Interface is a standard that allows a browser to execute a program on a server. The program processes the data and returns the results to the browser.

clickable image See *image map*.

client A computer program that requests data from another program called the "server."

composition The image you create in Microsoft Image Composer from a variety of elements, including text, hand-drawn art, and clip art.

controls Fields you use to create a form on a page; each control lets the person reading the form either enter data, such as their name, or make a choice, such as selecting their country of residence from a drop-down menu. The types of controls available in a FrontPage form include the following: one-line text box, scrolling text box, check box, radio button, drop-down menu, and push button.

current web See *active web*.

download The process of receiving data; a browser downloads data from a server (see also *upload*).

element An HTML feature in a page, such as a heading, horizontal line, table, or bulleted list (see also *tag*).

external link A hyperlink that targets a file outside of its Web site.

form An HTML feature consisting of controls for entering data and making choices. A user can fill out the form in a browser and then push a button to send that data to the server. You can use this data, for example, to compile a mailing list of all visitors to your site who fill out the form.

form handler A program, normally on the server, that collects the data from a form when the user of that form clicks the submit button. The form handler then processes the data on the server, such as saving it in a database or HTML file. Setting up the form handler to deal with a form is a critical part of the form-definition process.

frame A separate window within a page that displays a page or image (see also *frame set*).

frame set An HTML feature that lets you display multiple pages or images in a single page; each is displayed in its own window (see also *frame*).

freeware Any software available for free, with no obligation to pay for it and, consequently, no guarantee of its precision or reliability. Often includes small utility programs created by amateur programmers or by professionals who are either being magnanimous or simply can't be bothered to try to charge for a small piece of work (see also *shareware*).

FrontPage Editor The word processor–like program in the FrontPage package in which you create Web pages.

FrontPage Explorer The program in the FrontPage package in which you work with Web sites. You can create new Web sites, delete or copy a site, manage the files and hyperlinks in a site, assign access rights to a site, and much more. In general, when you want to do any work in your Web site, you will start in the Explorer and then open the page in the FrontPage Editor. For example, when you want to edit a page in a site, you will open that site in the Explorer and then double-click on the page in question to open it in the FrontPage Editor.

FTP The File Transfer Protocol is an Internet protocol for transferring files from one computer to another.

GIF The Graphics Interchange Format is a file format for image files. The image is limited to 256 colors and is compressed in the file (without any loss of quality) to decrease transmission time over a network. It is a popular file format (with a `GIF` file name extension) supported by just about all browsers on the World Wide Web (see also *JPEG*).

home page The first page that a user sees when accessing a Web site, typically containing hyperlinks that can lead the user to all the other pages in that Web. The home page is normally the first page opened when a browser accesses a Web site without requesting a specific file.

host The computer that runs the server that controls access to a Web site and responds to requests for files on that site.

hotspot Text or an image in a page that you can click to activate a hyperlink and open its target. The term is often used to refer to a defined hyperlink region in an image map (see also *hyperlink* and *image map*).

HTML You create Web documents (pages) in the Hypertext Markup Language using tags to define structural or formatting features in the page.

HTTP The Hypertext Transfer Protocol is the protocol of the World Wide Web by which a browser requests and opens pages or other files.

hyperlink Also called a "link." In a Web page, text or a graphic image that you can click to access the target resource of that link anywhere on the Web. Most browsers signify text links by underlining them and displaying them in a different color.

image Just about any non-text object displayed in a Web page. It includes line drawings, photographs, geometric shapes, and textures suitable for page backgrounds.

Image Composer An image-editing program that is part of the FrontPage package. It is particularly well-suited for creating and manipulating images destined to be displayed on a computer screen, such as in a Web site (see also *composition* and *sprite*).

image map An image in a page that contains hidden, clickable hyperlinks called "hotspots." A client-side image map contains all the necessary information to make the link to the target, while a server-side image map requires the server to process the link (see also *hotspot*).

inline image An image that appears within a Web page; the image is actually stored in its own file, separate from the HTML of the page.

interlaced GIF A GIF image file in which the order of its scan lines have been rearranged. When the image is opened in a browser, it seems to come into focus within its box, rather than appearing line by line.

internal link A link that targets a file within the same Web site.

Internet A network of countless smaller networks, all of which use the same protocol—TCP/IP—in order to communicate. The World Wide Web is one method of communicating on the Internet, along with FTP, Gopher, Telnet, and e-mail.

Internet Explorer A Web browser produced by Microsoft Corporation; you may often see it called simply "IE" (see also *browser*).

intranet A private network that functions much like the Internet; the same client and server software can be used on both.

ISDN The Integrated Services Digital Network is a telephone service based on digital instead of analog signals. A computer can transmit data at a much higher rate (up to 128,000 bits per second) over an ISDN phone line than it can over a regular phone line (currently about 28,800 bits per second).

Java A programming language that allows you to create mini-programs executable on a Web client instead of a server. For example, when you open a Web page in your browser, a Java program might be downloaded along with it (much as images are).

The program could then run automatically when the page is opened, or it might instead run when you point to an object on the page. Once the Java program is on the client computer, it will be available the next time a page calls for that program.

JavaScript A scripting language for creating programs within a Web page. When someone with a JavaScript-aware browser opens a page, the commands run on that computer, not the server.

JPEG The Joint Photographic Expert Group file format is a highly compact way to store true-color (24-bit) images with up to 16.7 million colors in a file. The method used to compress the image actually lowers the overall image quality, but it does so only slightly compared to the huge savings in file size. It is a popular file format, which uses a `JPG` file name extension, supported by just about all browsers on the World Wide Web (see also *GIF*).

link See *hyperlink*.

lossless An image file format, such as GIF, in which the image information is compressed in the file while losing none of the image's information (see also *lossy* and *GIF*).

lossy An image file format, such as JPEG, that actually throws away some of the image's information so that the image can be compressed more, with only a small decrease in image quality (see also *lossless* and *JPEG*).

marquee An HTML feature that creates a message that scrolls across a page, much like a marquee on the front of a stock brokerage building that displays a live ticker tape.

modem An electronic device that allows one computer to exchange data with another over ordinary phone lines by using sound (analog signals) instead of a strictly digital network connection. The name is derived from the fact that a computer sends data by modulating it into an analog signal, while the receiving computer demodulates the signal back into digital data.

'Net Slang or a nickname for the Internet.

Netscape Navigator A Web browser produced by Netscape Communications Corporation (see also *browser*).

online A computer connected to a network and able to share in its resources. You might say, "When I go online, I'll visit your Web site."

page An HTML document (file) that you can view in a Web browser, much as you can view a word processing document in a word processor.

Personal Web Server A scaled-down version of a Web server that allows you to create a Web site in FrontPage, test the site, revise it, and even host the site while under the server's control. FrontPage comes with two: the FrontPage Personal Web Server and the Microsoft Personal Web Server (see also *server*).

plug-in Any of a variety of programs designed to work with a Web browser and give it enhanced capabilities. For example, a plug-in might give a browser the ability to display a non-standard file. Plug-ins usually work behind the scenes, so the user does not even realize they are working with the browser.

port A Web server connects with the World Wide Web through one of the input/output channels in the server's computer. This is a virtual addressable port, not a physical connection on the computer. When a computer has multiple servers running at the same time, each must use a different port.

protocol A method of communication among computers on a network, such as TCP/IP on the Internet.

relative URL An address on the Internet's World Wide Web based on another address. If a hyperlink in a page references the target `Images/picture.gif`, then it is assumed this folder and file are in the same folder as the page that contains the hyperlink. In terms of street addresses, it's the equivalent of a friend giving you his address but supplying only a street, house number, and his name, in which case you would assume that this address must be in the same city and country you are in.

resolution The density of the dots that make up an image. On a computer screen, the number of pixels per square inch or centimeter, or in the entire screen. In general, higher resolution (higher dot or pixel density) makes for higher quality images. A computer screen whose resolution is 800 by 600 has a higher resolution than a 640 by 480 screen.

Glossary of Terms

resource Any file within a Web site, such as an HTML Web page, an image, a video clip, or an executable program or script.

root web, FrontPage The folder that serves as the default FrontPage web on a server. FrontPage refers to it as `<root web>`. All other FrontPage webs on that server reside within the root web.

RTF The Rich Text Format is a file format for storing a text document and its formatting in a text-only file. It's one way to transfer documents between different word processors; the FrontPage Editor can open RTF files, as well.

server A computer program that makes data available to other programs on the same computer or on other computers—it "serves" them (see also *client*).

server extensions Add-on programs that extend the capabilities of a server. The FrontPage Server Extensions allow a server to work more closely with a FrontPage web.

shareware Software available for free but nonetheless comes with a license agreement describing how you may use the software, how many copies you can make of it, and so on. Usually, the license also states that if you continue to use the software after a trial period, such as 30 days, you have to pay for it (see also *freeware*).

sprite The basic component of every composition in Microsoft Image Composer.

table An HTML feature that lets you create a grid of rows, columns, and cells for organizing information on a page. You can also take advantage of the structure of a table while hiding its borders so, for example, you can easily create three columns of text on a page by entering the text in a three-column by one-row table.

tag An HTML code, always surrounded by angle brackets, that defines an element in a Web page. For example, the single tag `<HR>` creates a horizontal line in the page; the tag `<H1>` and its closing tag `</H1>` display the text within them in the level-one heading style.

target The object that is opened or accessed when a hyperlink is activated. For example, a Web page can be the target of a hyperlink, so when the link is clicked, the target page will be opened in the browser. A target can also include a named bookmark in a page, so when the target page is opened, the bookmark will be displayed at the top of the browser's window (see also *bookmark*, *browser*, and *hyperlink*).

TCP/IP The Transmission Control Protocol and Internet Protocol are the protocols (the "rules of the road") by which the various computers on the Internet communicate.

template A model from which you can make many copies. You create new FrontPage webs from templates in the Explorer, and you can create new pages from templates in the Editor.

TIFF The Tagged Image File Format is a bitmapped image file format (usually with a `TIF` file name extension). Most Web browsers cannot display TIFF images, so in order to display a TIFF image in a Web page, you will normally convert the image file into either a GIF or JPEG image file (see also *bitmap*, *GIF*, and *JPEG*).

transparent A color hidden in a GIF image, so whatever is behind the image in the page will show through.

upload The process of sending data. A server uploads requested data to a browser (see also *download*).

URL The Uniform Resource Locator identifies the address of a file on the World Wide Web, as well as the protocol by which to reach it. An absolute URL is the complete address, while a relative URL defines the address in relation to another address. For example, if a hyperlink in a page targets a relative URL that is only a file name, then the target is assumed to be in the same location as that page.

web, FrontPage A Web site you created or are managing under FrontPage.

Web site A collection of files hosted by a server and accessed with a Web browser.

WebBot A FrontPage web automation feature that you insert in a page (or is inserted automatically) to create the appropriate HTML code for its defined task.

Wizard A FrontPage feature that helps you create new sites or Web pages by asking you relevant questions, accepting your responses, and then proceeding to the next step.

World Wide Web The network on the Internet that uses HTTP to distribute files from servers to clients. It is also known as the "WWW" or simply the "Web."

WWW See *World Wide Web*.

WYSIWYG An acronym meaning "What you see is what you get." Traditionally, you create or revise a Web page's HTML code in a text editor and then you preview the results in a browser. The FrontPage Editor lets you work on the page in a WYSIWYG environment, where what you see on its screen is pretty much what the world will see in their browsers when viewing the same page.

Index

Note to the Reader: Main level entries are in **bold**. **Boldface** page numbers indicate primary discussions of a topic. *Italic* page numbers indicate illustrations.

A

<A> HTML tag, 148, 158
absolute URLs, 137, **148–149**, 319
Active Hyperlink option, 138
active Web sites, 319
    in Explorer, **24–25**
    opening pages from, **100**, *100*
ActiveX controls, 319
Add Choice dialog box, 258, *258*
Add Computer dialog box, 298
Add Editor Association dialog box, 60, *60*
Add File option, 35–36
Add Folder option, 35–36
Add Name and Value dialog box, 214, *214*
Add Names list, 296
Add option
    for browsers, 86
    for drop-down menus, 258
    for file associations, 60
    for spelling checker, 78
    for tag attributes, 83
    for To Do Lists, 65
    for users, 295–296
Add Task button, 63
Add to an Existing FrontPage Web option, 38
Add To Do Task command, 55
Add To Do Task dialog box, 65, *66*
Add to the Current Web option, 28
Add Users dialog box, 295–296, *296*
adding
    browsers, 86
    cells, **237**
    drop-down menu items, 258
    fields, **251–252**
    file associations, 60
    list items, 117
    tag attributes, 83
    To Do List entries, 55, **65–66**, *66*
    users to sites, 295–296
    words to dictionary, 78
Additional Information to Save option, 248
Address style, 133
Administration tab, 300
administrative tasks, 287
    changing home page names, **307–309**
    with Personal Web Servers, **299–307**, *301–305*
    security, **291–298**, *294–296*, *298–299*
    testing sites, **288–291**
administrator rights, 25, 293, 297
administrators, 291, 319
Advanced tab
    for form results, 249
    for image maps, 161, *161*
ALIGN attribute, 135

Align Left button, 135
Align Right button, 135
aligning
    captions, 229
    cells, **233–234**
    fields, **245–246**
    horizontal lines, 111
    images, **184–185**, *185*
    tables, 230
    text, **134–135**
All Pages search option, 61
Allow Multiple Selections option, 258
Alt+Enter keys for properties, 74
    for fonts, 127
    for forms, 253
    for WebBots, 210
alternate pages for frame sets, **270**, *270*
alternatives to images, **182–183**
ampersands (&) in headers and footers, 87
anchor tags, 148, 158
anchors, 320
And Must Be option, 257
angle brackets (<>) for tags, 9
Animations clip art category, 176
Appearance tab
    for hyperlinks, 165
    for images, 179, 184–185, *185*
applets, 320
Apply option
    for fonts, 128
    in Image Composer, 194, 196, 199
    for superscripts, 132
Arabic style for numbered lists, 119
Archive page, 28
arguments in HTML window, 81
Arrange ➤ Bring to Front command, 198
Arrange button, 196, *196*
Arrange tool palette, 196

arrow keys
    for Hyperlink view, 49
    for selecting text, 126
    for tables, 225
arrows in Hyperlink view, 50–51
As File page saving option, 104
As Template page saving option, 104–106
aspect ratio for sprites, 196
Assigned To field, 64
associations
    adding and changing, **59–60**, *59*
    deleting, 60
    extensions for, 58
    for Image Composer, 187
asterisks (*) for mask fields, 298
attributes for tags, 9, 320. *See also* properties
    for extended HTML code, 83, *84*
    in HTML window, 81
author
    in Folder view, 52
    updating, 54
Author option for WebBots, 212
author rights, 293, 297
Auto scroll bar option, 279
automatic hyperlink updating, 57, 167
automating
    Server Extensions for, 15
    WebBots for. *See* WebBots
AVI extension, 177

B

Back button, 106, *106*, 156, *156*
Background Color option
    for marquee messages, 283
    for tables, 231, 234

Background Image option, 139
Background Sound option, 137
Background tab, 137–141, *138*
backgrounds
    for cells, 234
    color for, **137–138**, *138*
    for GIF images, 181
    images for, **138–140**, *140*
    for marquee messages, 283
    from other pages, **140–141**
    for tables, 223, **231–232**
backing up sites, **288**
Backspace key, 73
Balanced Ramp option, 192
Base Location field, 137
Below Selection option, 237
binary language, 320
bitmap (BMP) files, 176, 320
bits, 320
black text in HTML window, 81
blank lines in HTML, 9
blank pages, creating pages from, 71
<BLOCKQUOTE> HTML tag, 135
blue attributes in HTML window, 81
Blue value in Image Composer,
    192, 199
<BODY> HTML tag, 83, 138, 141
Bold button, 129, *129*
Bold font, 129, 131
Bold Italic font, 129
Bonus Pack, 312, *312*
Bookmark dialog box, 157–158
Bookmark Name field, 157–158
bookmarks, 156–157, 320
    defining, **157–158**
    deleting, 158
    going to, 158
    for hyperlinks, 148, **151–152**
    revising, 158
borderless tables, 222, 227

borders
    color for, 232, 234
    for frames, 274
    size of, 224, 230
    for tables, 223–224
Bots. *See* WebBots
Bottom of Table option, 229
Bottom option
    for cells, 233
    for images, 184
bounding boxes, *189*, 190
**
 HTML tag**, 75
Bring Forward command, 190
Bring to Front button, 198
Bring to Front command, 190
broken links
    causes of, 169
    color for, 168
    creating, 57
    in Hyperlink view, 48
    repairing, **170**
Browse Folders option, 40
browser rights, 293, 297
browsers, 6, 320
    for filling out forms, **261–263**,
    261–262
    for previewing Web pages, **84–86**, *85*
    for testing sites, **288–289**
browsing pages, **106**
Bulleted List button, 115–118, *116*
bulleted lists, 115
    appearance of, **118**
    creating, **117**
    from existing text, **115–117**, *116*
Bullets and Numbering dialog
    box, 118
bullets in Hyperlink view, 51
Buttons clip art category, 176
buttons on forms, 243, 245, 252,
    259–261
bytes, 320

Caption Properties dialog box, 229
captions for tables, 223
    adding and aligning, **228–229**
    selecting, 227
case-sensitivity
    of HTML tags, 9
    of names and passwords, 25
CD-ROMs, 321
Cell Properties dialog box, 232–236, *233*, 238
cells in tables, 222–223, *222*
    adding and removing, **237**
    aligning, **233–234**
    color in, **234–235**
    header, **234**
    merging, 228, **237–238**
    selecting, 226–227
    spacing, 231
    span of, **238**
    splitting, **238**
Center alignment option
    for cells, 233–234
    for tables, 230
Center button
    for marquee messages, 283
    for paragraphs, 135
center of focus in Hyperlink view, 50
centering
    cells, 233–234
    horizontal lines, 111
    marquee messages, 283
    in paragraphs, 135
    tables, 230
CGI (Common Gateway Interface), 205, 321
Cgi-Bin folder, 31
CGI scripts
    folder for, 31
    as hyperlink targets, 148

Change All option, 78
Change Font list, 128
Change option, 78
Change Style list
    for headings, 114
    for lists, 116, 121
    for paragraphs, 132, *132*
    for tables, 228
Change To field, 78
changing. *See* editing
character sets for languages, 128, 137
characters
    deleting, 73
    formatting, **126–132**, *128*, *131*
    special, **76**, 77
Check Box button, 251, *251*
check boxes, 245, 251, **259**
Check Spelling button, 76, *76*
child frames, 274
Choose Alternate Content dialog box, 270, *270*, 274
Choose Technique dialog box, 268, *268*
Citation font style, 131
Clear option
    for bookmarks, 158
    for hyperlinks, 156
client-side image maps, **160–161**
clients, 4, 321
clip art images, 176
    for background, 139, *140*
    for horizontal lines, **112–113**, *113*
Clip Art tab, 113, *113*, 139, *140*, 176
Clipboard
    for Editor, 74
    for file commands, 55
    for HTML window, 80
Close button, 71
Close option
    for importing files, 36
    for printing, 88

closing
  pages, 71
  sites, **32**
closing tags, 9
Code font style, 131
codes, HTML, 9, 327
  essential, **10–11**
  evolving nature of, 11
  in HTML window, 81
color
  for background, **137–138**, *138*
  for cells, **234–235**
  for comments, 211
  for GIF images, 181
  for horizontal lines, 111–112
  in HTML window, 81
  for hyperlinks, 7, 138, 146
  in Image Composer, **191–192**, *193*, 194
  in JPEG format, 175
  for marquee messages, 283
  for tables, 223, 225, **231–232**
  in testing sites, 289
  for text, 130
  in verifying hyperlinks, 168–169
Color Format list, 192
Color list, 130
Color Picker dialog box, 188, 192, *193*
Color Swatch, 188, 192
Colors dialog box, 130
columns, 222–223, *222*
  aligning text in, 134
  in frames, 274–275
  inserting, 237
  selecting, 226–227
  width of, 223, 225, *226*, **236**
Columns option
  for frames, 275–276
  for tables, 224
Comma option, 256
Command field, 60

commas (,)
  as delimiters, 248, 263
  in numbers, 256
Comment dialog box, 211
<COMMENT> HTML tag, 211
comments
  adding, 57
  color for, 211
  in Editor, 74
  for files, 17, 54
  in Folder view, 52
  in Personal Web Servers, 308–309
  providing for, **290–291**
  in templates, 93–94
  for To Do List tasks, 66
  for WebBots, 204–205, **209–210**
Common Gateway Interface (CGI), 205, 321
Common Gateway Interface (CGI) scripts
  folder for, 31
  as hyperlink targets, 148
Complete option, 65, 67
Complete Task dialog box, 67
Completed field, 64
completing To Do List tasks, 67
Composition Guide dialog box, 199
composition guides
  saving, **190–191**
  using, **188–190**
Composition Properties dialog box, 194
compositions
  creating, **187–190**, *189*, 321
  saving, **199–200**, *200*
compression
  for compositions, 199
  for images, 175, 182, 325
Computers tab, 292, 297–299, *298*
Configuration tab, 43
configuration variables, 211–214

Configure Editors list, 60
Configure Editors tab, 59, *59*, 187
Configure Server Type dialog box, 305
configuring form handlers, **247–249**
Confirm Password option, 296
Confirm tab, 249
Confirmation Field WebBot, 16, 203, 206, 249
Confirmation Form template, 205, 243
connection types, 41
Content folder, 25
Control Panel
    for colors, 191
    for Personal Web Servers, 300
controls, 242–243, 321
    adding, **251–252**
    aligning, **245–246**
    properties for, **252–261**, *253*, *255*, *257*
    selecting, **244–245**
converting files, **101–102**
Copy Changed Pages Only option, 38
Copy Child Webs option, 38
Copy command, 55
copying
    files, **56**
    images, 179
    sites, 15–16, 38
Corporate Presence Wizard, 29
Create Hyperlink dialog box, 150–154, *151*, 156, 163
Create or Edit Hyperlink button, 150, *150*, 155, *155*
Cross File Spelling button, 63, *63*
Ctrl key
    in copying files, 56
    in Hyperlink view, 49
Ctrl+A keys, 188
Ctrl+B keys, 129

Ctrl+Backspace keys, 73
Ctrl+clicking, 33, 35, 54, 106
Ctrl+Del keys, 73
Ctrl+End keys, 74, 126
Ctrl+F6 keys, 106
Ctrl+Home keys, 74, 126
Ctrl+I keys, 129
Ctrl+K keys, 150
Ctrl+N keys
    in Editor, 92
    in Explorer, 25
Ctrl+O keys
    in Editor, 70, 99
    in Image Composer, 190
Ctrl+S keys
    in Editor, 103
    in Image Composer, 190
Ctrl+spacebar keys, 126
Ctrl+T keys, 188
Ctrl+Z keys, 74
Current FrontPage Web tab, 100, *100*, 139
    for hyperlinks, 150, 153
    for images, 175–176, *176*
Current option for HTML window, 81
current sprites, 188, *189*
current FrontPage webs, 319
    in Explorer, **24–25**
    opening pages from, **100**, *100*
curves for text sprites, **195–196**
Custom Color option, 130
custom frame sets, **273–274**
Custom installation option, 314
Custom ISAPI, NSAPI, or CGI Script option, 247
Custom Palette tab, 192, *193*
Custom tab, 142
Customer Support Web template, 29
Cut command, 55

Dark Border option, 232
Data Length option, 256
Data Required option, 259
Data Type option, **256–257**
data validation, **254–257**, *255*
Data Value option, 257
date of file modification
 in Folder view, 17, 52–53
 in Properties dialog box, 57
 updating, 54
 WebBot for, **217–219**
Date This Page was Last Automatically Updated option, 218
Date This Page was Last Edited option, 218
dead links, 13
Decimal character option, 256
Decrease Indent button, 118, *118*, 135, *135*
Decrease Text Size button, 129, *129*
Default alignment option, 230
Default Document option, 308
DEFAULT.HTM file, 15, 307
Default Hyperlink options, 165
Default Target Frame option, 137
defaults
 for border color, 232
 for fonts, 127, 129
 for frames, 137
 for home pages, 15, 24, 308
 for hyperlinks for image maps, 165
 for paragraph styles, 133
 for table alignment, 230
 for text style, 126
 for Wave effect, 196
Define Custom Colors option, 130
Defined Term option, 121

defining
 bookmarks, **157–158**
 hotspots, **162–165**, *162*
Definition font style, 131
definition lists, **121–122**
Del key, 73
Delete command, 55
Delete option, 86
deleting
 bookmarks, 158
 browsers, 86
 captions, 229
 cells, 237
 characters, 73
 drop-down menu items, 258
 file associations, 60
 hotspots, 166
 hyperlinks, **156**
 list items, 117
 resources, 12, 55
 sites, **43**
 templates, 106
 To Do List tasks, 65, **67**
Description field, 64
destination targets, **151–152**
Details option, 65
Dial-Up Networking connection option, 41
dictionaries, spelling, 77–78
<DIR> HTML tag, 121
Directories tab, 308
directory lists, 121
Disallow First Item option, 258
Discussion page, 28
Discussion Web Wizard, 29
Discussion WebBot, 16, 203
disk space requirements, 177, 313
Display Name field
 for radio buttons, 259
 for text box validation, **254–256**
Display option for Sprites Catalog, 197

Display Properties dialog box, 191
<DL> HTML tag, 122
Do Task option, 19, 65
documents
    HTML source, **11–12, 80–82**, *81*
    selecting, 127
double-clicking
    for opening files, 55, 70
    for selecting text, 126
downloading, 112, 321
dragging
    icons, 55–56
    images, 74, 179, 185–186
    text, 74
Drop-Down Menu button, 250, *250*
Drop-Down Menu Properties dialog box, 257–258, *257*
Drop-Down Menu Validation dialog box, 258, *258*
drop-down menus, 245, **257–258**, *257*

E

e-mail address links, 48
Edit ➤ Add To Do Task command, 19, 64–65, 75
Edit ➤ Bookmark command, 157–158
Edit ➤ Clear command
    for cells, 237
    for list items, 117
Edit ➤ Clear Selection command, 188
Edit ➤ Copy command, 74
    for files, 56
    for images, 176, 179
Edit ➤ Cut command, 74
    for files, 56
    for images, 179
Edit ➤ Find command, 78
Edit ➤ Font Properties command, 127

Edit ➤ Form Field Properties command, 253
Edit Frame Attributes dialog box, 273, 277, *277*
Edit Frame Set Grid dialog box, 273–274
Edit ➤ Hyperlink command, 150, 155, 170
Edit Hyperlink dialog box, 155–156, 166
Edit ➤ Image Properties command, 179
Edit Link dialog box, 170, *170*
Edit New Page Immediately option, 154
Edit ➤ Object Properties command, 74
Edit ➤ Open command, 70, 99
Edit ➤ Open With command, 60
Edit option
    for browsers, 86
    for images, 180
Edit Page option, 62–63, 170
Edit ➤ Paste command, 74
    for files, 56
    for images, 176, 179
Edit ➤ Properties command, 57
Edit ➤ Redo command, 74
Edit ➤ Replace command, 79
Edit ➤ Select All command, 188, 190
Edit ➤ Undo command, 74
Edit ➤ Undo Insert command, 224
Edit ➤ Unlink command, 156
Edit URL option, 36
Edit ➤ WebBot Component Properties command, 210
editing
    bookmarks, 158
    browser settings, 86
    in Editor, **73–75**
    extensions, 56
    file associations, **59–60**, *59*
    fonts, **127–132**, *128*, *131*

frame sets, **274–279**, *275–277*
home page names, **307–309**
hotspots, **166**
hyperlinks, **155**
marquee messages, 284
titles, 57
To Do List tasks, **66**
WebBots, **210**
Editor, 13, **17–19**, *18*, **69**, *72*, 322
   for browsing pages, **106**
   for converting files, **101–102**
   for creating pages, **92–98**, *92–93*, *95–99*
   editing process in, **73–75**
   for extended HTML code, **82–84**
   following hyperlinks in, **156**
   for headings, **114–115**
   for horizontal lines, **110–113**, *110*, *112–113*
   for HTML source code, **80–82**, *81*
   inserting files into pages in, **102–103**
   inserting paragraphs and line breaks in, **75–76**
   for lists, **115–122**, *116*
   for new pages, **71**
   opening files in, **99–103**, *100–101*
   for page sections, **110–113**, *110*, *112–113*
   previewing work done in, **84–86**, *85*
   for printing pages, **86–88**
   saving pages in, **103–106**, *103*
   for searching for text, **78–79**
   special characters in, **76**, *77*
   for spell checking, **76–78**, *78*
   starting, **70–71**
   and Word, **72–73**
Editor Name field, 60
editors
   in opening pages, 55
   for Web pages, **58–60**, *59*
effects
   for fonts, **130**
   for sprites, **195–196**
elements, 9, 321
<EM> HTML tag, 129
Employee Directory template, 93
Empty Web template, 29
End key, 49
Enter key, 73, 75, 133
Enter Network Password dialog box, 295
entering text, WebBots for, **211–214**, *214*
errors
   in Hyperlink view, 48
   with WebBots, 207
Errors tab, 207
Everyone Has Browse Access option, 295
Excel files, converting, 102
Exclude option, 33
existing sites, Web sites from, **32–33**
existing text, lists from, **115–117**, *116*
exiting Editor, 71
expanding
   Explorer folders, 52
   Hyperlink view, **49–50**
Expired Scheduled Include placeholder, 207
Explorer, 13, **16–17**, *17*, **23**, **45–46**, 322
   active Webs in, **24–25**
   for deleting sites, **43**
   file properties in, **54–58**, *58*
   Folder view in, 17, **52–54**, *53*
   Hyperlink view in, 16, *17*, **46–52**, *47*, *51*
   for importing and exporting files, **34–37**, *35*
   for moving sites, **43**
   for new sites, **25–33**, *27*, *30*
   for opening and closing sites, **31–32**
   for publishing sites, **37–42**, *38*, *40–41*

for renaming sites, **42–43**
for searching for text, **60–63**, *62*
for spell checking, **63**
To Do Lists in, **63–67**, *64*, *67*
for verifying hyperlinks, **168–170**, *168–170*
Web file editors for, **58–60**, *59*
exporting files, 36–37
Extended Attributes dialog box, 83–84, *84*
extended HTML code, 82–84
Extended option, 83
extensions, file
    changing, 56
    for file associations, 58
extensions, server, 13, **15–16**, 327
external links, 12, 322
    in Hyperlink view, 52
    in Verify Links, 169

F1 key, 317
F7 key, 76
FACE attribute, 129
Feedback Form template, 93, 243
Field Must Be option, 257
fields, 242–243, 321
    adding, **251–252**
    aligning, **245–246**
    properties for, **252–261**, *253*, *255*, *257*
    selecting, **244–245**
file associations
    adding and changing, **59–60**, *59*
    deleting, 60
    extensions for, 58
    for Image Composer, 187

File ➤ Close command, 71
File ➤ Close FrontPage Web command, 32–33
File ➤ Composition Properties command, 194, 199
File ➤ Delete FrontPage Web command, 43
File ➤ Exit command, 71
File ➤ Export command, 36
File for Results field, 247
File Format field, 248
File ➤ Import command, 29, 33, 35
File ➤ New command
    for frame sets, 267, 273
    in Image Composer, 194
    for pages, 92–93
    for templates, 71
File ➤ New ➤ Folder command, 54
File ➤ New ➤ FrontPage Web command, 25–26
File ➤ Open command
    in Editor, 99–100
    in Explorer, 24
    in Image Composer, 190
File ➤ Open FrontPage Web command, 26, 31, 306
File ➤ Page Properties command, 83, 87, 135
File ➤ Page Setup command, 86
File ➤ Preview command
    in Browser, 85, 290
    for video clips, 177
File ➤ Print command, 86
File ➤ Print Preview command, 87
File ➤ Publish FrontPage Web command, 37–38, 307
File ➤ Save command
    in Editor, 103
    for forms, 250
    in Image Composer, 190
File ➤ Save As command
    in Editor, 103, 105
    in Image Composer, 190

File ➤ Save Selection As command, 191, 199
File ➤ Send to FrontPage command, 187
File Transfer Protocol (FTP), 5, 39, 41, 323
File Type field, 60
files. *See also* Web pages
    commands for, **55–56**
    converting, **101–102**
    copying, **56**
    exporting, **36–37**
    in Folder view, 17, **52–54**, *53*
    for form results, 247
    for hyperlinks, 147–148, **153**
    importing, **34–36**, *35*
    inserting into pages, **102–103**
    moving, **56**, 167
    names for, 52, **54–57**, 167
    opening, **99–103**, *100–101*
    properties of, **54–58**, *58*
    renaming, **55–57**, 167
    saving pages as, **104**
    for sites, 30
    transferring, 5
Files of Type list, 101
filling out forms, **261–263**, *261–262*
fills for sprites, transferring, **198–199**
Find dialog box, 78–79
Find Next search option, 79
Find occurrences of dialog box, 62, *62*
Find What field, 61
Finding a Sprite File window, 197
finding text
    in Editor, **78–79**
    in Explorer, **60–63**, *62*
fixed-width fonts, 133
fixing targets, **167**
flattening compositions, 191
focus in Hyperlink view, 50
Folder view, 17, 46, **52–54**, *53*
Folder View button, 52, *52*

folders
    creating, 54
    for importing files, 36
    for installation, 314
    listing, 17
    names for, 31, 38
    in publishing sites, 41
    for sites, 26, 30–31
    for templates, 106
Follow Hyperlink command, 106
following hyperlinks, 106, **156**
Font dialog box, 127–132, *128*, *131*, 194
<FONT> HTML tag, 129
Font Properties command, 127
<FONT SIZE> HTML tag, 130
Font Style list, 129
Font tab, 127–128, *128*
fonts
    accessing properties for, **127**
    changing, **127–132**, *128*, *131*
    effects for, **130**
    with Image Composer, 194
    monospace, **133–134**, *134*
    size of, **129–130**
    styles for, **129**, **131–132**, *131*
footers
    in printing, 86–87
    in Project Web template, 28
Forever option, 184
Form Field Properties command, 245, 253
Form Field Validation option, 254
Form Fields toolbar, 249
Form Handler list, 246
form handlers, 244, **246–249**, *246*, 322
Form Properties command, 246
Form Properties dialog box, 246–247, *246*
Format ➤ Background command, 138

Format ➤ Bullets and Numbering command, 118
Format ➤ Font command, 126–127, 132
Format ➤ Paragraph command, 114, 132
Format toolbar, 73, 127, *127*
formats
  converting, **101–102**
  for form results, 248
  for headings, 114
  for images, **174–175**
Formatted style, **133–134**, *134*
formatting, 125
  characters, **126–132**, *128*, *131*
  page properties for, **135–142**, *136*, *138*, *140*
  paragraphs, 75, **132–135**, *133–134*
  table contents, **227–228**, *228*
forms, **241–243**, *242*, 322
  adding fields to, **251–252**
  aligning fields in, **245–246**
  check boxes in, **259**
  creating, **243–244**, **249–250**
  data validation in, **254–257**
  drop-down menus in, **257–258**, *257*
  field properties in, **252–261**, *253*, *255*, *257*
  filling out, **261–263**, *261–262*
  handlers for, 244, **246–249**, *246*, *248*, 322
  one-line text boxes in, 244, **249–250**, **253–257**, *255*
  push buttons in, **260–261**
  radio buttons in, **259**
  scrolling text boxes in, **260**
  selecting fields in, **244–245**
Forms toolbar, 244, *244*
Forward button, 106, *106*, 156, *156*
frames and frame sets, **265–266**, 322
  alternate pages for, **270**, *270*
  appearance of, **279**
  creating, **273–274**

  default, 137
  for hyperlinks, **152–153**, **280–281**
  for marquee messages, **281–284**, *282*
  modifying, **274–279**, *275–277*
  names and URLs for, 273, **277–279**, *277*
  number of, **274–275**, *275*
  saving, **271–272**, *271*
  size of, **276–277**, *276*
  from templates, **266–272**, *267–272*
  uses for, **266**
  viewing, **272**, *273*
Frames Wizard, **267–272**, *268–272*
FRCONTEN.HTM file, 271–272
freeware, 322
FRMAIN.HTM file, 271–272
From File field, 100–101
FrontPage-aware servers, **15–16**
FrontPage Editor. *See* Editor
FrontPage Server Administrator dialog box, 304–306, *304–305*
FrontPage Web Settings dialog box, 43, 214, *214*
FTP (File Transfer Protocol), 5, **39**, 41, 323

General tab
  for file properties, 57–58, *58*
  for image properties, 179–183, *180*
  for page properties, 136–137, *136*
  for Personal Web Servers, 300, *301*
Generate Client-Side Image Maps option, 161
Get Background and Colors from Page option, 140
Getting Started with Microsoft FrontPage dialog box, 26, *27*

GIF (Graphics Interchange Format), 174–175, 180–182, 323
glossaries, definition lists for, 121–122
Goto command, 158
graphics. *See* images
Graphics Interchange Format (GIF), 174–175, 180–182, 323
Greater Than option, 257
green links, 168–169
Green value in Image Composer, 192, 199
groups in Personal Web Server, 303
Groups option, 292
Groups tab, 303

H

<H1> HTML tag, 9, 114
handles
  for images, 163, 166, 178, 185–186
  for sprites, *189*, 190
hard returns in HTML, 9
<HEAD> HTML tag, 136
header cells, **234**
headers
  in printing, 86–87
  in Project Web template, 28
headings
  in HTML, 9, 114
  in pages, **114–115**
height
  of horizontal lines, 111
  of images, 186
  of scrolling text boxes, 260
  of sprites, 194, 196
  of superscripts, 132
Height field, 186, 194, 196
help, **317**
Help button, 317
Help ➤ Microsoft command, 317

Help ➤ Sample Sprites Catalog command, 197
Hide/Show button, 227, *227*
hiding elements in Hyperlink view, 49
Highlight Hotspots button, 166, *166*
histories for To Do Lists, 65, 67
hollow bullet style, 118
Home key, 49
home pages, 7, 323
  default, 15, 24, 308
  in Hyperlink view, 48
  names for, **307–309**
  Wizards for, **95–98**, *96–99*
Horizontal Alignment option, 233–234
Horizontal Line Properties command, 111
horizontal lines
  appearance of, **111**
  creating, **110**, *110*
  images for, **111–113**, *112–113*
  thickness of, 111
Horizontal Spacing option, 185
host servers, Personal Web Servers as, 14
hosts, 323
Hotspot Properties command, 166
hotspots, 159–160, 323. *See also* hyperlinks
  defining, **162–165**, *162*
  revising, **166**
  viewing, **165–166**
<HR> HTML tag, 110
HTML (Hypertext Markup Language), 7, **9**, 323
  extended code for, **82–84**
  learning, **11–12**
  source documents in, **11–12**, **80–82**, *81*
  tags in, **9–11**, 81, 327
HTML Encoding option, 137
HTML Markup dialog box, 82

HTTP (Hypertext Transfer Protocol), 6, 323
HTTP-EQUIV attribute, 142
Hyperlink option, 138
Hyperlink Points To label, 151–152, 155
Hyperlink Type list, 153
Hyperlink view, 16, *17*, **46**, *47*
    expanding, **49–50**
    map pane in, 16, **50–52**, *51*
    outline pane in, 16, **47–49**
Hyperlink View button, 46, *46*
hyperlinks, 7, **12–13**, **145–146**, 323–324
    bookmarks for, 148, **151–152**, **156–158**
    color for, 7, 138, 146
    creating, **150–154**, *151*, *154*
    deleting, **156**
    with Editor, **106**
    external, 12, 52, 169, 322
    to files, **153**
    fixing targets for, **167**
    following, 106, **156**
    frames for, **152–153**, **280–281**
    in image maps, **158–166**, *159*, *161–162*
    in importing files, 35
    internal, 12, 52, 324
    for moved and renamed files, **56–57**, 167
    revising, **155**
    for tables of contents, 216
    targets for, **146–148**, **280–281**
    text and images for, **146–147**, *147*, 155–156
    URLs for, **148–149**
    verifying, 13, **168–170**, *168–170*, **290**
Hyperlinks Inside Page button, 49–50, *49*
Hyperlinks to Images button, 49, *49*

Hypertext Markup Language (HTML), 7, **9**, 323
    extended code for, **82–84**
    learning, **11–12**
    source documents in, **11–12**, **80–82**, *81*
    tags in, **9–11**, 81, 327
Hypertext Transfer Protocol (HTTP), 6, 323

I

icons in Hyperlink view, 47–48
Ignore option, 77
Ignore All option, 77
IIS (Internet Information Server), 14, 299
Image Composer, 13, **20**, **186–187**, 324
    colors in, **191–192**, *193*
    creating compositions in, **187–190**, *189*, 321
    effects in, **195–196**
    importing images for, **197–198**
    order of sprites, in, **198**
    saving compositions in, **199–200**, *200*
    size of sprites in, **196**
    Sprite Catalog for, **197**
    starting, **187**
    system requirements for, 313
    for text sprites, **194**, *195*
    transferring sprite fills in, **198–199**
    workspace for, **189–191**, *189*
Image dialog box, 113, *113*
image maps, **158–160**, *159*, 324
    defining hotspots for, **162–165**, *162*
    Server Extensions for, 16
    types of, **160–161**, *161*
    viewing hotspots for, **165–166**
Image Properties command, 165

Image Properties dialog box, 155, 179–186, *180, 183, 185*
Image Source field, 155
Image Source option, 179–180
Image toolbar, 163, *163*, 166, 178, *178*
images, **173**, 323
    aligning, **184–185**, *185*
    alternatives to, **182–183**
    composing. *See* Image Composer
    folder for, 31, 33, 41, 175, 177
    formats for, **174–175**
    for horizontal lines, **111–113**, *112–113*
    in Hyperlink view, 47–49
    for hyperlinks, 7, **146–147**, *147*, 155–156
    importing, **197–198**
    inserting, **175–178**, *176*
    for page backgrounds, **138–140**, *140*
    properties for, **179–186**, *180, 183, 185*
    saving, 102, **177–178**, *178*
    selecting, 74, 163, 166, **178–179**
    size of, 178, **185–186**
    sources for, **179–180**, *180*
    speed of downloading, 112
    types of, **180–182**
Images folder, 31, 33, 41, 175, 177
<IMG> HTML tag, 176
Import File dialog box, 35
Import File to FrontPage Web dialog box, 35, *35*
Import Web Wizard, 29, 33, *34*
importing
    files, **34–36**, *35*
    images, **197–198**
    pages into sites, 28
    sites, 15
In Percent option
    for images, 186
    for tables, 235

In Pixels option
    for columns, 236
    for images, 186
    for tables, 235
Include Field Names in Output option, 248
Include Subdirectories option, 33
Include WebBot, **206–209**, *208*
included pages, spell checking, 77
including pages, **207–209**, *208*
Increase Indent button, 120, *120*, 135, *135*
Increase Text Size button, 129, *129*
indenting paragraphs, **135**
INDEX.HTM file, 15, 24, 307
Index tab, 197
Initial Value field, 254
inline images, 174, 324
Insert ➤ Break command, 75
Insert ➤ Comment command, 74, 204–205, 210–211
Insert ➤ File command, 102–103
Insert ➤ Form Field command, 244, 249
Insert ➤ From File command, 197–198
Insert ➤ Horizontal Line command, 110
Insert ➤ HTML Markup command, 82, 204–205
Insert ➤ Image command, 102, 113, 147
Insert Image File button, 197
Insert ➤ Marquee command, 282, 284
Insert Rows or Columns dialog box, 237
Insert ➤ Symbol command, 76
Insert Table button, 224, *224*
Insert Table dialog box, 224–225, *225*, 235, 252
Insert ➤ Video command, 102, 177

Insert ➤ WebBot Component command, 205–206, 212
Insert WebBot Component dialog box, 206, *206*, 208
inserting
    extended HTML code, **82–84**
    files into pages, **102–103**
    images, **175–178**, *176*
    paragraphs and line breaks, **75–76**
    special characters, **76**, 77
    table elements, **237**
    video clips, **177**
installation, **311–316**, *312*, *315*
Integer option, 256
Integrated Services Digital Networks (ISDNs), 324
IntelliMouse, 73
interlaced GIF images, 181–182, 324
Interlaced option, 182
internal links, 12, 52, 324
Internet, **3–5**, 324
    vs. intranets, **8**
    World Wide Web on, **5–8**
Internet Database Connector option, 247
Internet Explorer, 6, 324
Internet Information Server (IIS), 14, 299
Internet Local User Administrator page, 302–303, *303*
Internet Service Providers (ISPs), 41
Internet Services Administrator page, 302, *302*
intranets, **8**, 324
IP addresses, permissions for, **297–298**, *298–299*
IP Mask fields, 298
ISDNs (Integrated Services Digital Networks), 324
ISPs (Internet Service Providers), 41
Italic button, 129, *129*
Italic font, 129

Java language, 324–325
JavaScript language, 325
Joint Photographic Expert Group (JPEG) format, **175**, 180, **182**, 325
JPG extension, 175

Keep Aspect Ratio option, 196
Keep Window Open option, 65
Keyboard font style, 131
keywords with <META> tag, 142

languages, character sets for, 128, 137
Learning FrontPage template, 29
Left alignment option
    for cells, 233
    for images, 185
    for tables, 230
Less Than or Equal To option, 257
<LI> HTML tag, 116–117
Light Border option, 232
LIGHTNIN.MIC file, 197
line breaks
    in Editor, **75–76**
    in forms, 251
lines, horizontal
    appearance of, **111**
    creating, **110**, *110*
    images for, **111–113**, *112–113*
link arrows, 50–51
Linked To field, 64

links. *See* hyperlinks
listing pages, **16–17**, *17*
lists, **115**
    appearance of, **118–120**
    creating, **117**
    definition, **121–122**
    directory, 121
    from existing text, **115–117**, *116*
    manipulating, **117–118**
    menu, 121
    nesting, **120–121**
local servers, Personal Web Servers as, 14
Local User Administration link, 302
Local User Administrator page, 302–303, *303*
location
    of files
    of pages, 136–137
    of sites, **29–30**, *30*
Location field
    for default hyperlinks, 165
    for files, 58
Loop field, 184
Loop Delay field, 184
lossless compression, 175, 325
lossy compression, 175, 325
Low-Res image option, 182, *182*

M

main sections in pages, 96, *96*, 98, *98*
Make a Custom Grid option, 273
Make Transparent button, 181, *181*
manuals, 317
map pane in Hyperlink view, **50–52**, *51*
maps, image. *See* image maps
Margin Height option, 279
Margin Width option, 279

margins
    for frames, 279
    for pages, **141**
    for paragraphs, **135**
MARGINS attribute, 141
Margins option, 279
Margins tab, 141
marquee messages, **281–284**, *282*, 325
Marquee Properties dialog box, 282–284, *282*
mask fields, 298
Max Length option, 256
maximizing windows, 74
Meeting Agenda template, 93
Members page, 28
memory requirements, 187, 312–313
<MENU> HTML tag, 121
menu lists, 121
menus
    drop-down, 245, **257–258**, *257*
    in Editor, 73
Merge option, 276
merging
    cells, 228, **237**
    frames, 276
messages
    marquee, **281–284**, *282*
    from WebBots, 207
<META> HTML tag, 142
MIC extension, 190
Microsoft Image Composer. *See* Image Composer
Middle alignment option
    for cells, 233
    for images, 184
MIDI files, 137
Min Length option, 256
minimizing windows, 74
minus signs (-)
    in Folder view, 52
    in Hyperlink view, 49, 52
modems, 325

modification date of files
  in Folder view, 17, 52–53
  in Properties dialog box, 57
  updating, 54
Modified By option, 212
Modify option, 60
modifying. *See* editing
monospace fonts, 133
Move Down option, 258
Move to Center command, 50
Move Up option, 258
moving
  drop-down menu items, 258
  files, **56**, 167
  hotspots, 166
  images, 179
  main sections in pages, 98, *98*
  sites, **43**
moving images
  inserting, **177**
  properties for, **183–184**, *183*
multiple cells, selecting, 227
multiple hyperlinks in Hyperlink view, 50
multiple pages in Editor, 73

N

Name of Destination FrontPage Web field, 38
Name/Value Pair dialog box, 83
name/value pairs
  for fields, 244
  for HTML attributes, 83
named targets for hyperlinks, 151–152
names
  for attributes, 83
  for bookmarks, 152, 157–158
  for check boxes, 259
  displaying, 25, 32, 57
  for fields, 244
  for files, 52, **54–57**, 167
  for folders, 31, 38
  for frames, 273, **277–279**, *277*
  for home pages, **307–309**
  for meta-variables, 142
  for pages, 96
  for radio buttons, 259
  for sites, 26, 29–30, 38, **42–43**
  for text boxes, 253–254
  for To Do List tasks, 64–66
navigating tables, 225
** HTML code**, 75
nesting
  lists, **120–121**
  tables, 225, *226*
'Net, 325
Netscape Navigator, 6, 325
Network connection option, 41
networks, 5
New button, 71, *71*, 92–93, *92*
New FrontPage Web button, 25–26, *25*
New FrontPage Web dialog box, 26, *27*, 28
New Page dialog box
  in Editor, 92–93, *92*, 104–105
  for frame sets, 268, 273
  for hyperlinks to new pages, 154
New Page tab, 150, 154, *154*
Next Page printing option, 87
No Constraints option, 256
No Wrap option, 233
<NOFRAMES> HTML tag, 270
non-breaking spaces, 75
Normal Break option, 75
Normal Page template, 71, 92–93
Normal style, 133
Normal Web template, 28
Not in Dictionary field, 77
Not Resizeable option, 279
number of frames, **274–275**, *275*
Number of Rows option, 237

Number option, 256
Numbered List button, 116, *116*, 118
numbered lists, 115, *116*
    appearance of, **119–120**, *119*
    creating, **115–116**
Numeric Format option, 256

Object Properties command, 74
Office Directory template, 93–94, *93*, *95*
Office products, interfaces for, 72–73
<OL> HTML tag, 115, 117
On File Open option, 184
On Mouse Over option, 184
One-Line Text Box button, 249, *249*
one-line text boxes, 244
    data validation in, **254–257**, *255*
    inserting, **249–250**
    properties for, **253–254**, *253*
One Page printing option, 87
online status, 326
Only Registered Users Have Browse Access option, 295
Open button, 99, *99*
Open command
    in Editor, 70
    in Explorer, 55
Open File dialog box, 99–101, *100–101*
Open File As dialog box, 102
Open FrontPage Web button, 31, *31*
Open FrontPage Web dialog box, 26, 31
Open Pages list, 151
Open Pages tab, 150–153, *151*
Open With command, 55, 60
Open With Editor dialog box, 60
opening
    files, 55, **99–103**, *100–101*
    resources, **6–7**

sites, **31–32**
To Do Lists, **64**
opening HTML tags, 9
optional tag attributes, 9
Options dialog box, 59–60, *59*, 187
order of sprites, 190, **198**
ordered lists, 115, *116*
    appearance of, **119–120**, *119*
    creating, **115–116**
Original option, 81
orphan pages, 291
Other Location tab, 100–101, *101*, 139, 175
outlines
    in Hyperlink view, **47–49**
    lists for, 120
overlapping sprites, 190
overwriting in importing files, 35

<P> HTML tag, 75, 133
page layout in printing, **86–87**
page numbers in headers and footers, 87
Page Properties button, 57
Page Properties command, 135
Page Properties dialog box, 57, 83, 135–142, *136*, *138*, *140*
Page URL field, 154
Page URL variable, 212
pages, Web. *See* Web pages
palettes, color, 191
Paragraph Properties dialog box, 132–133, *133*, 135
paragraphs
    aligning text in, **134–135**
    creating, 73
    formatting, **132–135**, *133–134*
    indenting, **135**

inserting, **75–76**
selecting, 126
Parameters tab, 214, *214*
parent frames, 274
Password field, 254
passwords
    in Explorer, 25, 30, 32
    for sites, 41, 295–296
    for text boxes, 254
Paste command, 55
Patterns and Fills tool palette, 188, *189*, 198
patterns for horizontal lines, 112
pauses for images, 184
Period option, 256
permissions
    assigning, **292–293**
    for computers, **297–298**, *298–299*
    in Explorer, 24
    for sites, 26, **293–294**, *294*
    for users, **294–297**, *295–296*
Permissions dialog box, 292–298, *294–295, 298*
Personal Home Page Wizard, **95–98**, *96–99*
Personal Web Server Properties dialog box, 300–301, *301*
Personal Web Servers (PWSs), **13–15**, **299**, 326
    for home page name changes, **308–309**
    installing, 314–315
    migrating from FrontPage PWS to Microsoft PWS, **306–307**
    for registering users, **301–304**, *302–303*
    running, **300–301**, *301*
    Server Administrator in, **304–306**, *304–305*
    system requirements for, 313
Personal Web template, 29
PgDn key and PgUp keys, 73
Pick a Template option, 268

Pick Template Layout dialog box, 268–269, *269*
pictures. See images
placeholders for WebBots, 207
plug-ins, 326
plus signs (+)
    in Folder view, 52
    in Hyperlink view, 49, 52
point sizes, 130
Polygon button, 164, *164*
ports, 304–305, 307, 316, 326
pound signs (#)
    for bookmark names, 152
    for comments, 308–309
<PRE> HTML tag, 134
Preview in Browser button, 85, *85*
Preview in Browser dialog box, 85, *85*
Preview option, 85
previewing
    pages, **84–86**, *85*
    printing, **87–88**
Previous Page printing option, 87
Print button, 86, *86*
Print dialog box, 86
Print Page Setup dialog box, 86–87
printing pages, **86–88**
priorities for To Do List tasks, 64–65
Priority field, 64
Priority option, 65
_Private folder, 31, 41
processor requirements, 187, 312–313
Product or Event Registration Form template, 243
Programs ➤ Accessories ➤ Internet Tools command, 40
Programs ➤ Microsoft FrontPage command, 316
Project Web template, 28
properties. See also attributes for tags
    for characters, **126–132**, *128, 131*
    for extended HTML code, 83, *84*
    for fields, **252–261**, *253, 255, 257*

for files, **54–58**, *58*
for images, **179–186**, *180, 183, 185*
for one-line text boxes, **253–254**, *253*
for pages, **135–142**, *136, 138, 140*
for paragraphs, **132–135**, *133–134*
Properties command, 55, 57
Properties dialog box
for files, 57–58, *58*
for horizontal lines, 111
for WebBot errors, 207
protocols, 326
in publishing sites, 41
in URLs, 6
Publish FrontPage Web dialog box, 38, *38*, 40
publishing pages. *See* Web pages
publishing sites, 37
to FrontPage servers, **37–38**, *38*
with FTP, **39**
with Web Publishing Wizard, **39–42**, *40–41*
purple tags in HTML window, 81
Push Button button, 252, *252*
Push Button Properties dialog box, 260
push buttons, 243, 245, 252, **260–261**

Q

Quality field, 182, *182*

R

Radio Button button, 251, *251*
Radio Button Properties dialog box, 259
radio buttons, 245, **259**
RAM for Image Composer, 187

Recompute Table of Contents When Any Other Page is Edited option, 216
Rectangle button, 163, *163*
red attributes, 81
red links, 168–169
red status indicators, 62
red triangles, 207
Red value in Image Composer, 192, 199
Redo button, 74
registering users, **301–304**, *302–303*
Registration WebBot, 16, 203
Regular font option, 129
relationships in Hyperlink view, **50–52**, *51*
relative font sizes, 130
relative URLs, **149**, 326
Remove option
for drop-down menus, 258
for file associations, 60
for importing files, 36
for To Do Lists, 65, 67
removing. *See* deleting
Rename command, 55
Rename dialog box, 56–57, 167
renaming
files, **55–57**, 167
resources, 13
sites, **42–43**
Repeated Hyperlinks button, 49, *49*
repeating images, 184
Replace All option, 79
Replace command, 62–63
Replace in FrontPage Web dialog box, 61
Replace option, 79
Replace With field, 61, 79
replacing text
in Editor, **78–79**
in Explorer, **61–63**, *62*
Required option, 256–257
required tag attributes, 9

requirements, system, 312–313
resolution, 326
   for browser windows, 85, *85*
   in testing sites, **289–290**
resources, 327
   deleting, 12, 55
   listing, **16–17**, *17*
   opening, **6–7**
restrictions, security, 291–298, *294–296*
Results tab, 247–248, *248*
revising. *See* editing
RGB values in Image Composer, 192, 199
rich text format (RTF), 327
   converting, 102
   in importing files, 34
Right alignment option
   for cells, 233
   for images, 185
   for tables, 230
robots. *See* WebBots
Roman numeral style, 119–120
root webs, 25, 327
rows, 222–224, *222*
   in frames, 274–276
   inserting, 237
   selecting, 226–227
Rows option
   for frames, 275–276
   for tables, 224
RTF (rich text format), 327
   converting, 102
   in importing files, 34
rules, horizontal, **110–113**, *110*, *112–113*

Sample font style, 131
Sample pane for fonts, 128
Sample Sprites Catalog window, 197
Save As dialog box, 103–104, *103*
Save As Template dialog box, 105
Save button
   in Editor, 103, *103*
   in Image Composer, 190, *190*
Save Image to FrontPage Web dialog box, *178*
Save Page dialog box, 271
Save Results WebBot, 16, 203
saving
   compositions, **199–200**, *200*
   Editor changes, 24
   forms, 250
   frame sets, **271–272**, *271*
   images, 102, **177–178**, *178*
   pages, 92, **103–106**, *103*
   workspace and composition guides, **190–191**
Schedule page, 28
Scheduled Image WebBot, 206
Scheduled Include WebBot, 206–207
screen resolution, 326
   for browser windows, 85, *85*
   in testing sites, **289–290**
scrolling
   in Editor, 73
   in frames, 279
   in Hyperlink view, 49
Scrolling option, 279
Scrolling Text Box button, 252, *252*
scrolling text boxes, 244, 252, **260**
scrolling wheels, 73
SDK (software developer's kit), 203
Search page, 28
Search Page template, 205
Search WebBot, 16, 203, 206
searching for text
   in Editor, **78–79**
   in Explorer, **60–63**, *62*
security, 15, **291–298**, *294–296*, *298–299*

Select Background Image dialog box, 139, *140*
Select button, 166, *166*
Select Font button, 194
Selected Pages search option, 61
selecting
    fields, **244–245**
    files, 33, 35, 54
    images, 74, 163, 166, **178–179**
    list items, 117
    table elements, **226–227**
    text, 74, **126–127**
selection handles, 163, 166, 178, 185–186
send mail link, 28
Server Administrator, 304–306, *304–305*
server-driven WebBots, 203
Server Extensions, 13, **15–16**, 327
server-side image maps, 160–161
servers, 4, 30, **37–42**, *38*, *40–41*, 327
Settings for Saving Results of Form dialog box, 247–249, *248*, 262
Settings option, 247
Settings tab
    for colors, 191
    for permissions, 292–294, *294*
SETUP.EXE program, 312–316, *312*
shadow effects for lines, 111
shape of hotspots, 166
shareware, 327
Shift key, 74, 126–127
Shift+clicking, 33, 35, 54
Shift+Enter keys, 75–76, 251
Show Color Coding option, 81
Show Controls in Browser option, 184
Show Each Page Only Once option, 216
Show FrontPage Editor button, 70, *70*
Show FrontPage Explorer button, 71, *71*

Show/Hide Marks button, 76, *76*
Show History option, 65, 67
Show Image Editor, 187, *187*
Show Pages with No Incoming Hyperlinks option, 216
Show To Do List button, 64, *64*, 75, *75*
Simple Table of Contents template, 269, 272
single system meta-variable, 142
sites. *See* Web sites
size
    of borders, 224, 230
    of browser windows, 85, *85*
    of files, 17, 52, 54, 57
    of Folder view columns, 53
    of fonts, **129–130**
    of frames, **276–277**, *276*
    of horizontal lines, 111
    of images, 178, **185–186**
    of one-line text boxes, 254
    of scrolling text boxes, 260
    of sprites, **196**
    of tables, **235–238**
    of windows, 74
Size list, 129–130
software developer's kit (SDK), 203
solid bullet style, 118
sorting To Do Lists, 65
sound for pages, 137
source documents in HTML, **11–12**, **80–82**, *81*
Source URL option, 278
spaces
    non-breaking, 75
    in pages, 9
spacing
    cells, 231
    images, 185
span of cells, **238**
special characters, **76**, 77
Special Styles tab, 131–132, *131*
Specify Size option, 186

Specify Value option, 258
Specify Width option
    for columns, 236
    for marquee messages, 283
    for tables, 235
speed
    of downloading images, 112
    of marquee messages, 284
    in testing sites, 290
spell checking
    in Editor, **76–78**, *78*
    in Explorer, **63**
Spelling dialog box, 77, *78*
Split Cells dialog box, 238
Split option, 276
splitting
    cells, **238**
    frames, **276–277**, *276*
    paragraphs, 133
Sprite Catalog, 197
Sprite Texture Type list, 198
Sprite to Sprite tool, 198
sprites, **187–190**, *189*, 327
    catalog for, **197**
    effects for, **195–196**
    order of, 190, **198**
    size of, **196**
    text, **194–196**, *195*
    transferring fills for, **198–199**
stacks for sprites, 190
Standard toolbar, 73
Start At option, 119
Start Copying Files dialog box,
    315, *315*
starting
    Editor, **70–71**
    FrontPage, **316–317**
    Image Composer, **187**
Startup tab, 300
status bars
    in Editor, 73
    for hyperlinks, 146
    for sprites, 188, *189*

status indicators in text searches, 62
status of hyperlinks, 168
Status page, 28
Stop button, 156, *156*
<STRIKE> HTML tag, 130
Strikethrough effect, 130
<STRONG> HTML tag, 129, 131
Style tab, 118
styles
    for bullets, 118
    default, 126
    for fonts, **129**, **131–132**, *131*
    for numbered lists, 119–120
<SUB> HTML tag, 132
Subfolders option, 41
subheadings, **114–115**
subscript characters, **131–132**
Subscript option, 132
Substitution WebBot, 206,
    211–214, *214*
suggestions in spelling checker, 78
Summary tab, 57, *58*
<SUP> HTML tag, 132
superscript characters, **131–132**
Superscript option, 132
Survey Form template, 243
Sybex home page, **162–165**, *162*
Symbol dialog box, 76, *77*

T

Tab key
    for hotspot selection, 166
    for sprite selection, 188, 198
**Table ➤ Caption Properties
command**, 229
Table ➤ Cell Properties command,
    232, 234, 238
<TABLE> HTML tag, 223
**Table ➤ Insert Caption
command**, 228

Table ➤ Insert Cell command, 237
Table ➤ Insert Rows or Columns command, 237
Table ➤ Insert Table command, 224, 252
Table ➤ Merge Cells command, 228, 237
Table of Contents template, 93, 205
Table of Contents WebBot, 206, **215–217**, *215*, *217*
Table Properties dialog box, 228–232, *230*, 235
Table ➤ Select Cell command, 226, 233
Table ➤ Select Column command, 226
Table ➤ Select Row command, 226, 228
Table ➤ Select Table command, 226
Table ➤ Split Cells command, 238
Table ➤ Table Properties command, 229
tables, **221**, 327
　alignment in, 230
　borders for, 223–224, 230
　captions for, 223, **228–229**
　color in, 223, 225, **231–232**
　creating, **224–225**, *225*
　in Editor, 76
　formatting contents of, **227–228**, *228*
　for forms, 252
　navigating, 225
　nesting, 225, *226*
　selecting elements in, **226–227**
　size of, **235–238**
　spacing in, 231
　structure of, **222–223**, *222*
　width of, **235–236**
tables of contents
　lists for, 120
　WebBots for, **215–217**, *215*, *217*

Tagged Image File Format (TIFF) files, 176, 328
tags, HTML, **9**, 327
　essential, **10–11**
　evolving nature of, 11
　in HTML window, 81
targets, 327–328
　fixing, **167**
　for hotspots, 166
　in hyperlinks, **146–148**, **280–281**
　for pages, 137
Task Details dialog box, 65
tasks. *See* To Do Lists
TCP/IP (Transmission Control Protocol/Internet Protocol), 5, 328
<TD> HTML tag, 223
TEM extension, 106
templates, 328
　for forms, 243
　for frame sets, **266–272**, *267–272*
　for pages, 71, **92–94**, *93*, *95*
　saving pages as, **104–106**
　for sites, **26–29**, *27*
　for tables, 224
testing
　hyperlinks, 13, **168–170**, *168–170*, **290**
　sites, 14, **288–291**
text
　aligning, **134–135**
　for captions, 229
　fonts for, **127–132**, *128*, *131*
　in form fields, 250–251
　in HTML window, 81
　for hyperlinks, **146–147**, *147*, 155–156
　as image alternative, 183
　from lists, 118
　lists from, **115–117**, *116*
　for marquee messages, 283
　for push buttons, 260
　searching for, **60–63**, *62*, **78–79**

selecting, 74, **126–127**
spell checking, **63**, **76–78**, *78*
in tables, 223, 233
Text Box Properties dialog box, 253–255, *253*
Text Box Validation dialog box, 254–255, *255*
text boxes, 244
  data validation in, **254–257**, *255*
  inserting, **249–250**, 252
  properties for, **253–254**, *253*
  scrolling, **260**
Text button, 194, *194*
Text Color button, 130, *130*
Text Database Using Comma as a Separator format, 248, 262
text entry, WebBots for, **211–214**, *214*
text (TXT) files, converting, 102
Text Format option, 256
Text image option, 183
text-only pages, **289**
Text option, 256
text sprites, **194–196**, *195*
Text tool palette, 194
thickness of horizontal lines, 111
thumbnail sprite images, 197
TIFF (Tagged Image File Format) files, 176, 328
tiled background images, 139
time of file modification
  in Folder view, 17, 52
  in Properties dialog box, 57
  updating, 54
  WebBots for, **217–219**
Times Roman font, 127
Timestamp WebBot, 207, **217–219**
title bars, 73
<TITLE> HTML tag, 136
titles, 136
  adding and changing, 57
  in Folder view, 52
  for frame sets, 271
  in headers and footers, 87

in page creation, 96, *96*
for sites, 31–32, 43
in templates, 94
To Do Lists, 13, **19–20**, *19*, **63**
  adding tasks to, 55, **65–66**, *66*
  for broken hyperlinks, 170
  completing and removing tasks on, **67**
  in Editor, 75
  modifying tasks on, **65–66**, *66*
  opening, **64**
  viewing tasks in, **64–65**
tool palettes for sprites, 188, *189*
toolbars in Editor, 73
toolbox for sprites, 188, *189*
Tools ➤ Arrange command, 196
Tools ➤ Back command, 156
Tools ➤ Follow Hyperlinks command, 156
Tools ➤ Font Options command, 128
Tools ➤ Forward command, 156
Tools ➤ Options command, 59, 187
Tools ➤ Patterns and Fills command, 198
Tools ➤ Permissions command, 292–293
Tools ➤ Replace command, 61
Tools ➤ Show FrontPage Editor command, 70
Tools ➤ Show FrontPage Explorer command, 71
Tools ➤ Show Image Editor command, 187
Tools ➤ Show To Do List command, 64, 75
Tools ➤ Spelling command
  in Editor, 76–77
  in Explorer, 63
Tools ➤ Text command, 194
Tools ➤ Verify Hyperlinks command, 168, 170, 290
Tools ➤ Warps and Filters command, 195

Tools ➤ Web Settings command, 43, 161, 214
Top alignment option, 233
<TR> HTML tag, 223
Transfer Full option, 198
transferring
    files, 5
    sprite fills, **198–199**
Transmission Control Protocol/Internet Protocol (TCP/IP), 5, 328
transparent GIF images, 181, 328
triangles for WebBot errors, 207
true color images, 191–192
True Color tab, 192, *193*
<TT> HTML tag, 130
tutorials, 317
24-bit color, 191
256-color images, 191
Two Page printing option, 87
TXT (text) files, converting, 102
Typewriter effect, 130
Typical installation option, 314–315

<U> HTML tag, 130
<UL> HTML tag, 115–117
UNDERCON.GIF file, 31, 181, 186, *186*
Underline effect, 130
underlining for hyperlinks, 7, 146
underscores (_) in folder names, 31
Undo button, 74
Uniform Resource Locators. *See* URLs (Uniform Resource Locators)
unordered lists, 115
    appearance of, **118**
    creating, **117**
    from existing text, **115–117**, *116*
updating hyperlinks, automatic, 57, 167

upgrading Personal Web Servers, 306–307
uploading, 328
URLs (Uniform Resource Locators), 6, 328
    absolute, 137, **148–149**, 319
    for frames and frame sets, 271–273, **277–279**, *277*
    for hyperlink targets, 147–148
    in Hyperlink view, 48
    in importing files, 36
    listing, 17
    in opening pages, 101
    in page creation, 96, *96*
    in Properties dialog box, 58
    in publishing sites, 41
    relative, **149**, 326
    in status bar, 146
Use Background Image option, 231
Use Same Permissions as Root Web option, 293
Use Unique Permissions for This Web option, 293
User/Group tab, 303
user manuals, 317
user meta-variable, 142
User Registration template, 243
User tab, 303, *303*
usernames
    in Explorer, 25, 32
    in publishing sites, 41
users
    permissions for, **294–297**, *295–296*
    registering, **301–304**, *302–303*
Users tab, 292, 294–297, *295*

Validate option, 254
validation of text box data, **254–257**, *255*

Value/Label option, 260
values
  for attributes, 83
  for configuration variables, 214
  for fields, 244
  for meta-variables, 142
  for text boxes, 254
variables
  with <META> tag, 142
  for WebBots, **211–214**
Verify Links dialog box, 168–170, *168–169*
verifying hyperlinks, **168–170**, *168–170*, **290**
Vertical Alignment option, 233
Vertical Position list, 132
Vertical Spacing option, 185
video cards for Image Composer, 187
video clips
  inserting, **177**
  properties for, **183–184**, *183*
Video Source field, 183
Video tab, 179, 183–184, *183*
View ➤ Folder View command, 52
View ➤ Format Marks command, 76, 158, 227
View ➤ Forms Toolbar command, 244, 249
View ➤ Go To Composition Guide command, 190
View ➤ HTML command, 11, 80, 129
View ➤ Hyperlink View command, 46
View ➤ Hyperlinks Inside Page command, 49
View ➤ Hyperlinks to Images command, 49, 52
View ➤ Image Toolbar command, 178
View or Edit HTML window, 80–82, *81*
View ➤ Refresh command, 54, 213
View ➤ Repeated Hyperlinks command, 49
View ➤ Source command, 12

viewers. *See* browsers
viewing
  frame sets, **272**, *273*
  hotspots, **165–166**
  source documents, **11–12**, **80–82**, *81*
  To Do List tasks, **64–65**
Visited Hyperlink option, 138

Warp Transforms effect, 195
Warps and Filters button, 195, *195*
Warps and Filters tool palette, 195
Watermark option, 139
WAV files, 137
Wave effect, 195–196
Web pages, 326
  automating. *See* WebBots
  browsing, **106**
  closing, 71
  creating, **71**, **92–98**, *92–93, 95–99*
  editors for, **58–60**, *59*
  essential elements in, **10–11**
  formatting. *See* formatting
  frames in. *See* frames and frame sets
  headings in, **114–115**
  horizontal lines in, **110–113**, *110, 112–113*
  in Hyperlink view, 48
  images in. *See* images
  importing into sites, 28
  including, **207–209**, *208*
  inserting files into, **102–103**
  linking. *See* hyperlinks
  listing, **16–17**, *17*
  lists in, **115–122**, *116*
  location of, 136–137
  opening, 55, **99–101**, *100–101*
  previewing, **84–86**, *85*
  printing, **86–88**

properties for, **135–142**, *136, 138, 140*
sample, 10, *10*
saving, 92, **103–106**, *103*
searching for text in, **60–63**, *62*, **78–79**
sections in, 110, *110, 112–113*
sound for, 137
spell checking, **63**, **76–78**, *78*
tables in. *See* tables
in templates, 28
templates for, **92–94**, *93, 95*
titles of, 52, 57, 96, *96*, 136
Wizards for, **94–98**, *96–99*
Web Publishing Wizard (WPW)
    publishing sites with, **39–42**, *40–41*
    system requirements for, 313
Web Settings dialog box, 161, *161*
Web sites, 5, 7, **287**, 328
    active, **24–25**
    closing, **32**
    copying, 15–16, 38
    creating, **25–33**, *27, 30*
    deleting, **43**
    from existing sites, **32–33**
    folder view for, **52–54**, *53*
    folders in, 31
    Hyperlink view for, **46–52**, *47, 51*
    importing, 15
    importing pages into, 28
    listing pages in, **16–17**, *17*
    locations for, **29–30**, *30*
    moving, **43**
    opening, **31–32**
    permissions for, **293–294**, *294*
    publishing, **37–42**, *38, 40–41*
    renaming, **42–43**
    security for, **291–298**, *294–296, 298–299*
    templates for, **26–29**, *27*
    testing, 14, **288–291**
    wizards for, **29**

WebBot Discussion Component option, 247
WebBot Include Component Properties dialog box, 208
WebBot pointer, 205, *205*
WebBot Registration Component option, 247
WebBot Save Results Component option, 247–249
WebBot Substitution Component Properties dialog box, 212
WebBot Table of Contents Component Properties dialog box, **215**, *215*
WebBot Timestamp Component Properties dialog box, 218
WebBots, 203–205, 328
    for date and time stamping, **217–219**
    encoding, **209–210**
    FrontPage, **205–207**
    for including pages, **207–209**, *208*
    revising, **210**
    Server Extensions for, 15–16
    for tables of contents, **215–217**, *215, 217*
    for text entry, **211–214**, *214*
What's New section, 28
Where to Find These Sprite Files option, 197
width
    of borders, 230
    of columns, 223, 225, *226*, **236**
    of horizontal lines, 111
    of images, 186
    of marquee messages, 283
    of one-line text boxes, 254
    of scrolling text boxes, 260
    of sprites, 194, 196
    of tables, **235–236**
Width field, 194, 196
Width in Characters field, 254
Width option, 186

wildcards in mask fields, 298
windows in Editor, 74
Wizards, 329
    for frames, **267–272**, *268–272*
    for pages, **94–98**, *96–99*
    for sites, **29**
Word
    converting files from, 102
    and Editor, 19, **72–73**
    importing files from, 34
word processor, Editor as, 19, **72–73**
WordPerfect files
    converting, 102
    importing, 34
words
    deleting, 73
    selecting, 126
    spell checking, **63**, **76–78**, *78*
Works files, converting, 102
workspace for sprites, **189–191**, *189*
World Wide Web (WWW), **5–8**, 329.
    See also Web pages; Web sites

World Wide Web tab, 150, 153
wrapping text in tables, 223, 233
WWW Administration hyperlink, 308
WYSIWYG environments, 18, 72, 329

yellow hyperlinks, 168
yellow status indicators in text searches, 62

Zoom In printing option, 87
Zoom Out printing option, 87
Zoom Percent tool, 198

SYBEX BOOKS ON THE WEB!

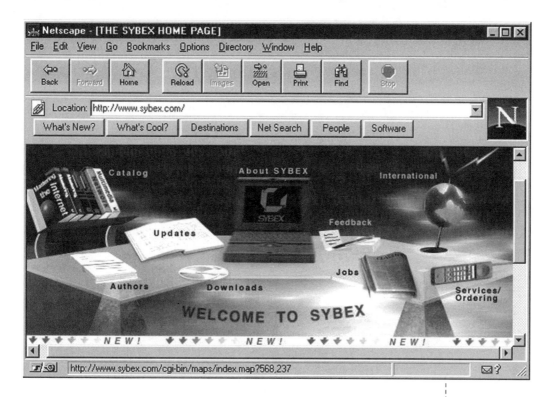

Presenting a truly dynamic environment that is both fun and informative.

- download useful code
- e-mail your favorite Sybex author
- preview a book you might want to own
- find out about job opportunities at Sybex
- order books
- learn about Sybex
- discover what's new in the computer industry

http://www.sybex.com

SYBEX Inc. • 1151 Marina Village Parkway • Alameda, CA 94501 • 510-523-8233